Heinrich Ewald, Edwin Johnson

Commentary on the Psalms

Heinrich Ewald, Edwin Johnson
Commentary on the Psalms
ISBN/EAN: 9783744779722

Printed in Europe, USA, Canada, Australia, Japan

Cover: Foto ©Lupo / pixelio.de

More available books at **www.hansebooks.com**

Prospectus of the
THEOLOGICAL TRANSLATION FUND.

As it is important that the best results of recent theological investigations on the Continent, conducted without reference to doctrinal considerations, and with the sole purpose of arriving at truth, should be placed within the reach of English readers, it is proposed to collect, by Subscriptions and Donations, a Fund which shall be employed for the promotion of this object. A good deal has been already effected in the way of translating foreign theological literature, a series of works from the pens of Hengstenberg, Haevernick, Delitzsch, Keil, and others of the same school, having of late years been published in English; but—as the names of the authors just mentioned will at once suggest to those who are conversant with the subject—the tendency of these works is for the most part conservative. It is a theological literature of a more independent character, less biassed by dogmatical prepossessions, a literature which is represented by such works as those of Ewald, Hupfeld, F. C. Baur, Zeller, Rothe, Keim, Schrader, Hausrath, Nöldeke, Pfleiderer, &c., in Germany, and by those of Kuenen, Scholten, and others, in Holland, that it is desirable to render accessible to English readers who are not familiar with the languages of the Continent. The demand for works of this description is not as yet so widely extended among either the clergy or the laity of Great Britain as to render it practicable for publishers to bring them out in any considerable numbers at their own risk. And for this reason the publication of treatises of this description can only be secured by obtaining the co-operation of the friends of free and unbiassed theological inquiry.

It is hoped that at least such a number of Subscribers of *One Guinea Annually* may be obtained as may render it practicable for the Publishers, as soon as the scheme is fairly set on foot, to bring out every year *three 8vo volumes,* which each Subscriber of the above amount would be entitled to receive gratis. But as it will be necessary to obtain, and to remunerate, the services of a responsible Editor, and in general, if not invariably, to pay the translators, it would conduce materially to the speedy success of the design, if free donations were also made to the Fund; or if contributors were to subscribe for more than one copy of the works to be published.

If you approve of this scheme, you are requested to communicate with Messrs. Williams and Norgate, 14, Henrietta Street, Covent Garden, London, and to state whether you are willing to subscribe; and if you are disposed to assist further, what would be the amount of your donation, or the number of additional copies of the publications which you would take.

We are, your obedient servants,

JOHN TULLOCH,	H. J. S. SMITH,
H. B. WILSON,	H. SIDGWICK,
B. JOWETT,	JAMES HEYWOOD,
A. P. STANLEY,	C. KEGAN PAUL,
W. G. CLARK,	J. ALLANSON PICTON,
S. DAVIDSON,	ROBT. WALLACE,
JAMES MARTINEAU,	LEWIS CAMPBELL,
JOHN CAIRD,	RUSSELL MARTINEAU,
EDWARD CAIRD,	T. K. CHEYNE,
JAMES DONALDSON,	J. MUIR.

The number of Subscribers is as yet far from that required to cover the cost of the undertaking. But it is hoped that a considerable accession will accrue as soon as the progress of the scheme is further advanced.

A Committee selected from the signataries of the original Prospectus agreed upon the works to commence the series. Of these, the following were published in

The *First* Year (1873):

1. KEIM (TH.), HISTORY OF JESUS OF NAZARA. Considered in its connection with the National Life of Israel, and related in detail. Second Edition, re-translated by Arthur Ransom. Vol. I. Introduction; Survey of Sources; Sacred and Political Groundwork; Religious Groundwork.
2. BAUR (F. C.), PAUL, THE APOSTLE OF JESUS CHRIST, his Life and Work, his Epistles and Doctrine. A Contribution to a Critical History of Primitive Christianity. Second Edition, by Rev. Allan Menzies. Vol. I.
3. KUENEN (A.), THE RELIGION OF ISRAEL TO THE FALL OF THE JEWISH STATE. Translated by A. H. May. Vol. I.

The *Second* Year (1874):

4. KUENEN'S RELIGION OF ISRAEL. Vol. II. Translated by A. H. May.
5. BLEEK'S LECTURES ON THE APOCALYPSE. Edited by the Rev. Dr. S. Davidson.
6. BAUR'S PAUL; the second and concluding volume. Translated by the Rev. Allan Menzies.

The *Third* Year (1875):

7. KUENEN'S RELIGION OF ISRAEL; the third and concluding volume.
8. ZELLER, THE ACTS OF THE APOSTLES CRITICALLY EXAMINED. To which is prefixed, Overbeck's Introduction from De Wette's Handbook, translated by Joseph Dare, B.A. Vol. I.
9. EWALD'S COMMENTARY ON THE PROPHETS OF THE OLD TESTAMENT. Translated by the Rev. J. Frederick Smith. Vol. I. General Introduction; Yoel, Amos, Hosea, and Zakharya 9—11.

The *Fourth* Year (1876):

10. ZELLER'S ACTS OF THE APOSTLES. Vol. II. and last.
11. KEIM'S HISTORY OF JESUS OF NAZARA. Vol. II. Translated by the Rev. E. M. Geldart. The Sacred Youth; Self-Recognition; Decision.
12. EWALD'S PROPHETS OF THE OLD TESTAMENT. Vol. II. Yesaya, Obadya, Mikha.

The *Fifth* Year (1877):

13. PAULINISM: a Contribution to the History of Primitive Christian
15. Theology. By Professor O. Pfleiderer, of Jena. Translated by
    E. Peters. 2 vols.
14. KEIM'S HISTORY OF JESUS OF NAZARA. Translated by A. Ransom.
    Vol. III. The First Preaching; the Works of Jesus; the
    Disciples; and the Apostolic Mission.

The *Sixth* Year (1878):

16. BAUR'S (F. C.), CHURCH HISTORY OF THE FIRST THREE CENTURIES.
    Translated from the third German Edition. Edited by the
    Rev. Allan Menzies (in 2 vols.). Vol. I.
17. HAUSRATH'S HISTORY OF THE NEW TESTAMENT TIMES. The
    Time of Jesus. Translated by the Revds. C. T. Poynting and
    P. Quenzer (in 2 vols.). Vol. I.
18. EWALD'S COMMENTARY ON THE PROPHETS OF THE OLD TESTAMENT.
    Translated by the Rev. J. Frederick Smith. Vol. III. Nahum,
    Ssephanya, Habaqquq, Zakharya 12—14, Yeremya.

The *Seventh* Year (1879):

19. KEIM'S HISTORY OF JESUS OF NAZARA. Vol. IV. The Galilean
    Storms; Signs of the approaching Fall; Recognition of the
    Messiah.
20. BAUR'S CHURCH HISTORY. Vol. II. and last.
21. EWALD'S COMMENTARY ON THE PROPHETS. Vol. IV. Hezeqiel,
    Yesaya xl.—lxvi.

The *Eighth* Year (1880):

22. HAUSRATH'S NEW TESTAMENT TIMES. The Time of Jesus. Vol.
    II. and last.
23. EWALD'S COMMENTARY ON THE PSALMS. Translated by the Rev.
24. E. Johnson, M.A. 2 vols.

Beyond these, the following Works are in the hands of Translators, and will be included in the next years' Subscriptions:

SHORT PROTESTANT COMMENTARY ON THE NEW TESTAMENT; including Introductions by Lipsius, Lang, Pfleiderer, Hilgenfeld, and others. Translated by the Rev. F. H. Jones, of Oldham (in 2 vols).

The Fifth Volume of KEIM'S HISTORY OF JESUS, translated by A. Ransom; and

The Fifth Volume of EWALD'S PROPHETS, translated by the Rev. J. Frederick Smith.

WILLIAMS & NORGATE.

14, HENRIETTA STREET, COVENT GARDEN,
LONDON, W.C.

THEOLOGICAL TRANSLATION FUND LIBRARY.

VOL. XXIV.

EWALD'S

COMMENTARY ON THE PSALMS.

VOL. II.

COMMENTARY

ON

THE PSALMS.

BY THE LATE

DR. G. HEINRICH A. V. EWALD,

PROFESSOR OF ORIENTAL LANGUAGES IN THE UNIVERSITY OF GÖTTINGEN.

TRANSLATED BY THE REV. E. JOHNSON, M.A.

COMMENTARY ON THE POETICAL BOOKS OF THE OLD
TESTAMENT. DIVISION I.

VOL. II.

WILLIAMS AND NORGATE,
14, HENRIETTA STREET, COVENT GARDEN, LONDON;
AND 20, SOUTH FREDERICK STREET, EDINBURGH.

1881.

LONDON:
G. NORMAN AND SON, PRINTERS, 29, MAIDEN LANE,
COVENT GARDEN.

TRANSLATOR'S NOTE.

THE present volume contains the exposition of the remainder of the Psalms, together with that of the alphabetic songs, called the Lamentations. At the suggestion of an esteemed correspondent, the section on Singing and Music from the first part of Ewald's *Poets of the Old Testament* has been translated and given in an Appendix at the end of the volume. Here will be found further elucidations of the section in Vol. I. on the inscriptions of the Psalms; and other references in the body of the work to pp. 209-233, *Dichter des A. B.*, I., point to matter contained in this Appendix.

In the correction of the proofs, as well as in the translation, the translator has striven to secure accuracy; and trusts that but few and unimportant *errata* will be discovered.

A complete Index of the Psalms, with the order in which they occur in the Commentary, is given at the end of this volume.

January, 1881.

CONTENTS OF VOL. II.

	PAGE
SONGS OF THE DISPERSION	1
THE BOOK OF LAMENTATIONS . .	99
SONGS OF RESTORED JERUSALEM	155
1. THE FIRST TIMES OF THE DELIVERANCE:	
A. IN THE VOICES OF INDIVIDUALS . . .	158
B. IN VOICES OF THE COMMUNITY AND INDIVIDUALS	176
2. ENDURING SENTIMENT	214
3. NEW DANGERS AND COMPLAINTS; NEW LIGHTS	224
LAST SONGS	267
APPENDIX: ON SINGING AND MUSIC . . .	328
INDEX	354

The Psalms explained in the present volume will be found as follows:—

Psalm		p.	Psalm		p.
,,	xiv.	143	,,	c.	198
,,	xvi.	10	,,	cii.	95
,,	xvii.	4	,,	ciii.	281
,,	xxii.	33	,,	civ.	284
,,	xxv.	90	,,	cv.	310
,,	xxxiii.	322	,,	cvi.	290
,,	xxxiv.	93	,,	cvii.	295
,,	xxxv.	50	,,	cviii.	309
,,	xxxviii.	56	,,	cix.	72
,,	xl.	60	,,	cxi.	299
,,	xlii.	23	,,	cxii.	299
,,	xliii.	23	,,	cxiii.	301
,,	xliv.	227	,,	cxiv.	301
,,	xlvii.	212	,,	cxv.	181
,,	xlix.	17	,,	cxvi.	183
,,	li.	77	,,	cxviii.	177
,,	liii.	143	,,	cxix.	267
,,	lxvi. 1-12.	213	,,	cxx.	148
,,	lxvii.	199	,,	cxxi.	150
,,	lxviii.	200	,,	cxxii.	169
,,	lxix.	66	,,	cxxiii.	151
,,	lxx.	65	,,	cxxiv.	159
,,	lxxi.	85	,,	cxxv.	161
,,	lxxiii.	126	,,	cxxvi.	163
,,	lxxiv.	230	,,	cxxvii.	164
,,	lxxvii.	133	,,	cxxviii.	166
,,	lxxviii.	255	,,	cxxix.	160
,,	lxxix.	233	,,	cxxx.	152
,,	lxxx.	235	,,	cxxxi.	153
,,	lxxxi.	264	,,	cxxxii.	239
,,	lxxxii.	141	,,	cxxxiii.	167
,,	lxxxiii.	252	,,	cxxxiv.	168
,,	lxxxiv.	30	,,	cxxxv.	314
,,	lxxxv.	250	,,	cxxxvi.	315
,,	lxxxvi	303	,,	cxxxvii.	173
,,	lxxxvii.	170	,,	cxxxviii.	186
,,	lxxxix.	242	,,	cxxxix.	218
,,	xci.	215	,,	cxliii.	305
,,	xcii.	188	,,	cxliv. 1-11.	307
,,	xciii.	190	,,	cxlv.	317
,,	xciv.	138	,,	cxlvi.	319
,,	xcv.	196	,,	cxlvii.	320
,,	xcvi.	194	,,	cxlviii.	325
,,	xcvii.	191	,,	cxlix.	324
,,	xcviii.	196	,,	cl.	327
,,	xcix.	193			

COMMENTARY ON THE PSALMS.

III.

SONGS OUT OF THE DISPERSION OF THE PEOPLE AND THE DESTRUCTION OF THE KINGDOM.

But in spite of all this later urgency and endeavour on the part of the better spirits among the people, the dissolution of the kingdom and destruction of the holy city could not be averted. Too great were the internal defects and corruptions, as these songs plainly show. Thus the exile was brought about, which had partly begun long before the destruction of Jerusalem; and with the exile first began that great turn in affairs which could alone entirely remove those profound deficiencies of the whole period.

For first of all there came, along with the exile, the deepest suffering of every kind, and the most manifold causes united to form a whirlpool of misery whence no deliverance seemed possible. Already the forced separation from the dearest associations of the fatherland, and the holiest associations of life,—from the Temple,—oppressed many with the sorest unappeasable longing. Earlier antiquity ever clave to its holy places with the most childlike love and devotion, because nothing could generally furnish such inner rest and serenity as the familiar participation in the sheltering delight and security of a sanctuary. (Pss. xxiv., xv., v., xxvi.) And the pious of Israel must have clung the more intensely to the Temple at Jerusalem the more purely they were there conscious of the nearness of the supremely Righteous and Gracious One, and the more closely that Israel by degrees attached itself ever more universally to this *one* sanctuary alone, and had assembled its spiritual possessions around this enclosure alone. The most grievous longing for the distant Temple, inaccessible only because of such oppression, and the most sorrowful complaint, is found, under these circumstances, amongst many of those first carried into exile. And this longing is all the greater the more, amidst the manifold distress of their circumstances, the solace of the sanctuary is missed, Pss. xlii., lxxxiv., lxi., lxiii.; and scarcely can we conceive an elegy nobler in mood, deeper in feeling than either of the two Psalms, xlii. and lxxxiv.—Besides, there was a mass of other sufferings and grievances, which in part are quite peculiar to the exile, as the rude contempt of the persecuted and suffering because of their very sufferings, scorn of Jahvé as the impotent God who helps not his most faithful worshippers, biting scoffs at prophetic truth and influence,—injuries in which frequently Gentiles concurred with the light-minded portion of the Israelites. Evidently the few in exile had the chief share of the suffering who maintained most firmly by word and deed the genuine old religion against every one, Gentiles and Israelites, amidst these extreme perplexities.

And in fact the troubles rush at times with such overwhelming force upon the faithful, that their song, incapable of maintaining a pure calm, passes at least transiently into imprecation and cursing (ix. 23, 29; cix. 6-20); as the like was noticed in several of the songs of the preceding cycle (Vol. I., p. 251).

But of what avail imprecation, glowing longings, urgent complaining and despondency? Either naught, or in this very chasm, this close of the ancient time, there must begin an entirely new elevation and the possibility of a new and better time; and the ancient religion of Israel had still enough of undeveloped truth and power in itself, to give to the few truly faithful ones endurance and victory. If all external resources which had been hitherto trusted in pass away, the pure and good temper is but the more brightened and strengthened, and so is it with genuine hope and joyous submission, Pss. lvi., lvii., xxii. If in extreme need all the greatness and dreadfulness of the old perversities is recognized with a certainty which it is vain to seek to shake off,—the sense of one's own and others' sins: then the new spiritual life will awake with the greater power, irresistibly. That which earlier seemed impossible, life amidst the heathen and a thousand corruptions of mankind, thus becomes even to the faithful gradually possible and easy. Indeed, the very remoteness of the Temple, and finally its destruction, now furthers the truth which earlier came to light (Ps. l.) that the true spiritual life and Divine blessedness still consists in quite other things than Temple sacrifices, Pss. xvi., xl., li., lxix. But hereby the ancient Israel is already born anew, and out of the midst of its fall and humiliation it gradually rises, ever stronger and more victorious, with prophetic intimations against the heathendom by whose means it had fallen, and looks with the greater confidence towards its new and certain salvation, Pss. lxxxii., xiv., cxx. sqq.

Thus there arise in exile most important songs. Many indeed bear most obvious traces of the great oppressive sufferings in the sorest time, their language and thought is in places more cramped, tedious and spiritless, Pss. xvii., xxxviii., li., lxix., cix.; but often the deepest thoughts and most eternal intimations flash forth with surprise, and towards the end even the language is evidently strengthened and rounded into greater poetical dignity, Pss. lxxxii., cxx. sqq.

We intended to place together here all songs from the dispersion of the people, including those which originated a longer or shorter time before the destruction of Jerusalem in B.C. 586. But the fine songs, Pss. lxi., lxiii., lvi.—lviii., which would, according to time, belong immediately to this place, have been already explained above in another connexion. The rest are, as far as possible arranged in order of time, the following:

A. 61-63. PSALMS XVII., XVI., XLIX.

We may easily convince ourselves that these songs are of the same poet, and of one who does not indeed speak of the Temple, but yet (xvi. 3) looks from a strange land very wistfully upon the Israelites dwelling in Kanáan. So great is their mutual resemblance, and their common difference from others. In the language, comp. חֶלֶד *world*, xvii. 14, xlix. 2; רָאָה שַׁחַת xvi. 10, xlix. 10, 11, comp. ver. 20 (repeated lxxxix. 49); סָבַב *surround*, of the wickedness of many persecutors, xvii. 11, xlix. 6; אֶל thus alone and directly for *God, Jahvé*, xvi. 1, xvii. 6, which in general is rare and only proper to certain poets, Pss. lii. 3, 7, lv. 20, the Book of Job, which has generally re-introduced this poetic usage, and a few still later Psalms; בַּל, xvi. 2, 3, xvii. 3, 5, xlix. 13: לְ "in what concerns," along with a proleptic noun, xvi. 3, xvii. 4, comp. § 310 *a*, and other instances of the kind. Still more salient is the resemblance of the stamp of the language, softly flowing, but in certain places rising to a clear fire. How similar is the fundamental tone is shown very clearly by the sharpness of the opposition, —well conscious of the inner difference,—of the worldly and Divine, of the aims of the great mass or of the world and of those peculiar to the poet, xvii. 2-5, xvi. 2-5, xlix. 7 sqq., the great inner anxiety and watchfulness for his soul's health, along with which he does not shun the stricter trial, xvii. 2, xvi. 7, 8; and the very singular joy (in this kind) with which he calmly looks into the future, xvii. 15, xvi. 9-11, xlix. 16. But they lie in point of time plainly somewhat far asunder; and if they are, as it seems we cannot doubt, of the same poet, Ps. xvii. must be the earliest.

Ps. xvii. is spoken from the midst of the first vivid fear of the tyrants who persecuted the poet without cause. The song announces itself as the first attempt to fly from the sudden danger to Jahvé and rest in Him. The persecutors belong, according to the clear description, vv. 9-14, to the party of the heathen and light-minded Israelites frequently elsewhere mentioned in writings of this time. They, merely pursuing pleasure and external power, made no scruple of falling on a peaceful, quiet fellow-citizen, because he would not pay homage to their principles and customs. In the confusion of later relations, such rakes could often long carry on their practices undisturbed; in opposition to the faith of the pious, accustomed to the rule of righteousness, they seemed to him in fullest comfort and prosperity ever to die surrounded by the highest human conditions of well-being, and thus to evade the Divine justice. How greatly the more conscientious took offence at such an experience is plain from several passages of the Book of Job. Our poet has also to contend with this new enigma of the time. Horribly beset by these impious ones, and seeing his life in danger, he cries with animation and energy to Jahvé for help against wrong, and this the more, as he cannot comprehend how such tyrants can be prosperous (ver. 14, comp. Job. xxi. 8, 11, and frequently elsewhere). And although he will not, cannot doubt of God,—but conscious of innocence, finally calms and strengthens himself in hope by Jahvé's help and light,—yet it first costs him some struggle to put away the contrary picture of the prosperous bad man; and the whole song shows an uncommon surging-up and straining of the noble mind, conscious of Divine leading, and yet so unusually suffering and experiencing such troubles, yea, transports of grief. The poet presses back the enigma as long as possible, as if he would not suffer himself to be thereby troubled. Only, his first wish is, may God hear the unvarnished right that is put forward,—He who alone is true Judge and known of men, and of the poet in particular, who, as he ever watches carefully over his thinking and doing, does not fear Divine trial, vv. 1-6, comp. xxvi. 1, 2. With confidence, therefore, he may cry to Jahvé, in the new and sore time which amidst the increasing frivolity and barbarity of men the more demands the mighty working of great Divine forces,—to deliver him from his insolent and raging persecutors (who are here for the first time further described), vv. 7-12; yea,—the address, after this long description of the wicked, is once more finally renewed with the greater energy—yea, may God save him from enemies whose worldly life was so bitterly opposed to the Divine working (and here only the sense of strangeness is entirely relieved); that the calm, never-failing hope of the poet may be soon fulfilled in the revelation of Divine salvation, vv. 13-15. Thus three strophés, but so that the discourse in its development and extension returns twice to its beginning, the address and the cry for help being twice interrupted by lengthy descriptions. Each of the two first strophés has twelve members, the last, seven; but the long formation of the members greatly predominates.

1.

1   O hear, Jahvé, right, bend to my supplication,
     Observe my prayer—without deceitful lips!
    From Thy throne goes forth my judgment,
     Thine eyes behold rectitude;
    Proved hast Thou my heart, searched me by night, tho-
                                         roughly purified me,
     Thou findest me not thinking ill, my mouth not
                                         offending;
    worldly deeds—no! through the word of Thy lips
     I have avoided the paths of a madman;
5   firmly my steps held to Thy tracks,
     my walk became not wavering.
    I cry to Thee, for Thou hearest me, God!
     bend to me Thine ear, hear my speech!

2.

Show Thy wonder-grace, Thou who helpest faithful ones
 before the rebels against Thy right hand!

Preserve me as the little man of the eye,
  in Thy wings' shadow concealing me,
from wicked men who have fallen upon me,
  the deadly enemies, who encompass me,
have closed their fat heart,   10
  with their mouth speak haughtily,
whither we go, now surround us,
  direct their eyes through the land to strike;
like a lion which longs to rob,
  and like a young lion sitting lurking.

3.

Up, Jahvé! prevent him, strike him down,
  my life deliver from wicked men by Thy sword,
from men, O Jahvé, by Thy hand, from men of the world,
  who have their pleasure in life and whose paunch Thou
                                    fillest with Thy good things,
who have sons in abundance and leave their substance to
                                    their children!—
I—may Thy face appear in salvation,   15
  awaking refresh me at Thy image!

1. Ver. 2 opens the reasons for the prayer, ver. 1, which were even begun, properly speaking, with the last words of ver. 1. *By night*, ver. 3, because the night is the time of stiller, deeper contemplations and counsels, comp. xvi. 7, iv. 5. Yet at the same time we learn from this that the poet composed in the evening, and to note this in connexion with ver. 15 is very important. At the end of ver. 3 פָּלֵיט is, in opposition to the Massôr. division, drawn to the preceding member, whereby the sense becomes most clear, and the arrangement of members proportionate. Ver. 4 runs literally thus: in what concerns the actions of the world (אָדָם acquires later the peculiar signification of men as they usually are, the world, the present corrupted, merely earthly-minded ones, in

opposition to the Divine life, comp. Job xxxi. 33, Hos. vi. 7; ὁ κόσμος, just so חֶלֶד, ver. 14)—I have, strengthened through Thy revelation, avoided the tyrants' paths, not pursued such worldly endeavours as the tyrants; rather my steps held fast . . . —Because of this sharp opposition תָּמֹה for תָּמְכוּ (§ 328 c); for that ver. 5 speaks out of experience is shown by the entire connexion and by the *perf.* בַּל נָמוֹטוּ. שָׁמַר, however, must as "guard" be here plainly an "avoiding," LXX correctly ἐφυλαξάμην.

2. They who rise against the Divine right hand, ver. 7, are precisely the men of violence, who out of self-seeking ever disturb the Divine order where they, on reflection, might see this directed against themselves, the same whom the supplicator, ver. 9, must call his *death-foes* (comp. Ez. xxv. 6, 15). חֶלֶב, ver. 10, "fat" for a hard and unfeeling heart, is here for the first time so used, afterwards repeated, lxxiii. 7, cxix. 70. Whilst they from hardness have shut their unfeeling heart against compassion, their haughty mouth is the more loudly opened for abuse. The frequent short use of the accusative פִּימוֹ, ver. 10, אֲשֻׁרֵנוּ, ver. 11, חַרְבָּם, יָדָם, vv. 13, 14 (§ 281 c), is, further, in this style, peculiar to the somewhat more artificial and elegant expression of this and some other songs of the time. Ver. 11 describes then plainly how jealously they spy through the whole land to get at defenceless saints, the poet and others of his kind, and everywhere to dog their heels.

3. In ver. 13 the figure is at first plainly retained of the lion, ver. 12, so that on this account it is unnecessary to refer ver. 12 to a single foe, possibly the leader, for רָשָׁע, ver. 13, stands undefined, and therefore generally. דִּמְיֹנוֹ is thus: *the likeness thereof*, of this thing, this appearance, the suffix taken as *neut.* The figure is only not carried out so far here as in the manifestly later song, x. 8-10. *Come in front of his countenance*, already the enemy comes running up like a raging lion; the strong hero and victor must throw himself upon his

face. חֶלְקָם, ver. 14, is: *their portion is in life*, they have in life their share, their lot, in the good that has fallen to them, and hence also their pleasure; but in what the faithful ought to have his part and his pleasure is stated in xvi. 5 sqq. The whole description of these people bears the greatest resemblance to that in the Book of Job xxi. 7-14: only the idea of the *world* already in the sense of the New Testament is new in our poet.—But with the last words, ver. 15, the poet manifestly tears himself free from the troublous recollections of these prosperous wicked, bringing to his mind his hope in God. But this hope is the last and highest: that the full clear light may finally shine on the faithful, or that the faithful may yet behold the face of God in salvation, may in the beholding of the pure light enjoy the highest pleasure, as xi. 7, iv. 7; comp. with the higher historic representation of Moses, Num. xii. 8. The image of the pure, bright, clear, the everstriven and longed-for, shall finally become once for all firm, and intense to the mind of the faithful, he shall once for all seize it, so as from that moment onwards eternally to hold it, and eternally refresh himself by it. The countenance, or rather the image of God, therefore, shall he behold (so far and in the way in which a human being can do this). This fundamental view of Hebrew antiquity seeks in this later time, because the unsettlement of all external possessions and of the sensuous life itself was ever more certainly recognized, a still higher or clearer expression. The spirit, becoming conscious of its inward force and stability, strives to raise itself above the appreciation of all earthly possessions, even of the sensuous life, and the purest intimation of true immortality which man cannot lose, powerfully emerges, as we see still more plainly in our poet in the following song, xvi. 9-11. It might, indeed, now appear as though at least in the present song, so strong on the whole, and particularly in the short final word, this wondrous *new thing* does not yet appear, but as if the poet here hopes still simply for the highest in the earthly life, and the more zealously, the sooner and the more certainly. In the evening (for it is an evening song, ver. 3), lying down amidst a thousand dangers, he yet hopes on awaking to refresh himself with the Divine image, then already so to have received the Divine salvation and light, that he may feel himself entirely irradiated and seized by the sublime picture as of the countenance of God. Comp. what is feebler but similar, iv. 9. Of an awakening after death, which at the first glance by no means suits in this connexion the order and clearness of the thoughts, the poet cannot apparently here be thinking. But it must be borne in mind that our poet, considering his age, may very well have read the Book of Job, and have accepted its true meaning. In that case, such higher, bright hopes, were not so strange to him that he could not even here, after the outbreak of stormy passions at the view of the present world, have been able to quell the storm of his bosom. And precisely in proportion to the sharp distinction in his contemplation of the *world* as possibly entirely separate from God and opposed to Him, does he consequently flee at the end to the Divine eternity alone. Moreover, it is the same poet whom we retrace, as already become fully familiar with such higher thoughts, in Ps. xvi.

For how far from fruitless the urgency of the preceding Psalm had been, is shown by nothing more clearly than by Ps. xvi. Hardly can true resignation, conscious of itself, to the will of Jahvé, be more complete; quiet, soft contentment, and inner serenity in spite of all life dangers and of the evil example from without, more noble, true hope, clearer and more sublime than we here see, all this as at a single stroke appear. Here is from the first no revolt, no fear, no sore struggle any longer. The serene splendour of a higher peace and the hearty intensity of a completed life-experience rises above everything. And if one would learn upon what ground the dependence of the true saint of those times in Jahvé rests, let this Psalm be pondered, and let it be seen how the poet becomes conscious of his trust in Jahvé, because he in Jahvé alone—in His revelations and in remembrance of Him—finds an invincible spring of clearness, joy, hope, and consolation. For if the religion of Jahvé is distinguished from all others by clearness and truth, if God is known and felt in it in His spirituality as nowhere else,—then he who wholly devotes himself to it and is ever anew stimulated by it, must become ever clearer in himself, ever more related to spiritual blessings. Thus we here see the poet already at that high stage when he feels alone in Jahvé and the possession of Him His highest good and his true delight and hope, overcoming in this blessed state with equal calmness the evil example of those hastening to idolatry, as in this hope under all sufferings (probably he suffered at that time from severe illness, vv. 1, 9) unwearied and undistressed,—in Divine joy experiencing that if his spirit be ever with God, as he feels that it is, God will send him no true sorrow, but will preserve and save him among all dangers, even in the midst of death. Therefore, as there is in the poet's soul but *one* great passion, the song also is but *one* gentle flowing gush, without storm, or harsh transitions, whilst the inner fire gradually glows and kindles. After a brief very subdued cry for protection, ver. 1, there is developed as the most important theme, the consciousness of the suppliant,—to possess Jahvé is the highest good, vv. 2-8, whence also the true hope in Jahvé, glancing tranquilly over all times and fortunes —because He is infinitely rich in grace and salvation, vv. 9-11. The cry for help therefore scarcely gains strength in the presence of the predominant blessed consciousness and serene hope.

Again, the structure of the strophés reveals the blessed rest and evenness of mood out of which the short and yet inwardly full song flows; three strophés, each of eight lines, the last only shorter by one. The long formation of the lines prevails here as in the preceding song.

1.

1 Preserve me, God, for I trust in Thee.—
I say of Jahvé: my Lord art Thou,
Thou art my highest good!
The saints who are in the land,
and nobles who have all my love—
many are their idols, they exchange strange ones
—they, whose bloody libation I will not sacrifice,
nor take their names upon my lips.

2.

5 Jahvé is the portion of my substance and cup;
Thou art the possession of my lot!
lines fell to me in the fairest spot,
and my heritage also pleased me well,
I bless Jahvé for the way He hath counselled me,
through nights also my reins warned me;
I have set Jahvé before me continually;
when He is at my right hand, I waver not.

3.

10 Therefore my heart rejoices and my spirit exults!
my body also will dwell in quiet!
For Thou wilt not leave my soul to hell,
nor suffer Thy pious ones to see the grave;
wilt teach me the way of life;
fulness of joy is before Thee,
pleasures in Thy right hand ever!

1. Ver. 2. Many ancients, Symm., Targ., Hieron., translate *my substance is not without Thee* or *outside of Thee*. It might be supposed they read בַּל בִּלְעָדֶיךָ, but there is no ground for this. עַל must therefore here denote "over and beyond something," therefore not touching it, remaining without it, as Gen. xlviii. 22, § 217 *i.* and *ely*, *Gr. ar.* ii., p. 81, *Syr.* xvi., 109,

clearer in a somewhat different way, עַל כִּי כָּבֵד *before* a person, so not touching him, but rather obscuring him and thrusting him back, i.e., *outside* of him, beyond of him, Ex. xx. 2, παρὰ with the accusative.

To other Israelites, indeed, proceeds the poet with grief, ver. 3, other gods are endeared, and they of horrible, bloody religions (*e.g.* of Moloch, as is well known from history). But he finds alone in Jahvé his joy and delight and feels the possession of Him or confidential relation with Him his highest good. This is plainly the connexion in the main. As the poet cannot avoid touching on this opposition of the time—*this* seems most profoundly to distress him, that the very Israelites, who ought to be the saints and pass for such (Ex. xix. 6, Deut. xxxiii. 3, Ps. xxxiv. 10, Dan. viii. 24, xii. 7), the noble, princely men, whom he especially so intensely loves (comp. l. 5; Jer. xi. 15) that even these begin to betake themselves increasingly to heathenism. Hence the names of honour with which he comes, ver. 3, to their mention, and which so far are not utterly unsuitable since the corruption is beginning, not yet completed. So: *in what concerns the saints* (*i.e.*, Israelites) *who are in the land* (whence it obviously follows that the poet at that time lived outside Kanáan, and therefore in exile) *and the nobles* (perhaps precisely the *princes* for the most part) *on whom all my pleasure depends* (on אַדִּירֵי § 332 c): *their idol-images multiply, strange gods they exchange* instead of Jahvé, a wretched barter! as it is expressed further, vv. 5 sqq. Thus the figure of the *possession* is retained from v. 2 to 6. אֶת signifies readily of itself when religion is spoken of, idols (Ex. xx. 3, Isa. xlii. 8), and the indefinite *sing.* of this word appears also elsewhere for our indefinite *plur.* § 310 a. The last two clauses, ver. 4, appear most readily to be understood as relating to the gods just named, so that the full opposition only follows in ver. 5, these subordinate propositions merely incidentally prepare for it; for the poet loves such longer evolutions, xvii. 14. That the suffix of נִסְכֵּיהֶם is to be referred to the idols is clearly shown by the corresponding שְׁמוֹתָם, because the poet can only mean he would not pollute himself by the solemn utterance and laudation of the names of the idols at their sacrificial feasts. עֲצָבוֹת must therefore = עֲצַבִּים, perhaps the former plays with the signification, "griefs, delusions," as the false gods are elsewhere frequently named in many applications, Am. ii. 4. The attempt to explain " they must ever increasingly suffer sorrows (sufferings) and *therefore* they hasten (from מָהַר *hasten*) to the idol-worship,"—whereby the name " saint," ver. 3, would be yet more readily intelligible,—breaks down under too great difficulties, for the transition would be too harsh and short even for this poet.

2. The opposition of the poet to that last said is so thoroughly understood of itself and is from his first word onwards, vv. 1, 2, so clearly indicated, that he, in the beginning of the second strophé, ver. 5, even without any word of an opposition, immediately continues to make further plain the good which to him is the only highest good. But also the figure itself of the *highest good* lies, from that very first word, ver. 1, so near to him, and governed already the whole first strophé so strongly, that it cannot but recur here, and be ever more widely extended in its entire significance. On the division of the conquered land, the property, according to the number of the conquerors, is divided into like parts, measured with lines and distributed by lot,—so that to the one a less, to the other a more fruitful and pleasant heritage falls. But in the overflowing fulness of blessed thoughts and words of the poet, there mingles with this predominant figure, vv. 5, 6, of the property in land, in the beginning the similar one of the cup, the contents of which the house-father holds out to every guest according to his proportion, xi. 6. Yet the first figure only, as that alone predominating from the beginning of the song onwards, is here also further maintained, *Jahvé is the portion of my substance and cup*, i.e., the good and the enjoyment which fell to my share as in the heritage which fell to me, or in the

cup held out to me. The חֶלְקִי forces its way in from the main figure. The תּוֹמִיךְ cannot be part. act. Qal. To punctuate תּוֹמִיךְ is (§ 151 a) impossible. But to the connexion and to the completion of the figure it suits rather to take it as an abstract substantive, § 156 c. The sense is then simple: Thou art to me a *possession* or heritage, as if fallen to me by a *fortunate lot*, on account of which figure of the lot, it runs in ver. 6 : lines, meaning cords, *fell* to me, as the lot by chance falls, *and* actually also *my heritage pleased me well*; for the נַחֲלָת may be regarded most aptly according to the connexion of the language as abbreviated from נַחֲלָתִי just as this poet dialectically says אֲמָרְתְּ, ver. 2, for יתי (§ 190 d). But the whole figure of the property fallen to him is the more appropriate because the Divine grace is ever the first to arouse and awaken man, thus anticipating him; especially in the community, where higher truths as already given and known meet the individual. But the poet is willingly followed, he feels also in himself the Divine operation, to him Jahvé remains no dead property, but has become something beloved and dear; because he feels Jahvé's voice working in him to his own salvation,—continually urging and exhorting him, and thus he blesses, as it is further expressed, vv. 7, 8, Jahvé, as his oracle, ever living in him, with whose clearness and desired continuance he cannot waver. On יָעַץ, comp. Isa. viii. 11, the יִפַּר only expresses the same thing more strongly,—namely, how powerfully the oracle awoke in him, ever urging him through the night. But how this is possible is then explained with brevity and aptness by the first member, ver. 8. But the golden words, ver. 7, are only fully understood when we reflect that אֲשֶׁר here (§ 333 a) denotes *how* and governs all the following words : *I bless Him for the way in which He has counselled me,*—how *even nights through my reins,* as awoke and led by Him, *warned me* not to do the seductive evil, 3, 4. Comp. also similarly Ps. xl. 7.

3. The hope, or rather in the first instance only its expres-

sion, vv. 9-11, now surpasses by so much more that wherewith the preceding Psalm closed, as this whole later Psalm stands higher. The truth has here unfolded out of that small germ wherein it there lay closed, and come to its full blossom; and there is hardly to be found a more beautiful or clearer declaration concerning the whole future of the individual man than the present. For the calm glow of the highest inner expansion and serenity here lifts the poet far above all the future and its menaces, and it stands clearly before his soul that in such continued life of the spirit in God there is nothing to be feared, neither pains of the flesh (body) nor death; but where the true life is there also the body must finally come to its rest; because deliverance also of the soul from the grave is possible through him who wills only life, with whom infinite joy and delight stand ever ready that He may lavish them on whom He will. When such hints and ideas of the true life come forth,—then in fact the veil of the whole future of the individual becomes so far lifted, and true hope is as clearly dispensed as is possible without using new figures. There is far from being dogma as yet here, and of the immortality of the spirit there appears here certainly the true anticipation and necessity, but not yet so ready and firm a conception with such enthusiastic, rapturous pictures as later. But this is precisely the noble feature: that we thus see in some songs, the higher intimation in its self-necessitated formation and rise, spring forth for the first time. For when it is most recent, when it is obtained in struggle and strain as the prize of the sorest conflicts, there it is freshest, there its essence is most necessarily formed, there the germinating revelation is purest and clearest, still without disguise and without exaggeration, without gloom and superstition. Comp. xlix. 16, Job xix. 26, 27, and in its beginning already above, xxxvi. 10, as well as Prov. xii. 28.—The *plur.* חסידיך in the K'tîb, ver. 10, is not incorrect,—probably the original reading: for the language may here at the end very well pass over into generality, because the truth does not hold good merely of the individual poet, and likewise passes in the latter half, ver. 11, into generality.

And finally, the poet in Ps. xlix. becomes even the inspired teacher of this (at that time) still unusual higher view of life. This extremely important song forms a certain contrast to the above explained Ps. i. For the simple teaching of that Psalm did not always suffice. Experience seemed, in the confusion of things during the seventh and sixth centuries, soon to show, on the contrary, even more certainly and universally, that might and good fortune stood at the command of godless and oppressive men. Divine justice and equity in human affairs seemed ever to tarry or utterly to pass away. The firmer the hope among the faithful of a great and speedy Divine judgment had become, the greater the despondency even of the more conscientious at its delay. Here was a hard riddle imposed by the time, and no true rest was possible until a new light had dispersed this thick darkness. But as the solution of the enigma could only come to pass by means of a penetration into the inner nature of dark things, the severity of the time now forced several spirits to pierce through, in this sphere, the external show, by deeper insight into the true and necessary, in order that in the midst of the dread view of the enduring power of vain men they might draw from a closer consideration of its nature comfort both near and safe. One of these is the author of this Psalm. While he sharply contrasts the outwardly splendid life and proud pomp of the mighty and rich, but corrupt ungodly, with their inward state and their hopelessness in death, and reflects that they with all earthly treasures and joys can purchase no serenity in God, and no deliverance from dreaded death, their fate must justly present itself to him as the more mournful and the less deserving of envy, the more horrid and painful this contrariety between the inner and outer in them may by themselves be felt; and the more certainly the pious man feels that he, even if he is bare and empty of all these external goods, has yet an inward imperishable and eternal good, consoling and strengthening him in all times and circumstances, even in the approach of death not forsaking him (ver. 16, comp. p. 16). Thereby the ancient hope, *e.g.*, that the just shall at last ever rule again, is not removed (see on the contrary, ver. 15), but loses the trouble and disquiet readily attaching to it, whilst thus attention is drawn before all to the inward life. The poet having thrown this deep glance into the true principle of nobility, and the glory, outlasting all external changes, of the human spirit that rests in God, and having so clearly recognized the difference of external and internal goods, feels himself not merely free from all earlier fear and unrest in a sore time, but also so full and inspired with the truth breaking forth in him afresh with power and light, that giving way to an inner impulse, he stands forth as its bold teacher and interpreter, and here, even to the great mass, yea, to all without distinction, resolved to impart his insight,—he begins, with art and selection, a didactic song, serious where the matter demands it, castigating folly with fine scorn. But the proper feeling of the poet, newly enlightened by this truth, is still so fresh and living, that the language proceeds with genuine lyric power from him, and he makes himself so far in thought the type of all faithful ones. Thus the didactic song, after a dignified preparation for the well-considered object, in a preliminary strophé, vv. 2-5,—is executed in two nearly uniform strophés; whilst the description in the midst, along with a main kernel-saying expressing the whole in brevity with sharp and sufficient force,—only rests, to begin again with new energy and, after complete exhaustion of the thought, to return to the above leading proposition, vv. 6-13; 14-21. The verse-structure is, as becomes so subtle a didactic song, very pleasing and light. Each strophé of sixteen members, the first as a mere prelude of only half the extent, but all the lines so arranged, that the long structure seems intentionally avoided. But to this elegant (as is best in a didactic song) and throughout uniform structure corresponds finally also the didactic verse with its two members; and almost in all these particulars this song yields fairly the direct contrast to Pss. xlii., xliii.

1.

Hear this, all ye peoples,   2
   hearken all world-inhabitants,
sons of men as well as heroes' sons,
   rich and poor together!
wisdom shall my mouth speak,
   my heart's sense is insight;
will bend my ear to the proverb-song,   5
   open with the cither my didactic word:

2.

Why should I fear because the evil one rules,
   because sin of the lurkers surrounds me,
of them who build upon their substance,
   boast of the fulness of their riches?
but safely none will buy himself free,
   nor give to God his ransom
   —for so dear is the ransom of the soul
      that it fails for ever—
that he may live yet further,   10
   not to see the grave:
no, he will see it! wise men die,
   together, fool and simpleton perish,
leave to others their substance,
no, their grave their eternal houses are,
   their seats for generation, generation,
   —they who were everywhere extolled!
And man in pomp but without insight
   is like to cattle, so they perish!

2 *

3.

This is their way who have folly,
and after them of those who love to say the like.
15   like to the flock, destined to the pit, death shall pasture
on them,
and just men lord it over them;
soon—so must their beauty rot,
hell becomes their abode.
But God will redeem my soul
from the hand of hell, when it seizes me.—
Fear not when any becomes rich,
when his house's might increases:
for all that he takes not with him, dying,
not after him does his power go down;
though then in life he bless his soul,
and men praise thee that thou doest good to thyself:
20   it will come to the race of his fathers
till the light is seen no more!
And man in pomp but without insight
is like to cattle, so they perish!

1. On ver 3 comp. above lxii. 10; the doubled גם must here plainly put contrasts on one level, and cannot here be simply repeated in a merely rhetorical way as Judg. v. 4; Job xv. 10. The poet does not shun then to call even those to his song whom his bitter censure must strike, the potentates. But also the poet would turn his whole attention to the beautiful production and presentation of the deeply meditated material, turn his ear to proverbial poesy, in order to watch for the most suitable form, ver. 5, similarly to the former poet, Ps. xlv. 2.

2. The connexion of thoughts of the first greater strophé is simple: why fear before the power of the evil man, vv. 6-7, since he with all treasures and all pride therein cannot redeem himself from death, because he has not the incorruptible God, exalted over all, for his friend, vv. 8-12. Therefore it must be

said: men who glitter in the highest splendour, but with this are devoid of (higher) insight, therefore know not how to protect and preserve themselves, because surrendered to blind chance and death, are in fact like to stupid cattle, *e.g.*, well-fattened young bullocks, which, in spite of their fine form and great strength, are strangled by wiser hands, and merit no better fate,—and this becomes the kernel-saying of the song, ver. 13. The clause—עֲוֹן, ver. 6—depends on בְּיָמֵי (§ 333 *b*). Ver. 8, אָח in this connexion cannot possibly be "brother;" for it comes to this, that no one can redeem *himself*, because every proud man stands nearest to himself alone, and seeks only to save himself, which all the following presupposes; also it is always elsewhere expressed אָחִיו with אִישׁ in the signification *brother*, for the words Ezek. xviii. 18 are of another kind. Nothing appears here so clear as that אָח is but another form (as Ezek. xviii. 10, xxi. 20) or rather false rendering for אַךְ, comp. ver. 16, according to which it then becomes necessary to read יִפְדֶּה. The second member explains it: God can be corrupted by the treasures of no man,—none can give Him, if in danger, ransom-money for his life. But if—in an intermediate clause it is almost ironically explained—God stands generally so high above men, that these, even if it were allowed, could not with all their treasures give a ransom sufficient for Him,—so that it must necessarily for ever cease, fail because of the too great cost (the כִּי in כְּשֵׁם as iv. 6); ver. 10 is then the true continuation to ver. 8, comp. § 347 *a*, and above, lxxii. 13-15.* Sharper contrast, ver. 11: if wise men even die (but how in the spiritual sense otherwise than fools, is very beautifully explained presently, ver. 16), how much more fools! But were קִרְבָּם, ver. 12, "their inward part," the sense must be: "their heart, their mind, their opinion is, their houses would be everlasting," to which then ver. 13 suited, in the sense:

---

* How far the language may be here used of an atonement-fine or *weregelt*, even in reference to God, is well explained from the Gentile customs, as the Egyptian in Herodot. ii., 65, comp. Diod. Sic. *Hist.*, i., 83.

but man remains not in pomp. But to begin with the last, this sense would be here plainly false; for thus the comparison with dumb cattle is not apprehensible; the kernel-saying must stand for itself and essentially run as in ver. 21, so that a ן more or less may be found, but the sense must not substantially be changed. In short, ver. 13 is, after ver. 21, unquestionably amended by יבין. This granted, then the above explanation of ver. 12 is not appropriate, and moreover would be in itself very strange and false. For קִרְבָּם or נֶפֶשׁ does not thus appear, there is no question of the duration of the houses, i.e, of the dwellings, and the last member would be superfluous. According to the old translation, קרבם is unquestionably = קברם, whether it be exchanged by the poet, or rather by copyists; for the whole Psalm has an unusually corrupt text; comp. *Koh.* xii. 5. More might be said for this, but this may suffice.

3. The last strophé proceeds from this equally dreadful and instructive end of the fools, and all who in the future follow their words and habits of thought, vv. 14, 15, but only the more briefly to set over against this the blessed end of the faithful, ver. 16; and thus concludes with energy, recurring to the beginning and end of the first strophe, vv. 17-21. Ver. 15 is divided quite against the Massôr. accentuation, and כִּמְבוּל or מִמְבוּל read as = זְבוּל. But as the shepherd drives the unwilling flock, which is already destined to the pit, = to death (שִׁית), xliv. 12, 23, death rules over them, without their being able at all to resist his power, comp. on the other hand Hos. xiii. 14, and here immediately ver. 16; in addition to this ver. 16, above, xvi. 9-11, and as a more ancient continuation, Hos. xiii. 14, and legend, Gen. v. 24. On ver. 19 comp. the further description of such a scene, Luke xii. 19, 20. On this כִּי see § 362 *b.** But it is quite to the purpose that

---

* I will not now further speak of this Psalm,—in our days much tormented and quite unnecessarily, since all that is above set forth is refuted by nobody. Comp. the *Jahrbb. der Bibl. Wiss.*, v., p. 255; xi., p. 308.

the poet towards the end of his didactic word, v. 19 *b*, for once, interrupting the ordinary calm of didactic speech, addresses the listener himself. This once occurs to him as in the zeal of his discourse, but immediately and properly he returns, ver. 20, back to the more tranquil language, and completes what he had begun, v. 19 *a*, to say concerning the *soul* of such men. Ver. 15 *b*. The Messianic hope flashes through.

64, 65. PSALMS XLII.—XLIII. AND PSALM LXXXIV.

evince themselves, by the stamp of the language, by arrangement and art, by the ebullient fulness of strange figures, finally by higher softness and tenderness of thought, to be so similar, and yet of the two songs each is so thoroughly original, and neither has proceeded from imitation of the other, that we are brought to the view that both belong to the same poet. And on comparison it is readily deduced that Pss. xlii.—xliii. must be the earlier by a wide space of time. But that the poet is a king driven into exile, is clear from lxxxiv. 10 (comp. xxviii. 8); and from xlii. 5 it follows at least, not in contradiction with this, that he was once a very conspicuous man in Jerusalem who led the festal train that yearly journeyed to the Temple. But we know of no king who before the destruction of Jerusalem was led over the Northern Jordan (xlii. 7) into exile, except Jechonja, a not inconsiderable man, according to Jer. xxiii. 28, 29, who after long sojourn in exile finally again comes to honour, 2 Kings xxv. 27. If these songs are from him, they teach us to recognize him more plainly than all historical information.

In Pss. xlii.—xliii. we see the poet violently detained by insolent foes on the other side of Jordan on the north-eastern boundary of Palestine, xlii. 7, 10, xliii. 2; and since the journey to Babylon has this direction, nothing prevents us from supposing that he at that time was detained there only temporarily,—perhaps, according to xlii. 9, only a night,—to be dragged further into exile. The circumstances are the most mournful and oppressive; all waves and floods of suffering are felt by the poet to be incessantly streaming in upon him.

He is most grievously wounded by the rash contempt of his foes against his God, who seems to have forsaken him, xlii. 4, 11, and whose lingering help he has long sadly missed, xlii. 10, xliii. 2; so that in the night he (ver. 9 comp. ver. 4) through this reflection sinks into the deepest melancholy, distressed by the stormy, scarce-to-be-soothed wish that he may finally escape from this flood of suffering to rest in the distant sanctuary. But if despondency thus moves most dangerously the surface of his soul, there lies on the other side in the depths of this soul another truth concealed, which strives not less to break forth and to dominate: the consciousness that there must be no doubt of God, becoming clear as the voice of the higher reflection and encouragement. The two opposite feelings here come into conflict with all violence and highest strain. But as in the divided soul grief and longing under the profound sufferings of the present is the most violent and prevailing of itself, against which the higher reflection maintains itself with difficulty,—despondency and revolt burst forth first, and longest, and with the greatest languor. But when this has had its way, and has become clear and manifest to itself in its outburst,—the more emphatically and earnestly then does the voice of the higher contemplation and reflection rise, as if chiding the too soft, too weak and distressed soul, encouraging and reviving, clothing itself in a brief, mighty kernel-saying of consolation, as the Divine voice rising against the human. But with the one rapid course of this excited struggle, the bosom of the poet is not yet fully calmed; still the nearest feeling of the uncommon griefs and sufferings is too strong, and the revolt and despondency, with difficulty repressed, recurs, by its outburst however calling forth also the counter-voice of reflection and encouragement. Thus the voice of despondency is repeated and alternately that of reflection three times, before reflection and encouragement alone remain dominant as the fixed disposition. Hence three quite equal strophes result, vv. 2-6; 7-12; xliii. 1-5. In this threefold removal of despondency there is at the same time an inner process, whilst by the influence of the ever-recurring deeper voice of reserve, despondency itself is gradually relieved and soothed. First the most grievous, bitterest outburst of despondency, ending in complete exhaustion and darkness, vv. 2-5; then, because grief, though repressed, nevertheless troublously recurs, it is lessened and softened by recollection of the Divine giver, so that he seeks to lose himself in a sad prayer for help, vv. 7-11 (despondency thus begins in itself to subside, and to clear away); finally, complete passing away of revolt in a prayer, even more restful, soft and joyous, xliii. 1-4. But while thus in three stages the rage of grief is more and more self-dissolved, and the troubled voice continues to change, the voice of solace, thrice resounding with mighty power, remains ever like to itself, because it contains the unchangeable Divine truth, to which the sufferer needs but to strive, to retain it finally as the permanent. And actually the two voices—which at first appear in complete disharmony and suggest opposition to one another, vv. 2-6, are at last resolved into a lovely harmony, feeling and understanding, excitement and reflection being entirely reconciled and inwardly coinciding, xliii. 1-5. All this without artificiality and violence: the faithful impression of the struggle of two principles waged in a mind of tender feeling no less than of balanced strength after reflection. The art is, at the same time, of the highest naturalness and purest inspiration. The particular points of description are also highly elegant and poetical.

In a poetic point of view this Psalm is perhaps the finest of all; but also the structure of its strophé is distinct. The long structure of the verse-members is indeed found not altogether rarely elsewhere in such songs as give rather severe contemplation than sudden movement of thoughts. But here it is carried through almost with complete uniformity, so that each strophé consists of ten such members, whilst the recurrent verse continually repeats its three so constructed verses.

1.

2 As a hart longs after water-brooks,
  so longs for Thee my soul, God!
  my soul pants for God, the living God;
  when shall I come and appear before God?
  tears were my food day and night,
  as they daily say to me, "where is Thy God?"
5 When I think of it, my heart must overflow,
  as I marched through thick throngs,
  led them away to the house of God,
  with clear jubilation, the festive-joyous multitude!—
  Why dost thou bow down, soul, and ragest in me greatly?
  wait for God! for yet shall I praise Him,
  my head's salvation and my God!

2.

My God! my soul bows down so greatly;
  therefore I think of Thee from Jordan and the
    Hermôn land, from the mount Miss'ar,
Flood calls to flood at the thunder of thy waterspouts;
  all Thy waves, billows streamed over me.—
In the day Jahvé appoints His grace,
  but by night the song abides with me, prayer to
    the God of my life;
10 I say to the God of my rock: "why hast Thou forgotten
    me?
  why go I mourning in foe's oppression?
  as it were shattering in my bones, my oppressors
    revile me,
  as they daily say to me, where is Thy God?"—
Why dost thou bow down, soul, and ragest in me greatly?
wait for God! for yet shall I praise Him,
my head's salvation and my God!

3.

1 Judge me, God!
  and lead my cause before the impious people,

from men of deceit and wickedness delivering me!
Thou art God of my defence; why hast Thou rejected me?
why go I mourning along in foe's oppression?
Send Thy light and Thy truth! let them lead me,
bring me to the sacred mount and Thy seat!
that I may come to the altar of God,
to the God of my highest joy,
and with the cither praise thee, O God, my God! 5
*Why dost thou bow down, soul, and ragest in me greatly?
wait for God! for yet shall I praise Him,
my head's salvation and my God.*

Ver. 3 *living God*, comp. ver. 9, lxxxiv. 3, at the same time as a contrast to the idol-images, by which the poet as given into the power of the heathen sees himself surrounded. On בְּאָמֹר ver. 4, comp. § 304 a; on עָלַי ver. 5, § 217 i: *I must gush forth my soul over me*, i.e., allow its free course over me, that it may bring me to despondency, comp. Job x. 1, xxx. 16. The present scorning of his God, ver. 4, which he must ever unwillingly listen to, drives the poet rather to flee to the recollection,—however mournful under present circumstances, and provocative of violent longing—of the proud pleasure he earlier enjoyed in the festal trains to the Temple of this very God,—which he now so grievously misses. The אֵלֶּה placed forward with emphasis,—*this*, is explained by the following כִּי, *as, since* with its clause (wherein אֶעֱבֹר, &c. is *imperf. præteriti*, § 136 c) and אֶדַּדֵּם forms by the power of the cohortative a kind of protasis, and עָלַי, אֵ an apodosis § 357 b, comp. lxxvii. 4. The ־ם in אַדַּדֵּם, whereby in passing allusion is made to the Israelites, the whole people, whom the poet as king led in the slowly solemn train (דדה) is in the following member more closely explained by הָמוֹן חוֹגֵג. But whilst with this sad recollection the speech of despair breaks off abruptly in the highest tension and excitement, there is gathered from this very recollection a hope in his deepest soul.

For if the poet could earlier praise God so joyously and serenely in the Temple, why should he not, when delivered, again be able to do so? So that the higher voice, after a moment of reflection, turning the thought to the future, breaks in upon the same ground, encouraging and consoling, ver. 6: whence it is clear that the kernel-word of consolation, precisely in this form is only here most appropriate, and afterwards is merely repeated. *My head's*, properly face's *salvation*, because it is a matter of life and death. Between ver. 6 and 7 אלהי has certainly fallen out, and the text at the end, ver. 6, is to be restored as ver. 12, xliii. 5; for also in the beginning of the following strophé the anxious אלהי would be ill missed.

2. In the impassioned half of the second strophé the strife between grief and endeavour after consolation is to be noticed, where the latter breaks through up to the framing of the prayer, but not yet restfully and permanently. First ver. 7, in reference to ver. 6: nevertheless the heart will not become tranquil; therefore I think on Thee, seeking consolation with Thee, ver. 5. The designation of localities, ver. 7, is involuntarily made with such exactness because they the more sadly awaken in him the recollection of the distant sanctuary. Because the Jordan in the north rises out of a confluence of many waters, between high mountains, the high northeast of the land may readily be called *the land of Jordan and of the Hermons*, for חֶרְמֹן originally denotes simply a high mountain summit. Such a plural was formerly found in the B. Hénókh vi. 6 ('Ερμονίν in G. Synkellos), comp. also the *Jahrbb. der Bibl. Wiss.*, iv., p. 170. (The accents separate the וחרמנים incorrectly.) When the poet here names the mountain Miss'ar not elsewhere found, this must be the more definite place where he at that time sojourned.

Indeed (ver. 8) sufferings incessantly stream over me, sent by Thee, or from heaven streaming down upon me, so that, like as a storm following the repeated thunder-voice, streams

down in increasing waterspouts and cataracts (מִשְׁבָּרֶיךָ LXX
τῶν καταρρακτῶν σου) so at the command of thy crashing
thunder-storm, as Thou sendest it from heaven, infinite floods
of sufferings come over me, one calling on the other, in ceaseless competitive sequence (the figure xviii. 5, 17, xxxii. 6) is
thus heightened by the fact that to the poet the flood-mass
wherein he seems to be perishing, seems as if sprung from a
Divine storm rolling over him and discharging itself; how
the thunder was conceived with the storm, comp. above
(Ps. xxix.) : but (ver. 9) not now, namely in the night time,
does Jahvé send His gracious help, for the day is the time of
action, of saving and of being saved, in the night I would
rather sing and pray in meditation to God; therefore I say
(ver. 10) even now in this night to the God of my rock,
my firmness and security (so distinctively God was not previously named, except in ver. 6) praying, pouring forth my
trouble in confidence. But the prayer begun passes over
once more, ver. 11, in the recollection of the keenly-wound-
ing speeches of the foes into sadness, so that no full relief and
calm follows, and after a fresh exhortation the prayer must
begin anew.

3. xliii. 1-4.—For בְּרֶצַח perhaps better because of the
following בְּ according to Symm. and a few Codd., כְּרֶצַח "as
if there were a shattering," as if I felt shattering in my bones,
so keenly striking through marrow and bones, wounding the
innermost man, are the slanders. Further, there are present
to the mind of our poet in xliii. 3, Ps. xxvii. 1, in xlii. 8 the
still simpler words of Jona ii. 4 (I., p. 155, *Dichter des A. B.*);
but it does not follow from this that he lived later than was
above indicated.—The שִׁירֹה xlii. 9, would necessarily according to this expression denote *his* (God's) *song;* but more
readily does שִׁירָה, found elsewhere, agree with the written form
of this piece and with the progress of the thoughts,=*song* is
with me, stands freely with me, namely *prayer to God,* as the
song here exactly conforms to this.

In Ps. lxxxiv. we see the poet on the other hand already a longer time in exile, settled, as vv. 5-8 makes clear, with many other banished ones, in the strange land. In him too here the glowing fire of the first passion and revolt is already quelled into gentler confidence and higher calm. But in quiet and in composure the hidden fire gleams forth the more intensely, unquenchably and powerfully, sparkling up in the king familiar with song and lyric strain, and incessantly breaking forth, however quelled by higher reflection. Such a warm outbreak from sadly-joyous recollection of the (still standing) Temple and from the need to moderate anew the oppressed grief, and ever anew to kindle the torch of hope—is this short, highly pregnant and suggestive song, which permits us to cast a refreshing glance into the depth of the tenderest and at the same time strongest soul. Here indeed no longer prevails the violent struggle of two opposite principles, as in the preceding song; but in this the present is like the preceding song, that the poet only by the outburst of sad and more widely deviating feelings and views opens the way to prayer, in the rest and composure of which the song blessedly and loftily ceases. First, then, the sadly-joyous, enthusiastically-yearning recollection of the Temple and of the true God; the banished one might almost envy the birds that nest in the Temple, vv. 2-4. Then, because the poet cannot now reach the goal of his longing, at least a congratulation of those who dwell at the place of the sanctuary (now unhappy, yet certainly once more happy) or those who have the Divine confidence, nobly self-rewarding, to journey thither, though under sore distress, vv. 5-8. Thus finally the thought falls back into the first joyous personal prayer, vv. 9-12, from which the singer, already strengthened, finally rises, ver. 13.

The first two strophes contain each eight verse-members. But justly the third is distinguished from them as that of pure prayer: it comprises ten members. Comp. for other particulars, I., p. 170, *Dichter des A. B.*

1.

How lovely are Thy seats,
    Jahvé of Hosts! 2
my soul longs, yea faints for Jahvé's courts;
    my heart and body—cry out to the living God.
Even the sparrow finds a house, and the swallow a nest
                                            for herself,
    where she sets her young,
at Thy altars, O Jahvé of Hosts,
    my king and my God!

2.

Hail to those inhabiting Thy house: 5
    still will they praise Thee!   *
Hail to men rich in strength in Thee,
    who gladly think on pilgrimages;
who passing through the balsam-vale make it a spring:
    yet a first rain covers it with blessings!
they go on from strength to strength,
    appear thus before God in Sion.

3.

Jahvé, God of Hosts, hear my prayer,
    observe, O Jakob's God!
our shield, O behold, God, 10
    look upon Thine anointed's countenance!
For better is a day in Thy courts than a thousand;
    to lie on the threshold in the house of my God
    is to me dearer than in impiety's tents to sojourn.
Sun indeed and shield is Jahvé God!
    grace, glory will Jahvé give,
    happiness not refuse to those walking in innocence.

4.

O Jahvé of Hosts,
    hail to the men who trust in Thee!

1. משכנת, ver. 2, corresponds to the rare expression, xliii. 3. The mere mention of the *courts*, ver. 3, shows that a layman is speaking. He, wholly with heart and body, his heart and body, therefore, cries out of sad longing to the beloved object. That birds, especially swallows, doves, or storks were freely allowed to nest in the Temple, is plain from passages of the classics in Bochart, *Hieroz.*, ii., pp. 592 sq., Lps. and of the Asiatics, comp. Hdt. i., 159 ; Porph. *de abstin.* iii., 16 ; Sacy's *Chrest. arabe*, tom. iii., pp. 76 sq., I. A., *Journal Asiatique*, 1838, Août, pp. 206, 214 ; it is still the case at the Ka'aba, see Burckhardt's *Travels in Arabia*, i., p. 277, and in Stambul (Lynch's *Narrative*, p. 88). The דְּרוֹר is merely, according to the now usual meaning, so translated ; for צִפּוֹר might very well signify the swallow ; LXX, Pesch. Targ. have *turtle-dove*, as if תֹּר=דְּרוֹר, but Aq. στρουθός, as all ancient translations of Prov. xxvi. 2.

2. Both the objects of congratulation, vv. 5-8, have indeed now to struggle with many sufferings, yet for both the poet anticipates final blessing. Those dwelling in the holy city, ver. 5, were at that time, in the last years of Juda, *not* happy ; but the poet thinks and hopes they would *yet* again be able to rejoice in the Divine victory, quite as xvii. 6. Those who, dispersed in the strange land, think of pilgrim-journeys to the Temple, on whom the poet, because they are nearest to him, longest dwells, have indeed also infinite sufferings and griefs in the recollection of the separation, hindrances, and restraints in the foreign land, and the dangers by the way ; but he who is rich in strength and trust in God overcomes them all. The poet accompanies with his full longing and love these pilgrims, whom he himself may not follow,—at least in his eager fancy, —through the dangers of the way up to the final arrival at the place of highest delight. Passing through the driest valley (the *Baka-vale*, *i.e.*, the dry ground wherein the balsam-plant grows, comp. Burckhardt's *Syr.*, pp. 977, 1081,—at the same time the name alludes to בְּכִי, " weeping," as will immediately

follow), they wash the waterless vale by the ceaseless stream of their tears, as at a spring, flowing ; but this stream of tears in Divine sorrow becomes at the same time a fructifying *rain*, *yet a first rain covers with blessings the dry vale* (in the beginning of winter) so that they, instead of wearying on the way, when out of their tears finally blessings spring forth, *ever more strongly* and boldly *advance*, finally attaining the wished-for good. Comp. the figure more simply, Hos. ii. 17, Isa. xxxv. 7, and the observations in the *Gesch. des V. Isr.*, iii., p. 385, of the third edition. The entrance to Palestine is actually dry and desert. On גם, ver. 7, see § 354 *a*.

3. Ver. 10 : *behold the countenance*, turned in humble supplication to Thee, *of Thine anointed*, who, therefore, can be none but the speaker: this lies unmistakably in the whole connexion ; comp. below cxxxii. 10. The הסתופף, LXX correctly παραῤῥιπτεῖσθαι, is properly to cast oneself on the threshold, into the dust, like the humblest servant (comp. an example in Burckhardt's *Travels in Arabia*, ii., p. 270) : he who according to his royal dignity would have the highest honour in the Temple, will rather appear there as the humblest servant than dwell among sinful heathen (דהר, *door*, Syr., here only, a rare word). Also the figure of the *sun*, ver. 12, nowhere further appears; elsewhere earlier the more general *light* stands for it ; comp., however, lxxii. 5, 17.

B. 66. PSALM XXII

is in this period one of the most important songs. So vividly does it set forth the struggle with the extremest sufferings, and how, nevertheless, in them the faithful does not lose all hope, that nothing greater in this kind can be expected. That the Temple still stood, follows from the mention of the sacrifices (then) to be brought, and vows to be paid, ver. 27, comp. with ver. 4. But the poet seems to be quite peculiarly persecuted by the heathen ; he was therefore already in exile. The whole song bears such a stamp and style as if the poet sharply separated the two, the heathen and Israelitish nature, and suffered from the former, by the latter lived and hoped, as he also, vv. 28-30, expects the final victory of the latter over the former. More closely to get upon the poet's traces is not now possible. Thus much is clear from ver. 9, that the very boldness of his confidence in Jahvé's religion, and his open confession of it, together with the honesty and virtue therewith connected, of his behaviour, have drawn upon him the keenest scorn and the sorest sufferings; he is already surrounded by sanguinary men, taken prisoner, ver. 19, and, according to unequivocal signs, threatened with death, vv. 14, 19, 21, 22. And although he, in his prolonged distress, has already often cried to the faithfully honoured Jahvé, he has remained without deliverance, and thus weaker and more worn down, the more exposed to the scorn of his foes, vv. 3-9, 15, 18. There actually gleams from the whole an amount of suffering such as can hardly be surpassed in severity, along with a state of mind in the hour of crisis, most free from guilt, and from ill-will to his foes; and there is no cursing even in the bitterest agony. So prays here the noble sufferer on the approach of death, carefully preserving himself from the last despair and urgently desiring to become conscious of all grounds of hope in Jahvé, without, indeed, a definite prospect of obtaining an escape from those great sufferings,—only sadly languishing and complaining, but at last,—at least in the taking of a sincere vow of true thanks after deliverance, and in the joyous picture of the fair consequence of his release,—obtaining some tranquillity and repose, and intenser hopes for the more remote future. Thus the long languishing song falls into three similar strophés,—at first the outbreak of despair in troublous urgency is gradually somewhat softened and so far driven away, that it is resolved into the burst of supplication to God, vv. 2-12; then, after the prevailing disquiet has come, at least as far as this beginning of prayer, more calmly the setting forth of the most horribly threatening dangers and gigantic sufferings begins,—causing the cry for help to be the more urgently repeated, vv. 13-22; finally, though no nearer hope and means of rest appears, yet at least some self-calming and strengthening in the taking of a sincere vow of true thanksgiving after deliverance follows,—until the picture of the bitter present is softened in reflection on the high thanksgiving then to be brought, and the other glorious consequences of deliverance. The spirit of the poet becomes as it were glowing in feeling and hope, dwells more fondly and longer,—more enthusiastically,—on the pictures of the fair and grand future, and therewith concludes; and the mightier thereby the calm consolation becomes, vv. 23-32. And here at least the intimation breaks in, clearly and unrestrainedly, that the very party, now so extremely unhappy, represented by the poet, will one day certainly prevail. In the general progress, the language is often meantime violently moved in the midst of its flow by extreme sadness and passionately strained or broken, vv. 9, 14, 16, 27.

No previous Psalm has such long extended strophes: but this is explained readily by its contents and nature, and the most important point under this head is only that in so wide a compass, so uniform a structure recurs. Of the three strophes the second and the third have each ten verses, but with twenty-four members each; if the first has eleven verses but twenty-two members, a two-membered verse has probably been lost from it.

1.

My God, my God, why hast Thou forsaken me,   2
    far my deliverance, words of my groaning!—
my God! I cry by day—Thou hearest not,
    and by night—and have no rest.
And Thou art nevertheless the Holy One,
    throned in the praise of Israel:
on Thee trusted our fathers,   5
    trusted—and Thou becamest their saviour,

complaining to Thee they were freed,
trusting in Thee they were not ashamed.
But I—a worm, no man,
scorn of the people, despised by the folk;
all who see me, scoff at me,
cleaving the lips, shaking the head:
"he trusted in God; let Him save him,
set him free, because He loves him!"
10 For Thou art He who drew me out of the womb,
who caused me to rest on my mother's breast;
on Thee was I cast since my birth,
from my mother's womb Thou art my God;
O be not far from me, for distress is near,
for help is none!

2.

Many beasts have surrounded me,
Basan's mighty ones encompassed me,
with gaping mouth against me;
—a lion tearing in pieces and roaring!—
15 Like water am I poured out,
all my bones stand out;
my heart is become like wax;
melted deep in my bosom;
like dry potsherds my skin in my mouth,
and my tongue cleaves to my palate:
—and to death's dust will Thou bring me?
For dogs have surrounded me,
the band of evil-doers environs me,
have bound my hands and feet;
I count all my bones:
they—look, feed upon me,
they divide among them my garments
and cast the lot over my clothing.
20 But Thou, Jahvé, be not far,
Thou my strength, hasten to my help,

free from the sword my soul,
 from the power of the dog my only one!
help me from the lion's mouth,
 and from the buffalo's horns hear me!

3.

I will tell Thy name to brethren,
 in the midst of the congregation praise Thee!
"ye fearers of Jahvé, praise Him,
 ye Jakob's children all, honour him,
  and bow before Him, all children of Israel!
for He hath not despised, shunned the sufferer's 25
     sufferings,
 hath not hidden His face from him,
 and when he cried to Him, He hath heard."
From Thee my praise shall proceed—in the great
    people's assembly,
 vows will I pay before His fearers;
that such sufferers shall enjoy and be refreshed,
 that they shall praise Jahvé who seek Him:
—may your heart live for ever!—
that mindful of this to Jahvé may turn—all ends of the
    earth,
 and do homage before Thee all heathen-tribes:
for Jahvé's is the kingdom,
 and He will rule over heathen.
In enjoyment all earth's mourners do homage, 30
—before Him bend all that are sinking into the dust,
 and he who prolonged not his life.
The children shall serve Him,
 the after-world is told of the Lord:
they come and announce His salvation,
 to the young people, that He wrought it!

1. The first strophé, beginning with the outburst of comfortless despondency, ver. 2, reaches its end with the

confident prayer, ver. 12. These opposites are connected by the agonized complaint concerning the endless vain cry for help, ver. 3, because Jahvé is nevertheless the Holy One (not enduring wrong), and as such rules in praise in the community, ver. 4,—as moreover, He on the testimony of ancient history, saved their forefathers, when they cried in confidence, vv. 5, 6; while the poet on the other hand is the most down-trodden and generally despised man, scarcely still man, most deeply scorned because of his very confidence in Jahvé, vv. 7-9; and in fact the senseless cruel scoffers must have a bitter justification in their demand that Jahvé shall help him; for certainly the poet from the first moment of his life as one born and grown up in the community of Jahvé was directed to Jahvé as his tutelary God: let Him then save him! vv. 10-12. So through deep grief and the most manifold and urgent thoughts preparing himself for confident prayer, the poet yet has not been able to describe more clearly the immediate dangers, or the foes that threaten his life: therefore, before the prayer is completed, the description of the foes stands apart, in a new, calm strophé, at the end of which then vv. 20-22, the more urgently the same prayer recurs. The name יֹשֵׁב תְהִלּוֹת is formed anew from the older more frequent יֹשֵׁב הַכְּרֻבִים *he who sits upon the Kerúbim*, i.e., dwells in the place of the ark of the covenant, throned above the K. (1 Sam. iv. 4, 2 Sam. vi. 2; later repeated, Ps. xcix. 1, lxxx. 2), so that it describes still more spiritually the relation of Jahvé to the Temple; "He who is seated on Israel's praises," or throned where these resound. The LXX: ἐν ἁγίῳ κατοικεῖς, ὁ ἔπαινος τοῦ Ἰσρ., less correct and easy. הֶפְטִיר "cleave," can, the more it metaphorically in such connexion, denotes scoffing (by indecent opening of the mouth), the more readily be connected immediately with בְּ: scoff with the lip, comp. Job xvi. 10. The *shaking of the head* is that passing over from astonishment into scorn,—hard, unbecoming, xliv. 15, cix. 25; Lam. ii. 15. The כֹּל, ver. 9, is in this connexion certainly best taken as perfect, LXX ἤλπισε, whether בל be taken as perfect, with intransitive force for the sake of the meaning "forsake oneself," properly wallow, cast upon any one his care, or whether גֹּל be read on the supposition that the Massoretes had taken the word here erroneously for an infinitive; but the first assumption is sufficient. In the second member, "because *he* loves" is, in conformity to the first, and because of the sharper scorn, to be referred back to the man.

2. In the second strophé, as far as the renewed cry for help, ver. 20, the description of the cruel and violent man, before whose death-threatening attack the poet sees no help, is the main matter; but with the feeling of this suffering coming from without there mingles soon that of the inward life, of the entire dissolution and wasting of all forces of the body and of the thereby threatening approach of death. Harassed by this twofold danger, the soul of the poet wanders in the description from one to the other, beginning in a subdued manner the description of each of the two sufferings, but soon becoming too agitated and concluding abruptly, vv. 13-14; 15-16. Only the third time does a new description running a somewhat calmer course, succeed, whilst now the two sufferings are taken in their reciprocal connexion,—namely, how the persecutors, through whose cruelty the poet has chiefly come into this sad bodily condition, again so bitterly mock at him, and because of the weakness of the wretched man, persecute him the more heartlessly, vv. 17-19, so that Jahvé alone can help, vv. 20-22. Yet as along with this current of thought the glance at the persecutors is here the principal thing, and firmly as the poet holds together again that which falls asunder, it is further clear that, as he from the first, ver. 13, had named the persecutors strong raging beasts (those of Basan) which rushed upon him like a bloodthirsty lion, then in the new addition, ver. 15, in respect of their shameless temper,—dogs, —so at the conclusion, rightly, in inverted reference, first protection from shameless dogs, ver. 21, then at last from the lion

and buffaloes is desired, so that the last words of the strophé, v. 22, recur to the figure of the beginning, ver. 13. Horrible is the picture here sketched in a few features of the inner dissolution: *like water is he gushed out*, without any inward firmness more,—his bones on the fainting, emaciated body, standing far out, so that they can be numbered (comp. above on cxli. 7), and the innermost life-force at the same time seems as if consumed by most burning fire. Hence also in consequence of the inner glow kindled by intense anguish, one dried of all life-forces, especially in the mouth, ever in vain complaining, xxxii. 3, 4 (but in the transition of the language from ver. 15 to ver. 16 it is necessary here to read for חִכִּי, *my strength*, not לֵחִי, *my sap*, after xxxii. 3, but חִכִּי, *my palate*, after the following member, as Saadia in the *Beiträgen zur gesch. der A. Tlichen Auslegung*, i., p. 24, thought. The more general word *strength* is here unsuitable to the figure). Must not then the poet for a moment at least be imposed upon by the fear that God will turn him into the dust of death, cause his already all but perished body entirely to crumble into death and dust (ver. 30) (שָׁפַת, bring, make לְ to something, as elsewhere שִׂים). But far worse than this is the view of those who scorn the miserable one because of his unutterable sufferings, who have bound him in narrow bonds, and because they have already condemned him to death, now cast the lot upon his upper garments, in order to divide them amongst themselves— as the custom was in the case of the condemned. In this connexion כארי, ver. 17, is quite plainly to be understood of the fettering of the hands and feet; anything else is not here suitable. The root כור, כאר, כחר denotes a compressing, enveloping, encompassing, therefore fettering; but related is also *kahar*, Arab., to tame, force. It is easiest to read in the *perf.* כָּאֲרוּ, for which many historical proofs offer themselves. Were כארי correct, in the *part.* כֹּאֲרֵי must be expressed, but less appropriately. The LXX have ὤρυξαν, as if it were = כָּרוּ from כרה; but it is by no means clear what the digging or piercing through of the hands and feet can here denote; for that the poet would say he is already in the last torture inflicted by his foes, perhaps on the cross, is against the rest of the connexion of the song, particularly against the just given description, vv. 15 sq. The vehemence of Christian-Jewish polemics, which were connected with this word, seems to have introduced into the existing impression of the text the reading כָּאֲרִי, which can alone be explained, "as the lion" (they surround) my hands and feet: but neither does the figure of the surrounding suit, nor does the figure of the lion generally in this place; for here the unabashed behaviour is to be marked.

3. Thus there seems in all the present to be no prospect of help at all remaining for him already as one hunted to death. It appears that he can but be dumb in despair, because that glorious hope does not immediately appear which we perceived in the case of the poet of Pss. xvi., xlix. But now he raises, after a short terrible pause, his eyes to the only spot at least of the more remote future to which his glance still is unfettered, —first gently, scarce taking breath, then ever more strongly; and wondrous is it to note in the last strophé the gradual glimmering and kindling of the fire of hope, under all the external hopelessness. A near prospect to which the sufferer ventures to lift his eyes, leads him on to the more remote, this again by itself to the still more remote and loftier; until, out of the first timid expression of a sincere vow, the fire of most glowing hope and presentiment is kindled, he revels in the secure hope of the final victory of the religion of Jahvé, and in this picture of the end of all confusions and sufferings upon earth, the long languishing song finds its rest and its end. In fact, the presentiments of the poet are not too enthusiastic. For if generally an endless chain of great consequences may be connected with an event, the poet had the justest cause to hope the most important consequences for his deliverance. For not only, it is evident, had it come with

the poet to that extreme that his example and fate must be a crisis and turning-point for the whole Jahvé-religion of that time, as it may be readily supposed that he was a very important person of that time; but the deliverance from the deepest sufferings must most powerfully impel him to become the most eloquent, boldest, and most active consoler and saviour of the many like sufferers. Already this design and this impulse breaks forth in a strong current, so soon as he, at present without any help and solace, turns to vows, and therewith to thoughts of the future; and the noble fire,—become through suffering still brighter and more intense—of the sufferer thus at last finds an issue for itself. Then soon there breaks forth ever more glowingly, the representation of the pure pleasure wherewith he then shall eloquently praise Jahvé, exhort and console all; refresh the mass of the sufferers in every way— yea, for ever, according to his wish! vv. 23-27. But once let there be so strong and general an exaltation in Israel, its power must break outward, and awaken the heathen to share in the salvation of Israel. If the poet's fancy has thus been warmed by the picture of that internal prosperity, it advances consequently further, and feeds itself still more on the picture of the conversion of the Gentiles, only possible after Israel's exaltation,—the heathen who now so cruelly persecute the poet; and of the fulfilment of the kingdom of Jahvé, all-embracing, poor and rich, heathen and Israelites,—Messianic presentiments, which awakened long before the poet, appear to him here in a strangely new connexion and with new truth, vv. 28-30; and concludes with *the* presentiment, that this exaltation, because of its very light and its strength, will have eternal issues, and will never pass away from memory, vv. 31, 32. The deepest, most comfortless sufferings, require the most exalted hopes or at least presentiments; and those here arising are truly the noblest and most modest, taking hold of the poet by a peculiar Divine power, and calming him in the most intractable grief. The אֶכְלַּיו, ver. 27, refers indeed in the first instance to the rich thank-offerings, but the outward eating and drinking is not the most important thing, and the object in thank-offerings at least should not be so. But with this sacred food and the physical enjoyment which the poet can by no means exclude in the case of the needy, the spiritual is to be united; the true satisfaction and refreshment is here also not described as merely bodily; and it cannot be doubtful in what the poet places true happiness (although he is also greatly concerned to remove bodily distress). *Mindful of this*, ver. 28, of the true salvation that they see in Israel, and of which also they have a repressed obscure presentiment, and for which a longing. On מוֹשֵׁל, ver. 29, comp. § 200, on וְנַפְשׁוֹ, ver. 30, comp. on the relative clause, § 350 b. With the אָכְלוּ וַיִּשְׁתַּחֲווּ, the poet, going back to ver. 27 (hence the *perf.* of that seen in fancy as already taken place), comprises the two figures hitherto separated; both all the rich of the earth, to whom, according to the conditions of that time especially powerful Gentiles belonged, and the languishing ones, then become blessed in the enjoyment of the holy peace and the truths of the Temple. But to take דִּשְׁנֵי, as *fat, i.e.,* rich ones, is harsh, and since the poet—although he hopes for the ultimate conversion of all—has immediately before his eyes the many deeply bowed down and persecuted generally—the word will be better explained as דִּשְׁנֵי, *covered with dust, i.e.,* mourning ones. What a grand spectacle,—to see *all* men of the earth, and pre-eminently the many, now utterly comfortless, united in such delight! לְדוֹר, ver. 31, "to the generation," *i.e.,* when older or riper men speak, to the forming generation, to the young contemporary world, or shortly (as we say) to the world, lxxi. 18; but more exactly, ver. 32; *they will come*, those not in existence, *and announce*, = future men will announce to the *born* people, *i.e.,* to those just born, therefore to the young, Ps. cii. 19, that He *wrought*, as in lii. 11.*

---

* On the gross mistakes which a later expositor commits in reference to this Psalm, see the *Jahrbb. der Bibl. Wiss.*, ix., pp. 165-168.

67-76. Psalms xxv., xxxiv., xxxv., xxxviii., xl., li., lxix—lxxi., cix., cii.

This considerable series of Psalms belongs again, according to all discoverable traces, to the same poet; in the case of Ps. cii. there might be a doubt whether it belongs certainly to this place; although with regard to it the probability predominates.—If we,—which is always the first point,—look at the particular personality of the poet, from all these songs there clearly appear the most peculiar traits of the same personality.

Nowhere do we behold the poet in the vicinity of the sanctuary, or even only of the Temple, full of wistful recollection; he vows to give public praise to God for deliverance and grace, xxxv. 9, 10, 28; xl. 4 sqq., 17; li. 15 sqq.; lxix. 31 sqq.; lxxi. 14 sqq.; cix. 30, comp. lxxxviii. 11-13, but nowhere does he take this vow in the way of the previously explained songs of the second period, that is, as if he would bring sacrifices in the Temple, and then sing thanksgiving and didactic songs. He had therefore from the first his situation far from Jerusalem, which he scarcely knows, probably among the Gentiles in exile, but survived the destruction of Jerusalem and of the Temple; for in his later songs he is jealous (as if the misfortune of Israel had been completed) for the honour of the destroyed Temple and of religion, and prays for the prosperity of Jerusalem and of Juda, and the redemption of Israel, li. 20; lxix. 10, 36, 37; lxxi. 20; xxv. 22; cii. 14 sqq. According to his position in the people, he is indeed from the first a very considerable and influential man, to whom many look with expectation, and who later, through the troubles of the time and the persecution of men, fell from his external dignity, lxxi. 21, comp. ver. 11; lxix. 7; and only from such a powerful, almost princely, position, is the peculiar Ps. li. completely explained. But nowhere is it clear that he has anything prophetic in himself or struggles against prophets.

He is manifestly a layman, probably a warrior from the royal house;* his song starts only from personal dangers or experiences, and although he vows as the best thanksgiving the loud public praise of Jahvé, and the instruction therewith related of the inexperienced, and not only so, but also confirms this (comp. the places before named), he nevertheless remains generally far removed from the peculiar prophetic height and position.

If the mind of the poet be examined, this mighty man shows an extreme softness, indeed tenderness of feeling, which leads him to take the most loving part in the weal or woe of others, and claims on this behalf also the compassion of others, xxxv. 12-14, xxxviii. 21, lxix. 10-12, 21, 22, cix. 4 sqq., and sorrowfully misses the friends who tarry, xxxv. 15, xxxviii, 12, lxix. 9, 21, cii. 7-9: in addition to this, the most hearty openness and honesty, xxxviii, 10, 18, 19, xl. 10, 11, li. 8 sqq., lxix. 6, 20; but partly also a very ready revolt and excitement of feeling, yea of passion and sinful haste,—to recall Ps. li. only. And certainly a warm open heart, such as the poet shows, precisely in these last extremely confused and immoral times could be very readily carried away to momentary revolt and passion. But sore was the conflict and the misery into which he thus fell; not merely with the world, with his acquaintances and friends he even falls out, and sees himself everywhere accused, despised and persecuted; not merely has he to struggle with weakness and sickness, the consequences of such a passionately disturbed and harassed life; but he

---

* Or perhaps even a king's heir, although not the Joachaz led away to Ægypt (*Gesch. des V. Isr.*, iii., p. 720, of the 2nd edition). The words, lxxi. 21, actually sound too lofty to allow us to think of a poet of a common rank. But if the poet was a man of such high standing, it is explained how his songs—although some of them are not precisely of the highest value—might have been nevertheless so carefully preserved.—The LXX have with Ps. lxxi. the superscription, as if it was composed "*by the sons of Jônadab, and the first who were led away.*" The inventor of this notion was not then deceived as to the age of the song, and sought for the poet only too limitedly among the Rekhabites, Jer. xxxv., as if these alone could at that time have been so pious.

has also soon to undergo the still sorer struggle with experiences of his own mind, and painfully to urge that he may not lose the holy spirit. In fact the poet stands in his long and thousand-fold oppressed life, often approaching to despair, the type of all sufferings of Israel in that severe transitional time. And as a nameless grief at that time befell the whole people, the poet often knows hardly aught but fasting and mourning garments, xxxv. 13, lxix. 11, 12, cix. 24. But again, *the* true God forsakes him not, to whom he in each trying situation directs the never long silent, never utterly troubled cravings and utterances of his spirit. He who has most deeply experienced in himself the nature of sin and guilt, obtains even in those most unhappy of times the victory still in God, advances from one wondrous deliverance and inner exaltation to another, and reaches finally, ripe in Divine strength and solace, to that higher blessed age, when he can be to the younger generation still an eloquent and happy preacher of the true Divine life, Ps. lxxi. Pre-eminently in the life and song of the poet the idea of guilt and sin is developed to an acuteness and clearness which is nowhere earlier or elsewhere found in the Old Testament. Nothing more is wanting here than what some time later, at the end of the exile, experience was to teach on a great scale,—namely that innocence may also be *for* other sufferings. And along with this the truth comes to full validity that true penitence and the genuine Divine life must show themselves quite otherwise than in the Temple-sacrifices, quite impossible to the poet, especially at that time, xl. 7-11, li. 15, 21, lxix. 31-33. Certainly one cannot wonder enough that by the side of such dull and gloomy pictures as Pss. xxxv., xxxviii., lxix., cix., the genuine pictures of that whole dreary time, such extraordinary noble elevations of feeling are found as in Pss. xl., li., lxxi., xxxiv. Thus this whole personality stands forth as unique in the Psalter, not indeed as one of the greatest, but as one of the most remarkable and most instructive; although hitherto we have not succeeded in tracing it to its place in the rest of known history.

The style too of the song is throughout the same, melting and diffuse, with difficulty collecting and rounding itself off, sometimes spasmodically broken off, xxxviii. 10-15, lxix. 6, 20, generally quite as the impress of the times was bound to form it in so soft an elegiac poet. Pre-eminently certain songs suffer from these long measures, Pss. cii., lxix., and still more, P's. cix. The language is entirely artless, while many poets, whose songs have been explained, are found of a certain intentional art. In details, the language has especially the following peculiarities: the poet is in the habit of terming his foes אֹיְבִי חִנָּם (שֶׁקֶר) (and the word חָנָם is generally a favourite expression with him) xxxv. 19, xxxviii. 20, lxix. 5; xxxv. 7, cix. 8, or such as requite him evil instead of good, hate instead of love, xxxv. 12, xxxviii. 21, cix. 4, 5, who seek or meditate his ill, or rejoice in it, xxxv. 4, 26, xxxviii. 13, xl. 15, 16, lxxi. 10, 13, 24, who secretly persecute him, שׂטם (a verb found nowhere else) xxxviii. 21. lxxi. 1, 13, cix. 4, 20, 29 ; they shall therefore blush and incur shame, comp. xxxv. 4, 26, xl. 15, lxix. 7, lxxi. 1, 13, 24, cix. 29, xxv. 2, 3, 20, xxxiv. 6. He, on the other hand, feels his mishaps to be divine blows, as heat and wrath from above, xxxviii. 3 sqq., lxix. 25, 27, cii. 4, 5, 11, or as a flood, a fountain wherein he is on the point of sinking, of swooning away, xl. 3, lxix. 2, 3, 15, 16 (lxxxviii. 7, 8, 18), figures which perhaps no poet elsewhere so marks with such preference and in such detail, and in which many rare words, almost peculiar to this poet, recur, מְצוּלָה lxix. 3, 16 (lxxxviii. 7) טִיט and יָוֵן xl. 3, lxix. 3, 15; he fears lest his foot may stagger, and feels it again at other times firm, xxxviii. 17, xl. 3 (xxxv. 7, 8, xxv. 15), comp. xxvi. 1, 12, lest his strength, the light of his eyes forsake him, xxxviii. 11, xl. 13, lxix. 4 (comp. vv. 24, lxxxviii. 10), Jahvé he loves everywhere to term *his* God, xxxv. 23, 24, xxxviii. 16, 22, xl. 9, 18, lxix. 4, lxxi. 4, 12, 22, cix. 26, xxv. 2, or

אֲדֹנָי יהוה, an expression which at least is not frequent with every poet, lxix. 7, cix. 21, lxxi. 16, and knows most vividly that he has sinned against Him *alone* and Him alone must praise, li. 6, lxxi. 16. Besides this there are found many words, partly of peculiar usage, partly rare, as תְּהִלָּה in this connexion, xxxv. 28, lxxi. 6, 8. 14, cix. 1, xxxiv. 2 and הָגָה xxxv. 28, xxxviii. 13, lxxi. 24, עָלַץ xxxv. 15, xxxviii. 18; אָגִילָה xxxviii. 6, 19, lxix. 6; בָּשֵׁת xl. 16, cix. 29, comp. lxix. 20, xxxv. 26 רָדַף persecute *that which is good*, xxxiv. 15, xxxviii. 21; and all previous songs עָנִי is not yet so frequent as here, xxxv. 10, xl. 18, lxix. 30, lxxviii. 16, cix. 16, 22, xxv. 16, 18, xxxiv. 7;—תָּמִיד is a favourite expression, xxv. 15, xxxiv. 2, xxxv. 27, xl. 12, 17, lxxi. 3, 6. cix. 15, as well as נֶגֶד xxxviii. 10, 12, 18, li. 5, lxix. 20, lxxxviii. 2, cix. 15, also *it is continually before me, i.e.*, I know it very well, xxxviii. 18, li. 5, cix. 15, where such more ancient passages as 1. 8, Jer. vi. 7 (comp. B. Jos. xlix. 16, lix. 12) may have passed before the poet's mind. Many others will be mentioned below. Conversely, there are wanting in this poet thoughts and words which elsewhere are the most customary, as *e.g.*, the phrase "hear my prayer!" which according to the Davidic iv. 2, is so frequent in the beginning of the songs of these times, scarcely ever appears here, comp. cii. 2, xxxv. 13, lxix. 14; or as רשע which in the Davidic and in other songs, especially Ps. xxxvii., is so endlessly frequent, appears here but very sparingly, and in the earlier songs of this series not at all, cix. 2, 6, 7, lxxi. 4, xxxiv. 22, הם and ישר only in the didactic poem, xxv. 8, 21.—In what concerns the position of these songs in the Psalter, at least xxxiv., xxxv., xxxviii., xl., and then lxix., lxx., lxxi. stand so together, that in this fact may be found a confirmation of this view of their common origin. Even Ps. lxx. is but the separated better half of Ps. xl., comp. Vol. 1., p. 8.

One might be tempted to bring Ps. xxii. also into this series, because it too shows a great resemblance in many ways, both in contents and in the style of the song (the structure of the strophés in Pss. xxii. and xxxv. is peculiarly similar) and as the language, e.g., יְחִידָתִי my only one, i.e., my dearest, irreparable good, my soul, xxii. 21; xxxv. 17: the vow to praise God בְּרַ־ בְּקָהָל xxii. 23, 26; xxxv. 17; xl. 10; cix. 30; the cry be not far! xxii. 12, 20 (comp. ver. 2); xxxv. 22; xxxviii. 22; lxxi. 12; comp. cix. 17 and the related haste to my help! xxii. 20; xxxviii. 23; xl. 14, 18 (lxx. 6); lxxi. 12; further שַׁאֲגִ of strong complaint xxii. 2, xxxviii. 9, אֱיָלוּת xxiii. 20, and אֱיָל lxxxviii. 5, and some other instances of the kind. But an unforced and thoroughgoing similarity is nevertheless not found. More original force, more intensity and concealed glow, more boldly poetical and striking elements are manifestly found in Ps. xxii.; and the mood is perhaps of a somewhat different kind. The historical pre-supposition of the Temple with its vows and sacrifices, xxii. 23-27, is entirely wanting in this poet. Just so, neither in Ps. xxii. nor Ps. xxxv. is it presupposed that the poet has already experienced a great deliverance from such sufferings, and yet these two songs manifestly belong to the same circumstances. Finally, it is decisive that lxxi. 6 is an unmistakable imitation and transformation of xxii. 10. The partial similarity appears rather explicable from the fact, that the fruitful poet of these songs had already heard that somewhat earlier and much more distinguished song, and had it deeply impressed on his mind. The great impression that Ps. xxii. early made, is also obvious from quite another source; much of it is re-echoed verbally in Isa. xl. sqq., as קָדוֹשׁ, xxii. 4, so shortly for קְדוֹשׁ יִשְׂרָאֵל, תּוֹלַעַת, xxii. 7, Isa. xli. 14, בְּזוּי עָם Isa. xlix. 7, liii. 3; this prophet must also have found patterns for his lofty pictures of the servant of Jahvé, and where did he find them so clearly as in Pss. xxii., lxix.?

To Ps. xxxi. also these songs have a certain resemblance, and they would then be derived from Jérémjá, in favour of which theory something may be said. But this is not a thorough resemblance, as *e.g.*, Jérémjá does not use the word יְשׁוּעָה of which our poet is fond along with תְּשׁוּעָה, xxxv. 3, 9; lxxxviii. 2; xxxviii. 23; xl. 11, 17; lxxi. 15. And further it is decisive that the beginning of Ps. lxxi. is manifestly a transformation of Ps. xxxi.—On Ps. lxxxviii. which also bears great resemblance, comp. Vol. I., pp. 307 sqq.

The situation which comes to light in Pss. xxxv. and xxxviii. is this: the poet, probably according to the figures xxxv. 2, 3, pursued by mighty warriors, has fallen into dangerous sickness, xxxv. 15, xxxviii. 2-9, 17, 18. Over this not merely do many of the particular friends and acquaintances of the poet scornfully rejoice, especially because he plainly belonged to the stricter adherents of the Jahvé religion (xxxv. 20), but seek also cunning pretexts for the complete destruction of him in his feebleness, partly beset by the superstition that the misfortunes of the poet show the guilt of his party and his own, partly from the wanton love of destruction. Incessantly they accuse him of crimes of which he knows himself to be entirely free; he is to confess that of which he is ignorant, and his innocence and quiet only invite their rash scorn and their rage, xxxv. 7, 11, 12, 15, 16, 21, xxxviii. 13. This cruelty vexes the poet, who feels himself entirely free from such culpability; and the more deeply, because he had ever shown the very men who now torment him because of his sickness, at an earlier date the sincerest compassion and the most hearty affection; when they were ill, he had deeply mourned and prayed on their behalf, xxxv. 12, 13, 14, xxxviii. 21. But nowhere else does he see help save in the eternal, righteous Jahve!

Ps. xxxv. is from the first period of these relations. The poet still feels less the pains, fears less the consequences of the sickness, than the cruel persecution of the scornful friends, who have changed into open foes, especially of a leader of them, ver. 8; and in violent embitterment at the unjust persecution, the rude slander, the wild, scoffing, shameful joy of the tyrants; he cries here—meekly and speedily overcoming despair—for help to Jahvé, promising for deliverance the warmest thanks. As the lament here for the first time gushes forth, it seeks entirely to exhaust itself in the long well-ordered song. Wishing for a forcible deliverance and a stormy repulse of the violent foe, the plaint to Jahvé opens in violent excitement, vv. 1-10, then more calmly and at the same time sadly the situation of the suppliant, according to its origin, and the cruelty of the thankless friends is described, till gradually the dejection again increases, and the cry for help powerfully recurs, vv. 11-19. Finally, there is yet a glance more into the general subject—how in truth those who now persecute the poet with such shameful delight, persecute in general all peaceful men, and so the most urgent, explicit prayer for deliverance of him with whose security that of many good men is connected, vv. 20, 28. Each of these three strophés unites at the end the vow of thanksgiving with the prayer for help, first most violently, vv. 9, 10, then recurrently, vv. 18, 28.

The song has, quite like Ps. xxii., three very long strophés, but somewhat differently, so that each embraces only nine verses with twenty members. To this measure the first only would not fully conform: but ver. 4 is probably only transposed to this place by an ancient hand from the words of the same poet, xl. 15; there it stands quite correctly, here it is better left out, considering the connexion of the words and figures of the strophé.

1.

Dispute, Jahvé, with them who dispute with me,   1
    fight those who fight me;
  seize shield and target
    and rise to help me,
  bare spear and battle-axe against the persecutors,
    say to my soul: thy help am I!

[let them blush, shame befall them who seek my life,
  ashamed let them fall back—who thus meditate my
    unhappiness!]
5   like chaff before the wind be they,
  thrust forth by Jahvé's angels;
  their way be darkness and slipperiness,
  by Jahvé's angels pursued!
    —because they without cause hid for me the hole
      of their net,
  without cause dug for my life.
  Let a storm fall upon him unawares,
  his net, that he concealed, take him,
  into the gulf let him fall!
  and my soul will be glad in Jahvé,
  leap because of His deliverance;
10 all my bones shall say: "Jahvé, who is like Thee,
  who savest sufferers from the stronger one;
  sufferers and needy ones from their spoiler?"

2.

  Cruel witnesses rise up
    what I know not is demanded of me,
  ill is requited me instead of good;
    —orphaned is my soul!
  I indeed, in their sickness, put on mourning,
    I tormented fasting my soul,
      and my prayer fell into my bosom;
  as if it were a friend, a brother to me, I went forth,
    as sorrowing for my mother I stole on my way
      mournfully.
15 but glad of my fall they assemble,
    scourges assemble against me—I know of nothing;
  they revile never keeping silence,
  with most impudent scoffs of slander
    gnashing their teeth against me!—

O Lord! how long wilt Thou see it?
snatch my soul from their throats
from the lions, Thou my only one!
I will thank Thee in the great assembly of the people,
in the full multitude praise Thee;
let not my lying foes rejoice over me,
those who causelessly hate me, let them not wink
with the eye.

3.

For never speak they peace,   20
and against peaceful men of the land they meditate
treachery;
and gape with their mouth against me,
saying, "haha, haha!
our eye has seen it!"
Thou hast seen it, Jahvé! be not silent,
Lord, be not far from me!
O rouse Thyself, awake to my judgment,
my God and Lord, to my cause!
judge me according to Thy right, Jahvé my God,
and let them not rejoice over me,
say not in their heart; "ha, our pleasure!"   25
say not: "we have destroyed him!"
blushing and shame together fall on those that rejoice
in my ill;
may disgrace and shame light on them who boast
against me!
let them jubilate and rejoice who love my salvation,
ever say: "exalted be Jahvé,
who loves the weal of His servant!"
and my tongue shall utter thy salvation,
every day Thy praise!

1. That the כִּלֹי, ver. 3, is a metal weapon, is clear from the "baring," whether it be compared with σάγαρις, a Scythian

battle-axe (Lat. *securis*), or in the Sanskr. *K'akra* (Discus) : it appears to have been well known as a new arm in the many wars of the seventh century in Palestine; comp. Xen. *Anab.* iv., 4, 10; v., 4, 6, and Bahrdt on the Kappadocian monument in the *Berl. Akad. Nachrichten*, 1859, Febr.; on the Persic-Armenian, comp. Whiston, *Pref. ad Mos. Chor.*, p. v., and on the *schagar* among the Beduins west of Egypt, Fresnel in the *Nouvelles Annales des Voyages*, 1848-9.—With this first cry of distress for help and defence, vv. 1-3, with its highly warlike pictures, are then connected others not less lively, with the wish that they who without cause seek to bring him to naught, —who would take him as in a deep lion-pit, below hidden with a net, above covered over—might themselves, pursued by the power of Divine punishment, fall into a gulf or deep precipice, —fall into their own net, that goodness may conquer! Jer. xxiii. 12. The propositions of state (§ 341 *a*) of the angel of Jahvé, vv. 5, 6, describe the power that is invisible, but incessant and fearful in its effects ; as if irresistibly driven by an angel from heaven, sent for the purpose, the wicked rush into destruction, are hunted into the precipice, which they desired to prepare for others. And while the figure of the net finally appears once more, vv. 8-10, with peculiar force, in order now for the first time to touch the main enemy, the language, ever growing more tumid, is now first completed with the glance at the joyous issue. But it is clear enough that the words, ver. 4, which would too early express the most extreme feeling, do not suit this connexion,—on the contrary would only aptly stand in ver. 26. The שׁוֹאָה, ver. 8 *c*, corresponds plainly to the שַׁחַת, ver. 7, and is properly the *cracking*, then the deep *gulf* (of which the *plur.* שׁוֹא ver. 17, according to § 176 *a*), the precipice into which one falls crashing, xl. 3, more generally, as all words of the kind, *ruin*, lxiii. 10. But it would be a very poor kind of language if the poet in the first member, ver. 8, only employed the same word as in the third ; also to the *striking* is much more suitable the word-play with שְׁאִיָּה *the storm* (Prov. i. 27; Ez. xxxviii. 9) wherewith the first figure from ver. 5 a is once more here repeated, and alone suitably.

2. The last words, ver. 12: *there is orphanage of my soul! my heart feels deserted of all friends,*—are very abrupt, spoken with great sadness; for already the poet here reflects how all friends forsake him in the life-danger, whilst he was farthest from forsaking men in their misfortune. But sickness is selected, ver. 13, because the poet now suffers from it, ver. 15. *My prayer also for them fell back into my bosom,* as I in distress could not lift up my head, but must let it fall in deep grief upon my bosom, comp. 1 Kings xviii. 42. The *fall,* ver 15, is the fall into dangerous sickness, the danger which hinders the poet from rising and from free action. נְכָאִים is understood by derivation (comp. נָכוֹן Job xii. 5) and signification by the LXX most certainly as μάστιγες, which denote scourges, but in such a connexion, where the poet recurs to ver. 11,—blows of the tongue (Job v. 21) slanders, or men wounding, slandering with merciless words. Ver. 16 describes the rude style of these men further: *with most unholy scoffs* (§ 313 c) of distortion (*i.e.,* intentional perversion, lying, slander) which therefore are entirely without foundation as petulance and scorn, *gnashing* (*inf. abs.* according to § 280 a) *against me their teeth,* showing their wrath against me. בְּעוֹג from עוג, *ûdj* Arab. be bent. Of the better known מָעוֹג, "cake," 1 Kings xvii. 12, the old translators have, with good grounds, not thought; the above word is here meanwhile selected also because of the similar sound with the לעג of like meaning. *Wink with the eye,* or distort the eyes, ver. 19, expressive of contemptuous scorn and of base joy.

3. Ver. 21: *our eye has seen it,* we ourselves have seen it,— namely, that the poet, who was ever so bold and strong, is now himself struck by the blow; he cannot deny that he repents and must further repent. But suddenly turning round the thought of shameful joy in remembrance of Jahvé, the poet exclaims, ver. 22: *Thou hast seen it* rather, namely, how deeply

they vex the feeble one. Comp. similar inversion of the thought in transition to God, x. 13, 14. Ver. 25, further an abrupt exclamation of shameful joy: *ha!* *our pleasure!* because all is attained that we wished, the inevitable fall of the constant man.

But in vain! deliverance did not immediately follow this first stormy supplication. Rather does the very sickness appear to have been aggravated by the violence of the complaint. At least in the following song, Ps. xxxviii., this appears so painfully enhanced, that the poet, because of the very excess, anew supplicates Jahvé. And already he is inwardly more serious and clear, he has become more collected in his mind. There is no longer the violent indignation about the external enemy, his slanders and his crafty designs, but a patient endurance. He has also become attentive to his own deficiencies, and prepared to remove them; and thus there strikes through the threatening despondency in raging grief over his sickness and external danger, a higher reflectiveness and calmness of mood, while the poet before everything feels himself impelled again to seek rest and hope in God—repressing the recollection of his foes, and only hoping at the very end, humbly and in confession of his own defects, for help from Jahvé, because otherwise with the victory of his prevailing foes, the party of frivolity represented by them would conquer. And thus three strophés: first the irrestrainable outburst of saddest prayer for at least milder, endurable punishment, vv. 2-9. Yet wherefore unending complaint, that still does not exhaust everything? Jahvé knows how the poet must mourn, he the deadly sick, forsaken by all his acquaintances, violently threatened by the enemy, himself opposing to all slanders and provocations the most silent calm; thus follows the higher reflection and calmness in opposition to all that is wrathful and excited, vv. 10-16; and because the poet places all hope alone in Jahvé, at last, with a repeated cry for help, a look is cast on all sides upon the whole situation and peculiarly upon his foes, who desire, though impotently, according to the Divine plan, to content their shameful joy! vv. 17-23. While in this way the glance back at the foes, which in the previous song was the main thing, is here much subdued and softened by deeper thoughts, this becomes one of the finer songs of this poet, as we at the same time recognize an important advance in the mind of the poet. Farther, the poet has here less I's. xxxix. than Pss. vi. and xiii. in recollection, see Vol. I., pp. 183 sqq.

The three strophés are here manifestly somewhat shorter than in the preceding song; and although the second and the third, according to the present arrangement of words, are somewhat too short, yet each, according to all indications, should have eight verses with sixteen members.

1.

Jahvé! punish me not in Thy zeal,
   and in wrath chastise me not!
for thy arrows have sunk into me,
   and on me Thy hand has fallen;
there is nothing sound in my flesh before thine anger,
   no peace in my bones from my guilt.
Yea, my punishments go over my head,   5
   like a heavy burden too heavy for me;
my stripes rot, they moulder
   for the consequences of my folly;
I am bent, bowed greatly,
   daily I go mourning,
because my loins are full of sores,
   and nothing is sound in my body;
benumbed and worn out too greatly
   I groan forth my heart's raging.—

2.

O Lord, before Thee is all my longing,   10
   my sighing not concealed from Thee!

my heart beats, beats, strength has forsaken me,
   my very eye-light is not with me.
afar stand my friends and acquaintances from my wound,
   and my relatives place themselves at a distance;
and they who seek my life lay snares,
   and those who wish my hurt bespeak destruction,
      and meditate only deceit daily.
But I like a dove hear not,
   and like a dumb man who opens not his mouth,
15   and became like a man who hears not,
      in whose mouth are no accusations,
because I hope on Thee, O Jahvé:
   Thou wilt hear, my Lord and God!

3.

I think indeed that they may only not rejoice over me,
   if my foot staggers, greatly-boasting against me,
because I stand near to falling,

        *   *

and always grief passes before my eyes,
   then I confess my sin,
      am troubled because of my guilt.
20   But my causeless enemies are numerous,
   and many are my lying-haters,
who requite only evil for good,
   persecute me for following after the good;
forsake me not, Jahvé,
   my God, be not far from me!
O hasten to my help,
   Thou Lord, my salvation!

1'. In the very first strophé the feeling of grief and that of guilt penetrates most closely, while the poet concludes the latter from the greatness of the former, and the more profoundly and seriously he thinks over his entire condition of soul, the more he feels himself harassed by grief. The same confession of sin therefore begins from the first which recurs more briefly and plainly, vv. 18, 19. On this account, however, the feeling of the Divine punishments is predominant, which the poet only wishes may be softened to endurableness, because the weight of punishment and grief bows him down too deeply, as in two clauses, vv. 3-4, 5-7 is expressed, and because the sickness is so severe and oppressive, vv. 8-9. The mere word "stripes," ver. 6, may be figurative, so far as it does not more closely designate the nature of this evil as sickness, but merely the deeply-rooted consequences of Divine chastisement: but ver. 8 speaks finally, plainly enough of the kind of sickness, without any figure. נִקְלֶה is that which is burnt, a brand, burning ulcer, *kaly*, Arab.; correctly so the Targ.

2. Ver. 11. On הֵם comp. § 311 a and above Ps. vi. 8. Ver. 12 runs properly: my friends and neighbours place themselves out of the neighbourhood of my torment, and my acquaintances stand already afar off, which again infers leprosy, Job xviii. 13-20. Because the mood of mind which the poet describes, ver. 14, lasts longer with him, his language, ver. 15, passes with וָאֵדַּע correctly into the past.

3. The thrice used כִּי wherewith the last strophé, according to its present arrangement of words—irrespective of the ver. 16, better to be attached to the preceding strophé— begins, must be so taken that the following ever explained something of the preceding; ver. 17, how the poet first of all hopes in Jahvé because he thinks or hopes deliverance will come, that the enemies may not have a godless, *shameful joy* in the fall of a good man; but he has this fear, ver. 18, because he feels himself near to death, or ready for the final *falling*; while he from the other side, ver. 19, also hopes, because he sincerely confesses his guilt, Ps. li. But we must not fail to recognize that between the two members of ver. 18 there gapes a chasm, because the first explains, correctly and more closely the *staggering of the foot* just mentioned, ver. 17; but the second touches on something quite different

which is then further elucidated, ver. 19. It is evident that here two members are lost, the first of which, completing the sense of ver. 18 a, still further marked the danger of death, the second with a new beginning introduced the confession of sin in the way that may be safely enough inferred from ver. 18 b, comp. with vv. 3, 4. Somewhat as follows :

because I stand near to falling
at the gates of death my foot tarries,
But blows of Thy wrath I bear,
and ever does grief pass before my eyes.

But, on the other hand, all this refers to foes such as requite, without repentance and remorse, proud in their numbers, the good deeds shown them with evil; therefore humble prayer for help, in the belief that such perversities cannot ever continue ! vv. 20-23.—On the *perf.* הִגְדִּילוּ in the second clause, ver. 17, see § 346 b. For חיּים, ver. 20, חַיָּם is, as others supposed, to be regarded as more original, both because of the connexion of this passage and of the usage of this poet.

The thank-songs which the poet might have sung after his deliverance from such sufferings, as he had vowed, are now indeed lost to us; but the substantial contents of one such have been marvellously preserved in Ps. xl. For Ps. xl. is, from the second half onwards, vv. 12 sq., a purely suppliant song; but the more unusual is the first half, which places a thank-song at the head. The mode of union can only be the following : the poet had lately been delivered from a great danger, and as he was only conscious of being saved through great constancy of spirit in confidence in Jahvé, he had then loudly before the great multitude praised Jahvé as the mighty safe deliverer of His servants. This thank-song had been probably according to the pattern of such given above, Ps. xxx.; but with some alterations. In the first place it had more surely and clearly flowed from the principle that the true and best sacrifice was not the sacrifice anciently offered, the external one, the more ancient meaning of which had now lost its inner force, but the new and spiritual, or the new life in the spirit; at that time a new truth, passing into the light, which had appeared in the poet with new force and peculiar Divine impulse—and therefore so overpoweringly taking possession of him, that he had not desired to appear in the Temple with sacrificial beasts and external splendour, but rather with the roll of the law or Divine revelation to be stamped on the heart, as it was now publicly acknowledged and generally accessible (the song is sung after the reformation of Josia); and had appeared before the congregation with the purer and freer praise of the spiritual deliverer. Secondly, the parties had separated more from one another, and the poet sung for a more restricted circle the more cordially and didactically. As now the memory of this deliverance through hope and of the fair inspiration of those times still lives quite freshly in the poet, he hopes to conquer by the like inner constancy; and as he, in the elevation which sprang up in that time, had most sincerely praised Jahvé, and offering the sacrifices of the spirit without fear and terror had sought to further His kingdom, he hopes that now conversely (according to the mutual relations of Jahvé and His own) Jahvé will help and save him. Hence he begins with the description of the earlier deliverance and of the hearty faithful thanksgiving of that time, the joyous recollection of which lives in him; and passes thence to prayer.

The first, second and fourth strophés have here manifestly each thirteen members; the last strophé appears besides in Ps. lxx. as a special song; and this is explained most readily as above in Ps. xliii., if it formerly—as easily recognizable—stood separate as a particular strophé. The third has thus manifestly lost at the beginning the first half; and hence we can understand how the transition to it may now sound so abruptly.

1.

I hoped firmly on Jahvé: 2
    and bending to me, he heard my complaint;

And drew me from the pit of ruin, from deepest mire,
and placed on a rock my feet, made firm my steps,
and put into my mouth a new song, "thanks to our God,"
that many, seeing this, might stand in fear—and trust in Jahvé.
5 " Blessed the man who made Jahvé his confidence,
not turning to the haughty and friends of lies !
in numbers didst Thou show, Jahvé my God,
thy wonders and purposes towards us,
O thou utterly incomparable One !
if I would praise and announce them,
too many are they to relate."

2.

Sacrifice and gift Thou didst not prefer,
—hadst opened my ears—
guilt—sin-offerings Thou didst not demand;
then spake I, "lo! I bring
the roll of the book prescribed to me;
to do Thy will I love, O my God,
and Thy law is deep in my inward part!"
10 joyously I praised salvation in the great people's assembly.
yea, my lips I restrained not,
O Jahvé, Thou that knowest it !
thy righteousness I hid not in my own heart,
of Thy truth, of Thy deliverance I spake,
concealed not Thy mercy and truth from many people.

3.

* * * * *

Thou, Jahvé, wilt not restrain Thy compassion from me,
ever will Thy mercy and truth protect me !
for evils have surrounded me—innumerable,
punishments have reached me—I cannot see—

more numerous than the hairs of my head,
and my heart has forsaken me.

4.

Be pleased, Jahvé, to set me free,
Jahvé, hasten to my help!
blushing and confusion together fall upon   15
   those who seek my soul to destroy,
back let them fall, feeling shame
   who delight in my misfortune!
let those be amazed at the consequence of their shame
   who cry to me: "haha, haha!"
let them leap and rejoice in Thee, all who seek Thee,
   ever say "high be Jahvé!" who love Thy deliverance!—
But I the poor helpless one—O Lord, haste to me!
   my consolation art Thou and my deliverer:
my God, O tarry not!

1. The first figure, ver. 3, is that of a deep pit dug for the wild beasts, vii. 16, xxx. 2, xxxvi. 7; with this is readily connected that of the deep mire, wherein it is possible easily to be submerged, lxix. 3; that all is figurative is shown by the counter-picture of the rock. From the words "new song" onwards, ver. 4, the poet manifestly begins to repeat briefly the main thoughts out of the same (comp. above on Ps. xli., Vol. I., p. 187), up to ver. 6, in the first instance; already in the change of the expression "*our God*" lies the transition to this recollection, since the poet began the thank-song somewhat as follows: "Thank our God;" the following וַיַּרְא to the end of ver. 1, is somewhat more clearly connected by indirect quotation; since the poet formerly sung: *see ye this in the multitude and fear;* but from ver. 5 onwards, the power of joyous recollection carries him away to the repetition in the same form wherein he had ever spoken. In the רְהָבִים and שָׂטֵי כָזָב, ver. 5, the direct opposition to Jahvé, the idols, cannot be found: it must then be proud, violent men, and frivolous, inclined to lies

(falseness, also idolatry), whose fellowship, according to the nature of that time, of itself leads further to idolatry. The words, ver. 6 c, may very well stand in the exclamation, and this last suits the connexion of the much complicated language; and on *d, e,* comp. § 357 *b.*

2. Ver. 7. In the beginning of the strophé the poet breaks in with a present consideration, but only, as vv. 8-9, again to take up the leading of the moods and words of that time. Wherewith could I have better thanked Thee? not with sacrifices of the old kind, for them Thou didst not love nor demand, as Thou hadst *bored through my ears, i.e.,* made me, who was earlier deaf to this, by Thy power, of clear hearing and understanding,—or *had* revealed to me (2 Sam. vii. 27; Isa. 1. 5): כָּרִיתָ, in the intermediate clause, is by the connexion *pluperf.* § 346 *c.* Two extremely important things at once: not merely the true insight in sacrifices, but also how such a new and higher insight arises in the poet by Divine revelation, which example one needs only to follow out in order to be certain about Biblical revelation. The insight itself is indeed already earlier indicated by prophecy; but also in our poet it came out with thorough independence and freedom, laying hold of him as an immediate certainty from God, and in his own affairs first of all powerfully leading him, as it in that time generally, although germinating here and there, was not throughout generally recognized nor heard. Ver. 8. Opposition. On בָּאתִי־בְ, comp. lxvi. 13, lxxi. 16, xc. 12, Hos. xiv. 3: it is plainly, since here for once the language is of sacrifices, "I bring not these sacrifices, but — ;" that the poet went with a Pentateuch into the Temple, or rather into the people's assembly, mentioned, vv. 10, 11, is not to be believed: that time was the first golden age of the written law, still without misunderstandings and abuses such as later, had been connected with it; and that the poet means it in an inward sense, he explains himself, ver. 9. On כָּרוּב עָלַי, *khâtab kâra ely,* Arab. "fore-read," "prescribe," is to be com-

SONGS OF THE DISPERSION.

pared, as Job xiii. 26 ; any *book* cannot indeed well be termed *prescribed*, but by a sacred book, as here, is understood as , such its contents, somewhat as immediately after in ver. 9. So freely and willingly did I then announce, vv. 10, 11, the Divine leading, without fear, before the great multitude.*

3. Ver. 13 only becomes plain when we reflect that "I cannot see," according to xiii. 4, xxxviii. 11, fully corresponds to "my heart has forsaken me," as עֲזָבַנִי to אֵין עַד, and finally, רְעוֹת to עֲוֹנֹתַי ; three ideas are thus merged in one another: (1) that evil and punishment have befallen the poet, and they (2) are countless; and besides (3) overpowering even to the weakness of death.—Ver. 18. Personal reflection, finally once more, according to the general thought, ver. 17. For יַחְשֹׁב, "the Lord will think on me," here according to lxx. 6, as according to the other similar places, חוּשָׁה is to be read, which also best suits the membering of this verse and the whole con nexion (for here is merely prayer).

The two halves are certainly somewhat loosely connected, and it might readily be supposed they did not originally hang together; vv. 14-18 appear as a proper song, Ps. lxx. Meanwhile this part may have been later separated, in order to form

---

* The above explanation of the words, vv. 7, 8, is to me, under all circumstances, that alone probable. Apparently ver. 7 might thus be taken :—

 Sacrifices and gifts Thou dost not prefer ;
 Thou hast pierced my ears,
 guilt and sin-offerings Thou demandest not,

as if these words bore the sense, external sacrifices "Thou demandest not as better, but open ears, i.e., obedience dost Thou demand as the best sacrifice." But such a sense would be here in itself not nearly so clearly expressed as 1 Sam. xv. 22 ; and although it is quite correct that God has bored man's ears, i.e., made and given them that he may use them, yet here plainly the language is of a quite peculiar revelation. Since here now, ver. 7 stands especially pure in the series of narration, vv. 2 sq., and this narration is continued vv. 8-11, it is self-intelligible, how the *perfects*, vv. 7 *a* and *c*, are to be taken, and that the *perf.* in *b* ought to give a mere intermediate clause. But the words, ver. 8, might at the most, according to the *Jahrbb. der Bibl. Wiss.*, v , p. 170, be thus understood, "I bring that prescribed to me in the book-roll," as the true sacrifice, but then the roll would be here useless, and it would rather be : "I bring that prescribed to me *in Thy book.*"

VOL. II.

of itself a suppliant song; and this is even singularly probable, because here between vv. 13-18 is the best connexion, the רָעָה, ver. 14, is badly wanting in Ps. lxx., and generally such a small suppliant song, wherein there is no inner completeness, may be more readily thought of as torn away from its context, than as an original whole. There is no want of easy transitions in sense and words from the first to the second half; comp. תִּכְלָא, ver. 12, finely echoing from אָכְלָא, ver. 10, רָצָה, ver. 14, from רָצוֹן, ver. 9. Thus this song appears actually in its present form to be original, and to form a readily explainable exception to the ordinary form of songs, because the poet certainly repeated to himself with pleasure the recollection of the thank-song, in order the more calmly at the end to speak anew words of an earlier prayer-song; for the whole conclusion of Ps. xxxv. again rings through this.

Further, the words, lxx. 2 a, yield, even after the removal of the first word, the at least tolerable sense, "God is here to save me" (*deus est qui me servet*), as in Hizqia, Isa. xxxviii. 28.

Ps. lxix. shows once more the poet sunk into extreme misery and into most fearful despondency. At a time when he for his very fidelity in the pure Jahvé-religion, and his zeal for it (ver. 10), suffers extreme trouble, painfully encountering with the softness and tenderness of his heart unfeeling rudeness, sick and helpless, despised and scoffed at, paying the debt of unheard-of sufferings for all time,—he is anew most keenly hurt as a countless host of rude slanderers press in upon him and accuse him of crimes, *e.g.*, of robbery, from which he is altogether free, vv. 5, 20-22, 27. But while thus a new violent distress, arisen through the mere blindness of arbitrary men, streams upon the poet, already deeply sunk into other distresses, as if it was not yet enough to endure in innocence the severest gloomy blows of fate and punishment: his soft and wounded heart is quite dissolved and scarcely capable of self-possession. In nameless grief he has (ver. 4) long in vain prayed for help to Jahvé; a new comprehensive attempt in the outburst of the most grievous and manifold feelings to become clear in his mind and obtain solace in Jahvé,—is this long languishing song. First the short, urgent cry for help in extreme distress and persecution breaks forth, vv. 2-5; since the language has come to the mention of the base accusation of the foes, sudden interruption from grief, fresh turn in woeful address to God, as He knows how severe and dark are the sufferings of the poet, and can help him, who for His sake alone and from zeal for His religion endures extreme distress and scoffing; yet patiently he will anew pray to Him, vv. 6-19 (6, 7; 8-13; 14-19). But as yet all is not cleared up in the mind of the poet; new and sad beginning, as the Jahvé, just appealed to so urgently, best knows all the bitter scorn, which the poet cannot possibly describe sufficiently, and will not (vv. 21, 22); and here, reflecting on the frightful bitterness of the scorn, the poet can no longer restrain himself, the strength of cursing breaks out (vv. 23-29), until at last complete rest returns, and hope for a better future of the poet and of all Israel (vv. 30-37).—The song falls, according to ver. 36, in the time after Jerusalem's destruction, and we hear the increased troubles of the time, through the echo of the language. But if we must pardon the long imprecation which finally breaks out, vv. 23-29, on account of the complete bewilderment of that period and the too gentle heart of the poet; it is on the other side plain that hardly can sufferings be greater and bitterer, and that the poet nevertheless still finally finds rest amidst them.

According to its structure, this long languishing song falls no longer merely into three simple long strophés, as above, Ps. xxii., xxxv., but, because it is extended into much greater length, into three different small songs,—the first seeking to exhaust the cry for help, and unable to do so; hence the second returns from historical relations, and the third from the curse, to prayer and hope. Since now six verses or twelve members

5 *

form the ground-measure, each of the three great sections in
the sorely-strained language ends with a short strophé, while
the main strophé is doubled in the second and third song.
But eleven to fourteen members alternate in the full strophé.

1 a.

  Help me, O God!
2   for already the water presses on my life,
  I sink in deepest mire, without firm footing,
   come into abysses of waters,
    the flood has streamed over me;
  weary am I crying, dry my throat,
   wasting my eyes
    in waiting on my God;
5   more than my head's hairs are those who causelessly
             hate me,
   more numerous than my bones my lying foes;
   what I robbed not, I am yet to make good!

b.

  O God! <i>Thou</i> knowest my punishment,
   and my sufferings are not hidden from Thee!
  let not those who wait for Thee blush for me,
   O Lord, Jahvé of hosts;
  let not those who seek Thee be ashamed of me,
   O Thou God of Israel!

2 a.

  For Thy sake I endure scoffing,
   ignominy has covered my face;
  I have become estranged from my brothers,
   a stranger to my mother's sons,
10 because zeal for Thy house devoured me,
   the scorn of those scorning Thee fell on me:
  I wept deeply, fasting—
   that became for a scoff to me;
  I made sackcloth my garment—
   and became a proverb to them,

.they that sit at the gate sing of me
and songs they who there drink wine.

b.

But—my prayer is to Thee, Jahvé!
at a favourable time, O God, through Thy fulness of
power
grant me the faithfulness of Thy help!
free me from the mire, let me not sink,   15
let me be free from haters and from water-depths;
let not the flood of waters stream over me,
shallows not devour me,
a well not close over my mouth!
hear me, Jahvé, for fair is Thy grace,
according to Thy fulness of compassion look on me
and hide not Thy glance from Thy servant,
because distress is near to me, hear me speedily;
come near to my soul, redeem it,
because of my foes deliver me!

c.

Thou knowest my scorn, the ignominy, the shame,   20
before Thee are all my oppressors!
scoffing broke my heart, that I became sick
and hoped for pity, it was nowhere,
for consolers,—found them not;
poison was put into my food,
for my thirst they give me vinegar to drink.

3 a.

May their table before them become itself a snare,
as a trap to the secure!
may their eyes be blinded, not to see,
and their loins, let them ever tremble;
pour out upon them Thy wrath,   25
and the glow of Thy anger, may it fall on them;

  may their precinct become desert,
    in their tent be no dweller!
  because they persecute those whom *Thou* hast so smitten,
    and increase the trouble of Thy sick ones :
  give guilt according to their guilt,
    let them not come into Thy gracious righteousness,
  be they blotted from the book of life,
    and not written with just men!—

b.

30 But I, wretched and full of grief—
    Thy salvation, God, will protect me!
  I will praise God's name singing,
    exalt him in thanks,
  which is dearer to Jahvé than bullocks, than young bull
    which has horns and hoofs!
  Seeing this, sufferers will rejoice;
    Ye who seek God, may your heart revive!
  for to the helpless Jahvé hearkens,
    his prisoners He has not despised.
35 Praise Him, heaven and earth,
    seas and all that moves in them!

c.

  For God will help Sion, build up Juda's cities.
    There will they settle, possessing them!
  and Thy servants' seed will inherit them,
    who love Thy name, dwell in it!

  The descriptions of the sinking vv. 2, 3, 15, 16 are, though very strong and dense, yet only figurative, as xl. 2, 3; Prov. xxiii. 27. For had the poet wished to express in no mere general terms the great distress into which he imagines himself to be falling, he must have spoken more plainly; but the plain language is forthcoming vv. 5, 15. But it seems as if the poet is so well acquainted with this picture and paints it, because he himself-like Jéremjá xxxvii., had been in such distress, in the cistern-prison, about to perish. But it does not follow that he was himself Jéremjá.—Ver. 4. The short connexion of the *part.* מְיַחֵל is noteworthy, § 341 *b.*—Ver. 5 as xl. 13, the end as xxxv. 11. אָךְ *nevertheless,* § 354 *a*. But manifestly מַצְמִיתַי *my destroyers* is not in place here, both as too strong in itself, and also because a word of comparison is wanting. Most readily מִצַּפָּתִי *than my locks,* may be read, comp. צַמָּה HL. iv. 1, 3, vi. 7 (something quite different is meant by צַמָּה Isa. xlvii. 2) to which *zeamta* or *zeaptā* (Syr.) *zabab* (Arab.) corresponds, and with which also צֶמֶר *wool* and צַמֶּרֶת *foliage* are more remotely related. Otherwise the reading of the *Peshito* מֵעַצְמוֹתַי *more numerous than my bones,* would very well suit, precisely in this poet, comp. xxxiv. 21, xxxv. 10, li. 10, comp. with Isa. xxxviii. 13; Jer. xxiii. 9, since certainly it was very well known at that time how difficult it is to count the human bones. This reading gives at the same time a word-play; but our poet does not altogether despise this, comp. ver. 28, xl. 4. Further, it is self-intelligible that the mode of expression, ver. 5 *c,* does not exactly express in figure the same thing that the two preceding members express by the *baseless* or *lying* haters.—Ver. 6. On לְ see § 277 *c*. אוֶּלֶת comp. xxxviii. 6, must here now immediately signify the consequence of folly and sin, punishment, comp. ver. 20, and foolish indeed it of course appeared to the world that this godly man was so greatly zealous.

2. Ver. 10 gives the explanation, begun ver. 8, of the reason in a more definite way. The *zeal for the Temple,* at that time destroyed and desecrated, or—since the Temple was regarded as the central spot and the firm support of religion,—the zeal for saving and defending the inviolable honour of religion and its holy usages,—despite the destroyed Temple—*has consumed me,* worn me out by its glow and the consequences of it, while the scorn of Jahvé and His Temple was turned against me; the mourning over this became again a

scoff for the unhappy one, who seemed so fruitlessly and mournfully to protect the betrayed thing. Ver. 11. נַפְשִׁי is subordinated to the verb בְּכָה (§ 281c). Ver. 14. עֲנֹת is connected at the end like lxv. 6.—Ver. 20, *are before Thee*, Thou knowest very well, how infinitely many oppressors surround me; just as xxxviii. 18.—Ver. 22 suits the figurative mode of expression very well, if we reflect how grievously bitter is scorn to the man requiring and longing for the opposite, compassion.

3. Since now the oppressors were men gormandizing in light-minded security and loving the lower comforts, the first words of the imprecation, ver. 23, lie all the nearer at hand after the figure with which the previous strophé closed; for in this very frivolous luxury their destruction, perhaps suddenly coming, must lie, whilst then, *e.g.*, a mighty foe or robber, somewhat as in B. Jes. xxi. 5 sqq., falls the more suddenly and crushingly upon them. Ver. 27. For יספרו plainly (also according to the LXX προσέθηκαν) יֹסִפוּ is to be read,—the poetic form of יָסַף=יָסַם; for that they tell of the Divine punishment is not nearly so punishable, as their increasing— as the connexion here requires—by their own actual attacks and blows in the most sensible way that punishment. Therefore, ver. 28: *give guilt*, punish *according to their guilt*, as much as the guilt deserves, a play of words and thoughts. Ver. 30 as xl. 18, vv. 31-32 as xl. 7, 8; an apt opposition of intelligent thanks by praise and of the dead sacrifice with horns and hoofs of unintelligent beasts. The words, vv. 33, 34, are plainly transformed according to xxii. 27; on רָיִי see § 348 *a* and 347 *a*.—But the final words, vv. 36, 37, bear great resemblance to those in 'Obadja, vv. 20, 21, as they proceed from the same time.

Precisely in the gloomy and dangerous portion of the last song, Ps. cix. now proceeds much further, presumably because under such a sad state of things a fresh severe persecution and calumny had been added. The bitter calumny proceeded probably in exile from the part of a religious associate; and the more highly piety in the religion of Jahvé was esteemed at that time among many of those later ones, the more deeply did the false charges of the opposite party work injury; for the firmer and more rigid the sacredness of an individual religion becomes, the greater this danger. So does the poet who is deeply trustful in God feel here; because of outward misery he is bitterly slandered and persecuted in his innocence by his own beloved religious associates, and feels so violently wronged that he,—scarcely depicting the guilt of his foes with sufficient plainness,—feels himself urged from the very first to thrust forth the strongest and longest imprecation, vv. 1-20. Only in a supplement does his language gradually become calmer and more collected in God, yea, at last joyously confident, vv. 21-31. The particular figures of the imprecation appear borrowed from his own experience,—for it may be readily wished that the frivolous persecutors might—in order to come to understanding—first pass through the same sufferings which they are preparing for innocence. And thus the song shows in this perilous point of view the extreme of that which in the case of the godly of that period might ever readily lurk in the background; all that is troubled is here discharged first of all without restraint; and hardly then comes, and only at the end, collectedness and hope!

The strophés appear here manifestly to bear the greatest resemblance to those of Ps. xxxv.: three on the whole, each in ten verses, or more exactly twenty verse-members,—the short member at the very beginning would be a surplus. The first two were then quite filled out by bitter lament, and only with the third would the language rise and return to intense recollection of God. But because in it, too, at last the power of the curse would again become mighty, the language returned at last as if spasmodically with the more decision, in a quite short strophé, vv. 30, 31, to the pure praise of God.

But the whole long contents of the song are divided still more fitly into six strophés of five verses each, of which two always stand nearer together. The rest as just stated.

1.

1   God of my praise, be not silent!
      because they opened wide against me the mouth of
                wickedness and deceit,
    the deceitful tongue spoke with me,
    with words of hate surrounded me,
      and assailed me without cause;
    for my love seeks to overthrow me,
      while I am altogether only prayer,
5   and lays on me evil for the good
      and hate for my love.

    Set a wicked man over him,
      and let an adversary stand at his right hand;
    if he is judged, let him go forth as guilty,
      and let his prayer become sin!
    few be his days,
      his office let another take;
    let his sons become orphans
      and let his wife become widow,
10   yea, let his children rove begging
      and seek bread from their fragments afar!

2.

    Let the usurer lay snares for all his possessions,
      and strangers plunder what he has gained!
    Let him have none who observe mercy,
      be there no gracious one to his orphans,
    be his posterity for destruction,
      in another generation their name be extinct;

his father's guilt be mentioned before Jahvé,
    and his mother's sin not be extinguished,
be they continually before Jahvé, 15
    that He destroy their memory from the earth!

Because he took not thought to exercise mercy,
    persecuted the sufferer and helpless man,
    and the heart-broken, to slay him utterly,
and even loved the curse—(and it smites him),
    and loved not blessing—(and it flees him);
and drew the curse on like his cloak—
    (it comes then also like water into his bosom
    and like oil into his bones):
so be it to him as a garment that he puts on,
    for a girdle which he ever binds around him!
this my adversaries' reward from Jahvé, 20
    of them who speak evil against my soul!

3.

But Thou, O Jahvé Lord—deal with me for Thy name's
                                                    sake;
    because good is Thy mercy, set me free!
For suffering and helpless am I,
    my heart overwhelmed in my bosom;
as a shadow, when it passes, am I passed away,
    am scared away, like locusts;
my knees stagger from fasting,
    my body is wasted away, without fat,
while I became to them for a scoff, 25
    they, seeing me, straightway shake their head.
Stand by me, Jahvé my God,
    help me according to Thy mercy,
that they may know this is Thy hand,
    that Thou, Jahvé, hast done it!
Though *they* curse—yet *Thou* wilt bless,
    stand they up—yet they blush for shame,

but Thy servant will rejoice;
my adversaries must incur disgrace,
as in a garment, clothe themselves in their shame!

4.

Praise I Jahvé greatly with my mouth,
and laud Him in the midst of Many,
that He stands at the right hand of the helpless,
to help him before his life's judges!

Ver. 1 as xxxv. 22, ver. 4 *b* as xxxv. 13, comp. cxx. 7 and § 296 *b*. Ver. 2 properly: *the mouth of a wicked man*, as a wicked man speaks, since they would still be Israelites; קָרְבָּם, ver. 3, connected according to § 283 *b*. From the beginning of the imprecation, vv. 6, 7, comp. with ver. 31, one would infer that the poet was innocently condemned under a heathen prince through the influence of an opponent and accuser, whose motive was mere hatred (to whom the place of honour belongs, Zakh. iii. 1). Comp. xxxvii. 33 and Zakh. iii., iv. Also that he had been deprived of his office (ver. 8). That an individual was his most violent foe, is clear also from the *sing.*, into which the *plur.* passes over in the most violent passages; and this individual was certainly himself an Israelite, as the very first word, ver. 2, brings out. Vv. 14, 15: that is, all sufferings now rush upon the poet, as if he must atone for his father's sins; comp. Isa. lxii. 2. Vv. 17-19: the curse, which he hurled against innocent ones, in which he completely covered himself, so that he only acted in it, in which alone as in refreshing strengthening food he had enjoyment and delight, may it ever return upon him, completely cover him-over, and hold him fast like a poisoned cloak and girdle, penetrate his bosom, like greedily devoured food. —On ver. 21 *b*, comp. lxix. 17; on ver. 22 *b*, comp. lxix. 21; on ver. 23 *a*, comp. cii. 12; *b* is from Nah. iii. 17, and ver. 25 from xxii. 8; on עַבְדֶּךָ, ver. 28, comp. lxix. 18, xxxv. 27. Most noteworthy here vv. 17, 18,

28 *b*, is,. the fact that the *perf.* is taken also as precative (§ 223 *a*), comp. lvii. 7, through the power of the *Vav. conseq.* : but this is not impossible according to the general spirit of usage, and is elsewhere found. But because such unusual modes of expression are not willingly long continued in Hebrew, the *prec.* ver. 19, passes over into the common *volunt.* —Further, the first words, ver. 1, immediately impress us with the fact that the poet had often before praised God.

The above is certainly not yet the mood in which the root of possibility for passionate rebellion and rashness could be cut away; and if this gloomier mood remains dominant, there comes in from without the power and opportunity of readily satisfying the indulgences of such a mood, perhaps for the moment evil. It might be in the case of a prince, a potentate; what offence is not here possible?—And thus we see the poet actually in Ps. li. fallen into heavy guilt, as it is not doubtful (ver. 16*) that he has now a blood-guilt (a murder) on his conscience. But if he had committed the dread deed which unquestionably was connected with other sins (ver. 11) in a moment of thoughtlessness, its consequences now oppress him, especially the pains of the conscience, so powerfully and dreadfully alarmed out of deepest security. These are now so intolerably severe, so utterly does he feel himself forsaken by Divine joyousness, serenity and strength,—so monstrously and singularly unhappy is his inner condition, that he here out of the deepest misery cries for deliverance and alleviation to God. This is precisely the most important point in which this Psalm is distinguished from the otherwise very similar Ps. xxxii., that we here still view the sin in the midst of its despondency

---

* דָּמִים may indeed, according to Ezek. xviii., signify generally and peculiarly, according to ver. 13, in the wider sense, any deadly sin ; but our poet supplicates in the whole song manifestly, not because he feels himself affected so severely only in general, but because he is affected thus immediately by the sin named, ver. 16, and its consequences.

and its misery, struggling most sorely with all pains and sufferings. But the sore agony and conflict is here not vain, unilluminated and obscure; the sorrow is not dull and godless, the prayer for help is no blind prayer; but when once the boldness is felt to behold the pure truth, and therewith the first ray of true perception has begun again to uplift and brighten the poet's heart, he becomes fit and capable for pouring forth this prayer. And exactly here is plainly shown the most beautiful and unique feature in this song. Nothing can be clearer and stronger than the inner light here arising, here beaming forth. For the poet has brought himself into such a state of mind that he, giving up all that is perverse and false, has desired only to see the pure truth, and with this sincerity and boldness appears before God (vv. 5, 6, 8). But having become inwardly so bold, and, in the midst of woe and sorrow, so clear and strong, he must equally feel the deepest and most grievous remorse for the recognized sin, and the most urgent, intensest longing for the new life in God, or for new strength and willingness in the Divine spirit. Thus the poet is filled by that *one* great feeling, and produces this sincerest and purest song, supplicating for new strength and purification, and revealing the deepest truths. And in this account it forms as the outburst of an unique, pure sensibility, an inseparable whole from vv. 3-19.

It follows from the poet's beginning his song in this highest truth and purest endeavour, that there necessarily occur to him in the midst of his agonizing sorrow, reasons for hope and claims upon the Divine grace and forgiveness,—reasons which cannot and ought not to excuse the sin, but which,—for him who in deepest repentance again strives after God—lighten this endeavour, and give him the support of the Divine audience. For once for all the individual man partakes of universal human weakness, of the germ and the possibility of sin, so that the sinner may,—not indeed defend himself for turning the possibility into actuality,—but yet, if he seeking again to conquer the actual, strives after God, he may hope for pardon from Him who knows human weakness and is exalted above it, ver. 7. And secondly, what is still nearer and more important, the poet places himself through the very truth of his bosom and the banishment of all deception again in a Divine disposition and in the genuine beginning of deliverance, so that he feels that God, who loves truth in the most secret part, will again brightly illuminate and encourage the man who strives after him, destroying the guilt of sin (so far as this is possible), vv. 8 sqq. Therefore in the very state of godly contemplation and sorrow, hope, confidence, and serenity ever come forth with greater power; at the close, vv. 15-19, the poet promises, already full of joyous anticipation, that after his deliverance he will instruct sinners with the greater force from the high experience of his life, and the light-minded ones who know not the Divine giver, and thus render the best thanks. Indeed, so free does his mind become at the end, that he adds a few words for the welfare of the kingdom, looking away from himself, vv. 20, 21.

This after-word casts the clearest historical light; it is thence clear that the song may belong to the time after the destruction of the Temple, and therefore be later than Ps. lxix., which, since according to this song, the discordance of the two preceding is hardly conceivable, might in itself be readily assumed. The song is first imitated, Ps. cxliii; much from it as from Ps. xxii. resounds, however, in the great Unnamed, B. Jes. xl. sqq. while that which Hezeqiel xi. 19, xviii. 31, xxxvi. 25-28, teaches in the sense of our poet, sounds entirely as from the mouth of a perhaps somewhat younger contemporary.

Although the song, as above stated, streams on until the after-word, vv. 20, 21, which strictly taken, might altogether be wanting, yet, more closely considered, it breaks up into four quite uniform moderate strophes, each of four verses, whose members bubble forth more freely in the highest degree at the end, while the last sounds out for a verse longer. And while thus in the midst of the overflowing stream of sensibility from which the song flows, firm measure is nevertheless preserved, it becomes all the clearer what higher rest from the first again prevailed in the poet's spirit, before he ventured thus to compose. Further, then stand, quite as in the preceding song, two of these strophés, according to the sense nearer together, so that the deepest reason of all the experiences of the song quite freshly gushes forth with the third strophé if as once more from the beginning; while the brief word of most urgent and glowing prayer breaks out in the last strophé, ver. 16, as if at the end it could not, in its entire force, be kept back.

1.

3 Be gracious to me, O God, according to Thy mercy,
  according to the fulness of Thy compassion quench
    my faults;
 wash me thoroughly from my misdeed,
  and purify me from my sin!
5 For my faults *I* know,
  and my sin is before me continually;
 only against Thee alone have I sinned, and done what
    appears evil to Thee,
 that Thou mayest be just in punishing, pure Thou
    as Judge.

2.

In sin was I indeed born,
 in guilt my mother conceived me.
Thou indeed lovest truth in the heart's chambers,
 and wilt teach me in secret wisdom,
 cleanse me with hyssop, that I may be clean,
  wash me, that I be whiter than snow,
10 cause me to hear pleasure and joy,
  that my bones may rejoice, which were crushed by
    Thee!

3.
O hide Thy face from my sins,
and all my transgression blot out,
a pure heart create in me, God,
and a firm spirit renew in my bosom!
cast me not away from Thy countenance,
and Thy holy spirit take not from me,
give me the delight of Thy help,
and support me with a willing spirit!

4.
I will teach the perverse Thy ways,   15
and sinners shall return to Thee:
free me from blood-guilt, God, Thou God of my salvation,
that my tongue may rejoice in Thy gracious righteousness;
O Lord, wilt Thou loose my lips,
my mouth will then announce Thy praise:
for sacrifice Thou lovest not, that I should give it,
burnt-offering Thou dost not desire;
the sacrifices of God are a broken spirit,
a broken and crushed heart—O God, Thou despisest not!

5.
Do good through Thy favour to Sion,   20
building the walls of Jerusalem!
Then wilt Thou love due sacrifices, burnt-offerings, full offerings;
Then come young bullocks to Thine altar!

1. In the great main division of the song, vv. 3-14, there follows upon the first outburst of prayer, vv. 3, 4, the ground for it, in which clearness and hope are calmly prepared, vv. 5-10, until by this very means the prayer is again resumed with the greater force and intensity, vv. 11-14. The nearest

and most necessary reason is the confession of sin, which is expressed, vv. 5, 6, with the greatest clearness, comp. with ver. 5, xxxviii, 18, 19 above, repeated B. Jes. lix. 12. The true consciousness of sin and its confession before God is this—that man, quite apart from all that is external, apprehending in the strictest and sharpest manner his relation to God, admits to himself before everything that the pure clear state and relation in which every man ought to stand towards God is in him now destroyed, and salvation is only possible in the restoration of this, and in the renewed rule of the purer and sacred impulse that lies in friendship with God. All other endeavours to make the consequences of sin harmless, and to soothe the conscience are vain and naught, so long as that fundamental mood is still injured and remains troubled. Separation and disease are only removed by the entire surrender of the spirit again to the Divine, and to His friendship and intimacy; and if the poet desired, *e.g.*, to give the most splendid satisfaction for the blood-guilt (which he could do as prince, and with which the mighty readily believe they do enough) it would be to him without the other vain, yea, hurtful. For the earthly substance which suffers through sin, *e.g.*, whether this or that one is put to death, is accidental and unessential; and the sin is not properly against matter, but every sin is in the strict and true sense a sin against the spirit or against God, a disturbance of the spirit, both of the individual human being in the body of the sinner and of the universal and the Divine. Therefore the poet here recognizes in the most serious and strenuous prayer to God, where the language cannot be of sin and punishment in the human sense, that he *only against God alone* has sinned, *from whom* he also conversely *alone* may expect to attain reconciliation and rest* Just as in another connexion, lxxi. 16,

---

* I leave this passage just as it stands in the first edition, because I have sufficiently expressed myself before about the dreadful misunderstanding which De Wette imported into my words; comp., however, the *Jahrbb.*, viii., p. 165.

he will ever praise *Him alone*). For this is necessarily the closely connected second truth, that because real sin, namely that of the spirit, is against God alone, only by the restoration of the disturbed relation to God, or by true inner intelligence and sincere repentance can pardon and peace be obtained from God. Yea, every sin leads and properly compels the man by the wretched consequences developed from it to the recognition of the Divine truth, which in every instance thus solemnizes its triumph ; and because the poet has come to this recognition as fruit and gain (sadly indeed obtained), and by it is enlightened, he adds : *That* Thou mayest be just and pure and as such mayest be recognized by men, whilst Thou ever anew punishest actual sin as Judge ;* therefore not that I may appear just in my own eyes, but that Thou again and afresh mayest be known as the only just one in punishment, who punishes that man may again turn to salvation.

2. The poet having thus purely known himself and God, there is in this very knowledge of the relation of God and of man a first ground for hope of grace on his behalf who is striving after God. Man is by birth (*i.e.*, by nature) exposed to the possibility of sin, but not God, who exalted above man can have pity and save; thus there lies in ver. 7, comp. Job xiv. 4, that which is true of the idea of hereditary sin,— namely, that sin as a germ and possibility comes not from without into man, but lies in him from the beginning,—as propagated from parents and so in endless succession to children. As the desires became later increasingly corrupt, while attentiveness to evil in them became increasingly awake and the horror of it became even stronger,—in ver. 7 there appears the first slight view of the essential sinfulness of

---

* If בְּדָבְרֶךָ ver. 6, means *in Thy speech*, regard would here be given to God in so far as He in His revelation especially for Israel, has long spoken concerning the mischief of sin, and that He would necessarily punish it. But that this explanation of the word is both unsuitable here and incorrect in itself, has been already shown in the *Jahrbb. der Bibl. Wiss.*, v., p. 171.

desire, which, here still merely poetic and tender, is far from appearing so one-sided as it does later, and suffers the thought, in itself certain,—that sin does not come from without into man (Job v. 6, 7)—still purely to glimmer through. The second ground of hope, ver. 8, touches the matter still more nearly, and therefore leads the more readily, awakening hope, back to prayer. Sincerity feels itself pleasing to God, and while the poet thus seizes and holds fast the purest truth of the present matter in the most secret working of his mind, he feels himself by this very means nearer to the Divine enlightenment, purification and serenity, and expects that soon again (ver. 10) the joyous serene Divine call will resound in Him (as Ps. xxxii.), and that thus a man crushed in all his members and bones may again loudly rejoice, comp. xxxv. 10, xxxiv. 21; תָּגֵלְנָה shorter, more abrupt for ותגלנה, as ver. 16, comp. § 347 b.

3. In the intensely renewed prayer, vv. 11-14, there then spring forth many new, very clear and exact, altogether apt denominations of the restoration or new birth; *conceal not*, as lxxxviii. 15, lxix. 18; *reject not*, as lxxi. 9.—In the closing portion, vv. 15-19, when (according to the custom of many songs of this period) vows are added, but here other than the ordinary and inferior, the language, already calmed, leaps hither and thither with more emotion from the new and joyous experiences. According to the ancient sacrificial usages, the hyssop was named, ver. 9, as a means of purification, but quite figuratively, for the language is of God. Ver. 16 *b* and ver. 17 as lxxi. 23, 24, ver. 18 as xl. 7. *Broken heart*, ver. 19, opposite of the hard, insensible, self-closing heart,— therefore one delicate, susceptible, become open to the Divine observation, because it has experienced the evils of its obstinacy and hardening in grief and mourning, xxxiv. 19, cix. 16, and after this passage frequently, Isa. lvii. sqq., just as ver. 20 *b* is re-echoed in Isa. lxii. 6, but in a strengthened form.

5. The sense, vv. 20, 21, is not that only now can the poet bring no thank-offerings, because Jerusalem and the Temple are destroyed, but that he would make it good, should they again be built up. For this connexion of thought is in nowise made clear, and to be proved from the poet himself; and our poet does not show himself so sensuous, as to say that he could bring no sacrifices, solely because the Temple was destroyed, which would be scarcely worth the trouble of saying; because the poet, like others of this time, may very well have the higher conception of the dispensableness of the outward sacrifices, and has this, according to his words, just as in Pss. xl. and lxix. But he thinks, if the weal of all Israel appears, he may then probably at the general feasts and sacrifices joyously sacrifice on his own behalf, and supplementally render the external thanks which it is unbefitting in present sufferings so splendidly to render; especially as it is better to offer spiritual sacrifices to God, if these according to inner and outer need, were more necessary and reasonable; for the outward sacrifice is not evil in itself, he thinks (as it is not), only quite unnecessary, even hurtful, without the inward spiritual sacrifices, and offered instead of them. In ver. 21 the poet glances, as is self-intelligible, to vv. 18, 19, but not conversely in vv. 18, 19, to ver. 21.

And in fact, as a movement, so extraordinary in its depth in the innermost of the spirit, cannot remain without an entire transformation of the man, Ps. lxxi. now shows historically what noble consequences spring from it in the case of this poet. Here he has become very old and weak, vv. 9, 17, and has survived the strangest fortunes, ver. 7; in the weakness of old age he is now anew threatened by vain men with death, vv. 11, 12. But he is so accustomed to clear reflection, serene resignation, and perpetual praise of the Divine deeds, so abundantly does his mouth overflow with perpetual thanks and praise, that in the prayer for deliverance, even the recollection of the nearest danger rather recedes, and scarcely here and there gleams through. After the first brief cry, vv. 1-3, a fresh and more definite cry for deliverance, but also already founding his hope on Jahvé, who from his youth up wondrously led him, is ever truly honoured and sung by him, vv. 4-9; then a somewhat nearer indication of the danger with renewed cry, but only the more strongly again to return to encouragement and self-exhortation, to everlasting celebration and praise of Jahvé the infinitely just one, vv. 10-18; till the long languishing song finally, as with an invocation of the Divine righteousness for all Israel and especially for the poet under all his sufferings most serenely closes, vv. 19-24. A fine monument of the serene and vigorous mood, looking out with joy on all, even troubled times, and habituated to the noblest comfort,—of one already far advanced in years. It follows from vv. 20, 21, that the song falls in the midst of the exile.

We have here plainly larger strophés of nine verses each, only that the third closes more briefly. But in the first, the growth of such a longer strophé of nine verses out of three smaller with three verses each, may still be clearly recognized; and in the second there is still at least a still stronger trace of this, vv. 15-18. The first two are alike especially in this, that each closes with the mention of the advanced age of the poet; just as the third still more permits the purely personal dignity of the poet to be seen.

1.

1 To Thee, O Jahvé, I flee,
   let me not be ashamed for ever!
   through the right of Thy grace freeing me and delivering
     bend to me Thine ear and help! *
   become a rock of refuge to me, ever to be entered,
     for a strong battlement to help me,
   since Thou my rock art and safe retreat!

   My God, deliver me from the hand of the wicked,
     out of the power of the sinner and devastator

for Thou art my hope, 5
    Lord Jahvé! my confidence from my youth;
have stayed myself on Thee from my birth,
    from my mother's womb Thou doest me good,
Thee ever celebrates my praise.

A wonder I appear to many;
    but Thou art my strong refuge:
my mouth overflows with Thy praise,
    every day with Thy glory:
cast me not away in the time of age,
    for my strength passes away, forsake me not.

2.

Truly my foes said of me, 10
    they who lurk for my life, took counsel together,
thus thinking, "God has forsaken him:
    pursue and take him, for there is no deliverer!"
(O God! be not far from me,
    my God, haste to my help!
cause to be ashamed, to pass away, those who hate my soul,
    to put on ignominy and shame, who seek my hurt!):
But I will always tarry,
    and all Thy praise yet increase;
my mouth will tell of Thy righteousness, 15
    every day Thy deliverance:
I know no bounds, truly!

I will bring the Lord Jahvé's great deeds,
    will boast Thy grace alone.
O God, Thou hast taught it me from youth,
    and hitherto I announce Thy wonders:
also even unto grey old age, God forsake me not,
    till I make known Thine arm to the generation,
to all those to come Thy power!

3.

In Thy righteousness, O God, which is heaven-high,
by that which Thou hast done,—it is great,
(O God, who is as Thou?
20 Thou who causedst us to see many and sore distresses,
Thou wilt again revive us,
and out of the earth's depths again exalt us!)
wilt Thou increase my greatness
and again comfort me:
so will *I* also praise Thee with the harp,
O my God, Thy faithfulness;
will play with the cither—to Thee, Thou Holy One of
Israel!
(O let my lips rejoice, yea play I to Thee,
with my soul redeemed by Thee!)
so will my tongue also sing Thy righteousness daily,
that shame, that ignominy fell upon those who thus
seek my hurt!

1. Vv. 1-3 plainly borrowed freely from xxxi. 2-3; the same poet would not thus repeat himself, and Ps. xxxi has more original connexion in the particulars of description. מָעוֹז ver. 5. might now possibly be a happy innovation for מָעוֹן, after Ps. xc. 1; but possibly too be occasioned by incorrect reading, and this in time occasioned the addition "ever to flee into;" and the צוית must then be explained just as the *perf.* above in vii. 7. Moreover, our poet is very fond of the תָּמִיד ver. 3, according to vv. 6, 14, and other places. But the words "be to me for a rock of refuge, that I ever flee in, having commanded to help me," are too unpoetical to admit of being ascribed to our poet; and as the LXX read the words entirely as xxxi. 3, an old reader seems only to have mistaken לבוא תמיד צוית for לבית מצודת. The sense is then harmonious with the whole contents of the song; because Thou in general art my refuge, help me also now! But it may be rightly supposed that the poet

added לבוא תמיד to the following להושעני to correspond, and that למעודה must merely be read for צוית. In regard to ver. 6, the figure is equally clear in xxii. 10, 11; for גחי the poet here gives—possibly in the first instance induced to do so by an obscure copy— גוזי (וז from ח) from גזח=djaza, Arab. " requite benefit" (LXX σκεπαστής, Vulg. protector), the more readily because he here would say not so much that he is directed to no other god from his birth, as, more practically, that he has ever stayed himself on no other, and has felt none but Him to be his benefactor, and thus has *praised* Him; there is thus a somewhat different turn to the sense from that in xxii. 10, 11. Vv. 7, 8, express the same thing in another way. A wonder, or *portentum*, he appears to many because of the incredible sufferings and fortunes he has known; but he knows Whom he has to thank for his wondrous preservation (on עי—מחסי comp. § 291b), and therefore on this account the more unweariedly praises Jahvé, justly expecting and begging for further deliverance. Ver. 8 is thus as little to be taken jussively as the last member of ver. 6.

2. The words, ver. 11 run like iii. 3; but the whole stream of this strophé is only understood when we firmly grasp the fact that the words, vv. 10, 11 (§ 362 b) form a mere *protasis* to those in 14, 15; while those in vv. 12, 13 form a parenthesis where the designations—elsewhere so novel with the poet—of his foes, may once again more freely burst forth. For, repressing his anguish, the poet would ever anew sing and praise, vv. 14, 15, as God indeed has taught him from early times, and may also further permit, that he according to his wish may first teach and rouse the later world, vv. 16-18, כפרות vv. 16, are bounds, ends, comp. *spór*, Syr., edge, prop. that which is ground off, separated; from the meaning of boundary is derived that of number. Ver. 16 as xl. 8; ver. 18 at the end after xxii. 31.

3. A strange and rare conclusion. The justice and the omnipotence of God the poet will ever extol, he has just so

strongly said; but hastening to his close, it is as if he cannot deny that much of the proof of them in the present condition of himself and of the whole people is still in arrears; and so he closes as with a conjunction of these two Divine powers, making his vows anew; for thus, in this firm expectation of deliverance, he on his side will never weary in song, for the next deliverance and for all, vv. 22-24, so that the contents return upon themselves and the song is fully concluded. The ן ver. 19, is clear from § 340 c; and all from c to the close of ver. 20 is again an intermediate proposition, comp. xl. 6. The clause of prayer, ver. 21, has the two dependent sentences, beginning with כי vv. 22 and 24, and the last, ver. 24, returns entirely to the sense of the beginning of the strophé, ver. 19; but ver. 23 is again a mere intermediate sentence, as the poet is greatly addicted to them, particularly in this song. Ver. 12 strongly recalls xxxvi. 6, comp. vii. 8; ver. 22—lvii. 8-11; the connexion of the כי quite as lxxvii. 12. Ver. 20. The K'tib is alone correct, because in these later times, when the individual increasingly passes away, very frequently our poet thinks at the same time of the sufferings of Israel, under which he more or less suffers.

And finally, we can happily still prove, how nobly the new-born poet kept his oft uttered vow,—to teach the inexperienced and sinners the true praise of Jahvé: according to all traces we have such songs from him in the alphabetic Pss. xxv. and xxxiv. For, in the first place, it is certain that these two didactic songs are from *one* poet. This follows from their quite peculiar alphabetic arrangement, by which they place —instead of the ו, which could merely appear as a copula—at the end of the alphabet פ again, in pronunciation now *f;* comp. *Lehrb.* p. 46, seventh edition. And in both each letter comprises a two-membered verse. But also in contents both stand in a close reciprocal relation: P's. xxv. contains the prayer of one striving after salvation and for holiness, for the relief of the outward life, with clear consciousness of the true inner happiness of the faithful. Ps. xxxiv. is then the corresponding thank-song for deliverance, passing from the beginning onwards, into the didactic and hortatory. The description has for alphabetic songs great coherence, the thoughts are noble and select. And in what concerns the poet, words and thoughts so completely agree with those of the preceding songs, especially of the later ones, that the sameness of origin may in many ways be proved in every verse. Pre-eminently the poet is occupied, here also, with the equally intense and serious thought of guilt and sin, and the songs tend entirely to the higher view of life and serene joyousness, which the poet according to the last·songs has obtained.

The individual lines, however, do not stand side by side in such a way that the poet expresses, for the sake of the alphabet, by each a thought not standing in connexion with its surroundings; rather does the same higher thought frequently pass over from one to the other, and the art demands only that each line by itself alone should readily give a sense included within itself. But as we saw on page 320, Vol. I., that even in such songs there may be larger strophés, so there stand here manifestly eleven lines exactly against eleven.

1

Aloft, to Thee, Jahvé,   1
    lift I my soul, O my God!
Believing in Thee : let me not be ashamed,
    my foes not rejoice over me !
Do not let all that hope in Thee be ashamed :
    ashamed must be the vainly faithless !
Enlighten me in Thy ways, Jahvé,
    O teach me Thy paths !
5   Further me in Thy truth, for *Thou* art God of my salvation,
    in Thee daily I hoped !

Give heed, Jahvé, to Thy mildness and grace,
   that they are ever of old ;
Have no regard to the sins of my youth,
   remember Thou me according to Thy grace, for Thy
            goodness' sake, Jahvé !
Is Jahvé good and upright,
   therefore He directs sinners, how to go;
Jahvé leads the meek in the right,
   and teaches the meek His way;
10 Known as grace and truth are all His ways
   to those keeping His covenant and exhortation:
Lord, for Thy name's sake, Jahvé,
   pardon my guilt, for it is great!

2

Men that fear Jahvé
   are directed by Him in the best way:
No good is wanting to their soul,
   and heirs of the land their seed become.
Open to Jahvé's fearers is His secret:
   his covenant is, to teach them.
15 Plighted in faith towards Jahvé I look,
   for *He* will free my foot from the net
Return Thy glance and favour to me,
   forsaken am I, suffering!
Sore is my heart; relieve it,
   and lead me out of my distresses.
Turn to me wretched and troubled,
   forgive all my sins!
Unnumbered, see, are my foes,
   and hate terrible hatred against me,
Undertake my defence, redeem my soul,
   let me not be ashamed, because I trust in Thee!
With innocence and honesty let me be preserved,
   for in Thee I hope, O Jahvé !—

Zealous to release Israel from all his distresses,
  O hasten, God!

From ver. 2 אלהי must be taken with ver. 1 : but owing to the peculiar alphabetic art and the similarity of xxxiv. 2, it is doubtful whether the possibility mentioned (I., pp. 115, sqq., *Dichter des A. B.*) has place here, and whether a few words sufficing for the fulness of the second member have not dropped out, just as, according tot he LXX, after the last word of ver. 21 a word יהוה was wanting; at least the excessive shortness of this member is more harsh in the case of ver. 21 than in that of ver. 22. Ver. 5. ולמדני is probably only repeated from ver. 4. Ver. 19. Read הָרָחִיב וּמִ׳; ver. 18, probably קְרָה or נִדַּס *come towards!* for ראה, for the alphabetic order must not be so greatly interfered with.—Ver. 10 *b* from Ex. xx. 6; ver. 15, comp. Prov. iii. 32 ; ver. 21, comp. xl. 12, ver. 22 an after-word like that at the end of Pss. cxxv., cxxviii., which cannot be accidental, but points back to a standing liturgical phrase.

Psalm xxxiv.

Awake! let me bless Jahvé at all times,
  ever be His praise in my mouth!   2
Blest let my soul call herself through Jahvé,
  that sufferers, hearing this, may rejoice!
Do honour with me to Jahvé,
  let us exalt His name together!
Enquiring of Jahvé, I was heard,   5
  from all fears He freed me.
For joy be radiant, ye who look up to Him ;
  your countenance shall not blush ;
Given ear hath Jahvé to this sufferer's cry,
  out of all distresses helped him.

Helpfully encamps Jahvé's angel
   round about His fearers.
In yourselves experience, how good is Jahvé,
   blessed the man who trust in Him!
10   Jahvé do ye fear, His saints,
   for to his fearers there is no want!
Known is hunger and want to the lions:
   they who seek Jahvé, want no good.
Let it be called to your minds, ye sons,
   the fear of Jahvé will I teach you.

2.

Mirth wouldst Thou have in life,
   would'st enjoy good for many days?
Notify thy tongue against evil,
   and lips, not to speak craft;
15   Omit ever the ill, do the good,
   seek peace and pursue it!
Present is Jahvé's eye with the righteous
   and His ears at their cry:
Returneth never Jahvé from evil-doers,
   not to destroy their glory from the land.
Sounded the cry of the just: Jahvé helped,
   freed them from all distresses;
True is Jahvé to the heart-broken
   and helps the bowed in spirit.
20   Unnumbered are the good man's ills:
   but out of all Jahvé frees him,
Upholds all his bones,
   not one of them is crushed,
Wickedness itself slays the wicked,
   the haters of the just man suffer for it;
Zealously Jahvé delivers the soul of His servants,
   they who trust in Him suffer no hurt.

Even the infrequent figure, ver. 8, strongly recalls the

same poet, xxxv. 6; just so the ver. 21, comp. on the above, p. 71. The tenor of the language is in the first half hortatory to all the faithful to thank and to fear alway along with him who here thanks God, but it changes in the second. Accordingly, the words, ver. 6, הַצְּבִי and יְהָרוּ are to be expressed, and then וּפְנֵי must be read. It seems striking that the mention of the unjust, ver. 17, interrupts the discourse concerning the just man, vv. 16 and 18; the LXX, however, correctly insert צדיקים after יַעֲקֹב.

Ps. cii. is probably also of the same poet, even if according to vv. 24, 25, from a somewhat earlier period than Ps. lxxi. He sings here a deep song of suffering and lamentation, with which so many of the dispersed and grievously crushed godly ones of those days could agree; and would according to his first words, ver. 1 (Vol. I., p. 57) really speak more in the sense and as out of the heart of all the similarly unhappy ones, than merely out of his own experience and sensibility; but can for this very reason,—in reflection on the sorrows of the Holy City—the more purely and freely draw his hope as that of all suffering in like manner from the Messianic expectation,—so that he pre-eminently in this song carries out further for the first time in this song what he had more briefly uttered in lxix. 36, 37. And so he sketches at the outset, vv. 2-9, a dread picture of all the sore sufferings of those days. But already the mere thought that they all proceed from the now heavily angered true God,—binds him to the thought of the eternity of God, who as ever, may in the future again send new salvation, and leads him over to the Messianic hope so quickly that he may abide alone by its entire consolatory content, vv. 10-16; 17-23. First in an after-song he is impelled to speak somewhat more closely of himself, but only to return from his own most grievous life-experiences and his own prayer for the Divine grace in virtue of the same fundamental thought of the eternity of God,—to the same Messianic hope, vv. 24-29.

The structure of the strophés is that of seven verses, and the second and the third both conclude with high Messianic pictures. If the first has eight, and the redundant fourth has six verses, they are only slight changes of the fundamental measure. That the poet, further, selects so general a tenor of his lament, and says this himself in an introductory verse, ver. 1—is all the less striking if he, as the two preceding songs show, were wont to occupy himself on other occasions as a didactic poet.

1   Prayer of a sufferer, when he is weak
       and pours forth his sighs before Jahvé :

1.

Jahvé, O hear my prayer,
    and let my plaint force its way to Thee !
hide not Thy glance from me for I am in distress,
    lend to me Thine ear for I now cry ;
       in haste listen to me !
For my days are passed away in smoke,
    burnt through are my bones like glowing hearth,
5   withered like grass, dried up is my heart,
       because I forgot to eat my bread !
because of my loud sighing
    my bones cleave fast to my flesh,
I am like the pelican of the desert,
    am become like the owl of the waste
am sleepless and become as
    a bird solitary upon the roof.
Always my foes revile me,
    they that are mad against me—swear by me.

2.

10   For ashes have I eaten like bread
       and mixed my drink with weeping

before Thine anger and Thy dread ;
   because Thou removedst, castedst me away,
my life's days are a shadow which bends,
   while I wither as the herb.
But Thou, Jahvé, art enthroned for ever,
   Thy glory is eternal to all generations :
Thou wilt, rising up, have pity on Sion,
   —for it is time to be gracious to her,
   yea the hour has come—
(Thy servants love her very stones,   15
   and are devoted to her dust)
that the heathen may fear Jahvé's name,
   and all earth's kings Thy majesty !

3.
For " again hath Jahvé built Sion,
   hath shown Himself in His majesty ;
hath turned to the prayer of the poorest,
   and not despised their prayer,"
be this written of the future generation !
   and let the young people then praise Jah
that He looked out of His holy height,   20
   Jahvé looked from heaven upon the earth,
to hear the prisoner's sighs
   to redeem the children of death,
that Jahvé's name may be glorified in Sion
   and His praise in Jerusalem,
when people assemble together
   and kingdoms to serve Jahvé !

4.
Bowed hath He in life my strength,
   shortened my days :
I say : my God take me not away in the midst of life, 25
   Thou whose years are to generation and generation !

Of old Thou hast founded the earth,
and Thy handiwork are the heavens:
they disappear—and Thou wilt continue:
they all grow old like the garment,
as raiment Thou changest them and they also change:
but Thou art the same,
and Thy years have no end.
The sons of Thy servants shall have rest,
and Their seed continue before Thee!

On ver. 4, comp. xxxvii. 20; ver. 6, according to Job xix. 20, also above Ps. cxli. 7, xxii. 15, 18. But the connexion of the thought is here: *because I forgot to eat*, from suffering and weeping could not eat at all (as with other figures is said also in the beginning of the following strophé, ver. 10); I am become so utterly weak and frail, vv. 4, 5; and *because I* always do nothing but *loudly sigh*, I have become so emaciated, so restless, and so forsaken and isolated from all men, vv. 6-8. Quite similarly the doubled series of thought is related in the beginning of the second strophé, vv. 10-11 *a*, 11 *b*-12. The forsakenness of all friends of which this poet complains so much in Ps. lxix., leads him then at the end of the strophé ver. 9, suddenly to a short word concerning the foes of whom he complains in a similar manner in his other songs,—especially Pss. lxix., lxxi.; but here comp. on *b*, Isa. lxv. 15, Jer. xxix. 22. So great is already his suffering and so famous, that those who rage against him (see on cxxxvii. 3), use proverbially his name in curses. Ver. 10 as lxxx. 6; the *ashes* on the head of the mourner, Job. ii. 8. According to ver. 11 it seems to the poet as if God had slung him forth with overpowering hand to a distance (Isa. xxii. 17), and crushed him so that he must soon pass away, comp. ver. 25. Ver. 12 as cix. 23. The Messianic figures vv. 16, 22, 23, are not loftier than as they had been announced by prophets of that time long before, comp. B. Zakh. xiv. 9, 16, 17: but ver. 16 is closely connected in sense with ver. 14 a, and two mediate thoughts find their way between; and from ver. 15 it may be concluded that the poet himself at that time mostly sojourned in the ruins of Jerusalem. It must be meant that the moving love of the faithful even to the stones of these ruins must call forth the Divine pity. Since now this says plainly enough that Jerusalem was at that time completely destroyed, the words vv. 17, 18 can only be introduced so as to point to ver. 19 a; may it be that God thus hearing the deepest prayers, shall soon have gloriously restored Jerusalem for everlasting praise and thanksgiving from the young generation, and may it be written down as for an everlasting monument! With this thought the poet would move the Divine compassion, vv. 17-19 a, and then further carries this out in its Messianic signification, vv. 19 b-23.* Ver. 18. בזה לא as lxix. 34, li. 19; ver. 19 b as lxxi. 18, according to xxii. 31; ver. 21, later applied, lxxix. 11.—Ver. 25 as lxxi. 9, 18. Vv. 26-28, as B. Jes. li. 6. Ver. 29 as Ps. lxix. 36, 37.

C. 77. The Book of Lamentations.

As the last songs carried us into the midst of the period of the destruction of Jerusalem, we may best place here the small Book of Lamentations, which might have been incorporated with the Psalter, had it not long been connected with the books of Jérémjá.

That these songs were not composed till after the destruction is shown by their entire contents. But they cannot have been composed immediately after this, and—as is usually thought—on the ruins of Jerusalem themselves. The grief at this destruction, and all the thousandfold sorest sufferings

---

* The connexion of clauses, vv. 17-19 a and 19 b-23, is therefore quite as above, in two instances in this song: and true it is that a later generation which sings such songs of praise, has the best pleasure in writing down also that which is worthy of praise.

7 *

connected with it was still fresh and unstilled when they were composed. Again, they are provoked by the most vivid and truest touches of recollection of the dread days of the siege and conquest. They stream in upon the poet, so that we can recognize many features of the history of those days much more closely and completely from these songs, than from other writings that have come down; and the poet was evidently enough one of those who himself had lived close at hand through those days of horror, and had tasted the highest sufferings of the time. But those days with their first dreadful consequences and with their first wildest grief were nevertheless at that time manifestly somewhat further removed; and according to the clear sense of the words, i. 3, iv. 18, 19, v. 5, 9, and of the similar v. 6, it admits no doubt that the poet at that time lived among the fugitives who partly before and still more after the destruction of the city, had fled in such great numbers to Egypt. They had fled thither under a thousand sore dangers and privations, and had thought to find there an effective protection against the Chaldeans; but found themselves soon greatly deceived in this, because the Egyptian rulers in their fear of a Chaldean irruption treated them very severely and almost let them starve (iv. 17, 18, v. 4, 8-10).

Meanwhile there was a greater mass of the people of the true religion in Egypt again brought together; and this host could move somewhat more freely than the dispersed at that time in the Chaldean empire; at least they could mourn and lament more openly, and none hindered them from holding a solemn feast of mourning and penitence. Thus we here see the poet taking up the art of plaintive song for a mourning feast of this kind, as it had never yet been applied in Israel; and the fact that this garland of song which he wove was designed from the first to have this higher meaning and to serve publicly for a congregation,—gives to these songs their true value, while it determines their tenor and their peculiar art. To lend words to righteous and profoundest grief, to glorify the trembling heavy sighs on the lips of individuals into the true prayer of the whole congregation, even to draw into the light thoughts of the deepest despondency, in order to relieve the too deeply oppressed bosom by their expression: all this the poet might attempt, as it befitted such a festival. Yea, in this direction the loud public lamentation cannot sound strongly enough, must ever begin anew and gush forth in a roar; but it is good that it should once for all become perfectly clear to itself, and once for all entirely exhaust itself. But if the poet desired by his art at the same time to introduce a mourning celebration which should be worthy of the people and of this congregation there assembled—although small and far-dispersed, yet representing the whole great people of that time—he was bound, in the midst of the streaming outburst of lamentation, to direct above all the heart so grievously afflicted to the quarter where it alone could now immediately find true solace. And that he now understands how to lead the deeply mourning ones, unobserved, to true self-acquaintance with their own great guilt, and thereby only to turn lamentation to sighing, and the wildly raging grief, ever more purely and fully, into true prayer, so that the Divine recompense and new strength may be resolved into the joy of the everlasting Messianic hope, and the most touching prayer for Divine compassion,—this is the best feature in this poet, and it is only by this means that his songs correspond to the object which they manifestly ought to serve. The poet attains this once for all by the fulness of genuine prophetic truths and impulses which lives in him. But he attains it also equally by means of his able employment of everything that could lie in the art of the plaintive song, and in the arrangement of a public solemnity of the kind.

The song of mourning admits (I., pp. 148-152, *Dichter des A. B.*) of a violent and somewhat raging outburst,—an endless flow; but also a reiterated beginning and an ever more complete exhaustion of the complaint, until it can be perfectly calmed and stilled. But the art of worthy celebration and good fulfilment of a public solemnity in the assembled congregation admitted (I., *Dichter des A. B.*, pp. 46 sqq., 82 sqq.) also of a manifold, changing representation by the prophetic poet and of a bringing-near of that which he had to offer; and a species of changing treatment (Drama) might very well consist with the public solemnity. And thus there are five lamentatory fragments in which the vast grief, as if it were too sore and to dense to be exhausted in one, repeatedly rises,—in which as if distributed and diffused, it thrice in ever higher floods gushes forth,—until they are gradually relieved with the grief itself, are shortened, and come to an end. But thus there are five particular treatments which here follow step by step upon one another, and with the changing series of which the first great treatment of true complaint and Divine mourning is completed. We look upon *Jerusalem first* herself (represented as a *woman*), as if condemned to deepest mourning, we look upon her actual present condition,[*] and we hear how she agonizes and complains:[†] but of what use is her incessant lament and her sincerest supplication for Divine grace to individuals? Thus the *prophet secondly* rises,—only the more deeply to begin his lament over Sion, to bewail, namely, the fact that none other than God his Lord Himself has so sorely afflicted, and implacably punished her; but of what avail his most burning complaints,[‡] his pointing to the fall of Jerusalem as the true and last cause of its present unutterable sorrow,[§] finally his despondent demand of the half-fallen, deserted walls that they themselves should bewail their sorrow before God?[||] Nowhere as yet will lament and despair pass

---

[*] Op. i. 1-6, 7-11.   [†] i. 12-17, 18-22.
[‡] ii. 1-6, 7-11.   [§] ii. 12-17.
[||] ii. 18-22. All that is grand and noble is only prized at its highest as it passes away; and such was the case with these walls, grey with age which seemed still more objects for protection than a common city, and which now in the midst of their ruins seemed to have become a mysterious power, comp. B. Jes. lxii. 6.

away. But now appears suddenly,—in the *third* place,—an *individual man;* the individual may, according to his most personal experiences, properly be the first in deepest lament, so that here despondency for the third time begins, still more sorely :* but the individual may also most readily come by his own deepest reflection on the eternal relation of God to man,† to the true knowledge of his own sins, and the necessity of repentance,‡ and therewith to believing prayer.§ Who is this individual who thus laments, and thus supplicates? whose *I* passes unobserved but quite in the right place into the *we*?‖ O man, he is thy own picture! every one ought now to speak and think as he! and thus, imperceptibly by this very speech, beginning most grievously, for the first time grief is resolved into true prayer. Thus this fragment shows how even in such wildest turmoil the Divine altitude may be gained; any one may gain this by the steeping of himself in the full and serious truth, and where *one* has not yet found it, there is generally as yet no true beginning of better things; therefore an individual is here put forward as carrying through the whole of this necessary action in himself. Now indeed with true penitence on the part of the individual little is as yet gained; and again there rises *fourthly* the lament of *man* over this unutterable suffering, proceeding rather from the nearest present, especially over the degradation of the highest and noblest men of Israel :¶ but the consideration that even the prophets and priests themselves are under the deepest guilt, and that the false confidence of the people would never be thoroughly removed,** here quells and shortens all his words into obscure complaint, so that the righteous complaints the more readily are converted into the Messianic hope, and for the first time again a beam of hope tends to brighten everything.†† Hence, *fifthly,* it rises once more as the lament of the *whole community,*

---

* iii. 1-18.   † iii. 19-33.   ‡ iii. 31-51.   § iii. 52-66.   ‖ iii. 40 sqq.
¶ iv. 1-6, 7-11.   ** iv. 12-17.   †† iv. 18-22.

to pass entirely into believing penitential prayer, and all glowing, becoming still shorter, to resound in the most moving sighs.*

But the poet desired to clothe the song-garland of the words of this mournful solemnity according to the fresh art of that time, in alphabetic attire: this required short, sharp-cut verse-members, streaming and gushing forth in long series; and nowhere are these so suitable as where the mournful feeling is poured forth in loose sobbing clauses. Thus he carries the long members through his songs, places each abruptly apart, and so forms in the two first of these five songs, out of every three members a set, or small strophé, at the head of which the alphabet takes it course. In the third song,—which as it breaks forth in the midst, introduces the most fluctuating but also deepest and most decisive language, and where all the sensibilities flow together into an extreme turbidity, in order finally to be the more readily relieved,—the art rises to its height, all three verse-members of the twenty-two sets beginning with the same letter. In the fourth song, where the high flood of complaint begins to fall, each set embraces only two, in the last only *one* long member. But with this last ceases also the external alphabetic chasing, as if suited no longer for this congregational song, quite otherwise occasioned; but the twenty-two members still remain, only in such a way that each two form a higher unity, and therefore the whole is rapidly unfolded in eleven double long members. But the *one* great strophé which thus fills this whole last song is the harsher for this and thus finishes the whole grave treatment of the solemnity with the greater weight.† Each of the first four songs is divided on the other hand into four great strophés, each of six and five verses, just as in the above-mentioned songs, pp. 320 sqq.

---

* Chap. v.

† All this solves the earlier suggested doubt as to whether the poet did not intend also in chap. v. the alphabetic series.

That the five songs are of the same poet,* is clear enough from the following facts: the whole five-parted poem is only *one* great song of lamentation, according to ancient genuine Hebrew arrangement and execution, which has here a grandeur found nowhere else. The same conclusion is yielded as certainly from the similarity of the style, the stamp of the language, and of the figures, thoughts and feelings. If the poet in the speech of the individual man, chap. iii., repeats many older poetic words, he does so only because this speech must be as it were more many-sided and reflective, and the poet did not allow the flight of his own thoughts to unfold so freely in it as in chapters i., ii., and especially in chap. iv. We have nothing further from this poet; he has as in several portions of the language, so also in the alphabetic arrangement, that which is peculiar, placing the פ before the ע. In chap. i. where this is not now seen, the ע may have been brought by later hands into its ordinary place in the series.† That the poet thus composed in Egypt is clear from the above; and equally, that he was a man of prophetic vein. But that he was Jérémjá can in nowise be proved; on the contrary, according to all indications of the style, it is impossible to think so. He might however be a pupil of Jérémjá, Barûkh or another. But if this small song-book originated in Egypt, and was destined in the first instance for the community there, it is very clear that it might be early more closely united with Jérémjá's writings, and at the same time be preserved by their means.

---

* As I always maintained; it is sad to see how often and how obstinately it has always been sought to deny this.

† Probably because a later reader thought the speech of Jerusalem, vv. 12-15, must continue with ver. 16; but the language might be interrupted cursorily by ver. 17, and it will be found that the sequence of the thoughts is rendered better if ver. 17 stands before ver. 16.

CHAPTER I.

1.

Ah! how she sits there desolate—the city so rich in people,
is become as a widow—the great one among the peoples,
the princess among the cities—become subject!
Bitterly weeping in the night, the tears on her cheek,
she has not *one* comforter—of all who loved her,
all her friends betrayed her—and became her foes,
Departed into the lands is Judah—from misery and much servitude;
she sat among the peoples—finding no place of rest,
all her persecutors overtook—her in the midst of distresses.
Empty, Sion's ways mourn—without any festive visitors,
all her gates desolate, her priests sighing,
her maidens led forth—she herself deeply troubled.
5 Foes became lords over her, too prosperous her enemies,
because Jahvé left her in grief—for her many transgressions,
her tender children went—in captivity before the oppressor.

Ver. 1. Here as elsewhere throughout where it is necessary, the rhythm of the three-membered verse is neglected because of the Massôr. accentuation.

Ver. 2. On the betrayal here intended and in ver. 19, through the peoples allied at that time with Jerusalem, comp. the *Gesch. des V. Isr.*, iii., pp. 741, sqq. of the 2nd edition.

Ver. 3. The word בָּלַךְ *roam the land, or wander forth* among the strangers, which here well fitted into the alphabetic succession, leads the poet to the mention of the numerous and yet unhappy multitude of fugitives who partly before and partly after the destruction of Jer. sought to withdraw themselves from the Chaldean rule; comp. the *Gesch. des V. Isr.*, iii., p. 750, iv., pp. 5, sqq. The same circumstance is treated of more fully below, iv. 19, v. 5, 6.

Ver. 4. The LXX read for בוּגֹרת which here expresses too little, נהוּגֹרת *led away captive*, which in itself is correct, and is perfectly safe and suitable.

Gone from the daughter of Sion—is all her glory:
her princes become like harts—which found no pasture,
so that they went powerless — from before the
pursuer.

2.

Hard are the thoughts of Jerusalem—the day of misery, of
expulsion.
when through oppressors her people fell, she was
without helpers,
the foes seeing her, laughed at her ruin.
In sin sank Jerusalem: therefore she became a horror,
all her honourers despised her, after they saw her bareness,
she herself also sighs, and turned backwards;
Jerusalem soiled her steps, thoughtless of her future!
so she sank wondrously, has no comforter,
"see, Jahvé, my misery! how proudly doth the foe
behave!"
Kings stretched out the hand — after all her ancient
treasures, 10
the heathen even she saw—come into the sanctuary,
whom Thou didst command that they should never
come into Thy congregation;

Ver. 7. The words מִימֵי קֶדֶם
כֹּל מַחֲמוּדֶיהָ אֲשֶׁר הָיוּ which
belong quite well to ver. 10, appear to
stand here incorreectly, although they
are found in the LXX. They are
brought with difficulty into the verse-rhythm; but what is still more important,
they give no genuine sense in this
verse. For they would have to be understood as follows: Jerusalem thinks in
the days of misery, i.e., now, of all her
old treasures. But this thought is in
nowise suggested here by anything elsewhere; still less carried out; the following members lead to other thoughts.

Ver. 9. For טֻמְאָתָהּ must be here
read טֻמְאָתָהּ (194 b), because the
verb better suits here both the mode of
expression and the whole connexion.
For the figures which predominate vv.
8, 9, are the same which find application in Isa. xxx., 22, and which are
explained if we bear in mind that the
city is likened unto a maiden, scorned
by all—therefore to one scorned for her
impurity: and in this comparison the
vileness is in the fact that this maiden
became thus unclean only through her
own sin and light-mindedness.

Long hath her whole people sighed—seeking bread,
gave up for food its dearest—to draw breath,
" see, Jahvé, and behold, how I am despised!"
" Men call to ye, all ye wanderers of the way, behold and see:
is there a sorrow like mine which was done to me,
whom Jahvé afflicted—in the day of His fiery anger?
Nay, He sent fire into my bones, glowed through them,
spread a net for my feet, turned me round,
made me quite waste, sick always;
O how by His hand—is the yoke of my sufferings fastened!
the withes have come upon my neck, my strength was
bent;
the Lord gave me into hands—which are irresistible;
15 Put away hath the Lord all my mighty ones whom I
had,
called out a feast hither, to break in pieces my warriors,
the Lord trod the wine-press — of the maiden,
daughter of Juda,

Ver. 10. The addition *ancient* adopted here from ver. 7.

Ver. 12, אליכם stands here only more shortly as in Prov. viii. 4; and לוא must stand here iii. 38 interrogatively, as is said in I., p. 144, *Dichter des A. B.*, on 2 Sam. xxiii. 5.

Ver. 13, רדה might here appear related to רצץ-רצח, דצה *shatter to pieces*; but this (although Tanchûm compares *raddadd*, Arab.) would not suit the figure of the fire; the word is better understood as related to רתח *glow*. Then it is not necessary here to read with the LXX יוֹרְדָּפָה or rather still 'better for the context הוֹרִדָהּ " from the heaven he sent fire, into my bones he cast it down."

Ver. 14, שׂקד seems related to the Aramæan סבד and to *dilaghat, dilaghad, dilaghath,* Arab., and to mean " press," but also " twine, weave," which best suits in the connexion of the two first members. The figure is then borrowed from a yoke harnessed with many cords, and the rare שׂקד was certainly the technical expression for it. Tanchûm explains it only according to the derivation by *t'lak, attached.* On the literal sense of בידי, see § 333 b.

Ver. 15, סָלָה *take up* or *take away,* cast away, here in the bad sense of our *give up*, be unwilling to protect, according to the Aramæan signification which the word has, Ps. cxix. 18. A *feast,* as ii. 7, 22; and as the *wine-press treading* points to the blood-bath prepared for the city and for its warriors (as B. Jes. lxiii. 2, 3) the figures of all these members, just as that of the last of the preceding verse borrowed from the wild festival of the autumn feast (the Dionysia). It is not then necessary to read with the LXX כִּמְקְרָבִי.

Running with water is my eye, over this I weep, weep,
    that far from me is a comforter, a reviver,
    forsaken are my sons, because the enemy hath gained
                                                the day!"
Sion stretcheth out her hands, yet she hath no comforter:
Jahvé hath round about Jakob—ordered his oppressors,
    Jerusalem became—a horror among them.

4.

" Truly, righteous alone is Jahvé, because I followed not
                                                His word!
    hear then ye peoples all—and see my grief:
    my maidens and young men—went in captivity!
Upon my lovers I called: they betrayed me
    my priests and elders—fainted away in the city,
        as they sought food for themselves, to draw breath.
View, Jahvé, my distress; my inward part seethes,   20
    my heart turns round in me, because I followed not;
    without the sword desolated, within as the pest!
Well heard they me sigh, "I have no comforter,"
    all my foes heard my trouble, glad that *Thou* hast done
                                                it:
    Thou bringst the day, thou call'st the time—that they
                                                become like me!

Ver. 19 *a* is explained from ver. 2; *b* and *c* as above, ver. 11. The addition of the LXX וְלֹא מָצְאָה is unnecessary if יכ is rightly understood.
Ver. 20 *like as* the pest, for the real pest did not at that time exist, but only something similar; thus כ stands like the Sanskr. *iva*, lessening, mitigating, through comparison.
Ver. 21 *b that Thou hath done it*, so said according to that old belief of the inseparableness of a people and its God,—expressed similarly in Num. xxi. 29; but what veiled and as if suppressed

sigh lies here at the same time in these two words!—Were the correct reading in *c*, and were קָרָאתָ actually the second person,—as the Massor. punctuation would make it—הֵבֵאתָ must be taken,—as Tanchûm proposed (§ 223 *b*)—as *precative:* "wouldst Thou but bring the day when Thou criest, that they should become as I!" Or the word might be uttered in shortened form as the first person (§ 190 *d*) qarât, and the whole clause *c* be thus connected with *b*: " glad that *Thou* hast done it, hast brought the day when I cry 'my

To (Zu) Thy throne may all their evil come
do to them as Thou hast done to me—for all my faults!
for many are my sighs and my heart sick."

CHAPTER II.

1.

1 Ah, how He over-clouds with anger—the Lord the daughter
of Sion,
has from heaven to earth—cast Israel's splendour,
and of His footstool—has not thought on the day of
wrath!
Blasted hath the Lord without sparing—all the pastures of
Jakob,
in His anger the strongholds—of the daughter of Juda
destroyed,
cast to the earth, desecrated—the kingdom with its
princes;
Destroyed in fiery anger—every horn of Israel,
turned back His right hand—before the enemy's face,
and burned Jakob, as fire-flame which devours around,
Enemy-like, horrible, bent the bow,
as an adversary, aimed with his right hand—and slew
that which feeds the eyes,
in the daughter of Sion's tent—as fire poured forth
His glow.

fate be theirs.'" But the *prec.*, which manifestly best suits the connexion,—particularly in transition to ver. 22,— is most readily placed here, if according to the reading of the LXX, עֵת is supplied after קִרְאַת.

Ver. 1. *His footstool*, the Temple, the same likewise called in ancient phraseology vv. 4, 6, *the tent*.

Ver. 2. If חִצִּיעַ לָאָרֶץ is taken with the last member, it fits more readily into the verse-structure, and it is then the less necessary to read with the LXX after ver. 9, מַלְכָּהּ *their*

king, for מַמְלָכָה. But because the language was of kingdom and princes, *every horn*, *i.e.*, every power, is mentioned in ver. 3 *a*.

Ver. 4. If נִצָּב is thus read correctly, it must have been taken in the first member with יְמִינוֹ כְצָר *standing there with hostile right hand* (prop. so

Foe-like was the Lord, annihilated Israel,   5
annihilated all its castles, broke the strong hold to
    pieces,
and heaped up in the daughter of Juda—sighing and
    groaning.
Grimly, like the vine, he destroyed His tabernacle, his
    strong place;
forgotten in Sion the Lord left—feast and sabbath,
rejected in his anger's rage—king and priest and
    prince.

2.

Harsh toward His altar, the Lord rejected His sanctuary,
gave over to the hand of the enemy—the walls of her
    castles ;
in Jahvé's house they clamoured—as if it were a feast!
In Jahvé's mind it was to destroy—the daughter of Sion's
    wall
he drew the line, kept not His hand from destroying,
left wall and rampart together—to sink into ruins
    and rue.

that his right hand is as an enemy's). But to the connexion better suits the *perf.* בָּעַם which is then best understood as *direct*, *i.e.*, *aim* (comp. Ps. xi. 2), and with which יָמִין is to be taken according to § 281 c. But at the same time after כְּאוֹיֵב in the first member, וְאֶבְזָר must probably be inserted, comp. iii. 4, to which the addition ὑπεναντίος LXX points. Thus the *right hand* of God forms here, ver. 4 b, the true opposition to ver. 3 b. *What feeds the eyes*, i.e., the dearest children, spouses, and other human beings of the kind.

Ver. 6. The reading כְּגַנּוֹ suits according to Isa. v. 1 sqq, Ps. lxxx. 9, and other passages better than כְּגַן as

the garden ; and the figure is the more suitable, as the *vine* is the sensuous picture as of all Palestine, so especially of its sanctuary, which is here named *the Tabernacle*, and is more closely designated by the *festive solemnity*. On שָׂבֵּךְ from a possible שָׂכָה=שָׂפָה see § 257 d. The addition וְשִׂי at the end according to the LXX.

7. *A feast*, comp. above i. 15.

Ver. 8. *He drew the line*, as one does in cold blood to measure off the territory to be destroyed.—*Mourning and ruins*, c (*ruin* and *rue*)—only to render as far as possible the play on words.— (Ger.: *trauer und trümmer.*)

Jerusalem's gates sank into the earth, He tore, broke
    asunder her bars;
her king, her princes are among Gentiles, there is no
    more law,
also her prophets found — no more a vision from
    Jahvé;
10 Keeping silence there sit on the ground—the eldest of
    Sion's daughters,
with dust cast on their head, girded with sackcloth;
hold their head sunk to the earth—Jerusalem's
    maidens.
Languishing in tears is my eye, my inward part seethes,
my liver poured to the ground—for the wound of the
    daughter of my people,
because child and suckling fainted away—in the streets
    of the city.

3.

Mothers were addressed: " where is corn and wine?"
because they as wounded ones swooned in the streets of
    the city,
because their soul was poured out—in their mother's
    bosom.—

Ver. 9. *There is no more law*, because the public power under which the Law of Israel had hitherto ruled, is now ruined. If in this way the two clauses *b* refer to the enduring present, *c* returns to *a* and to the whole previous history of the destruction to complete the picture of this history by that which, according to the feeling of antiquity is the gloomiest feature of all,—that at the end, during the last days of the siege and then during the destruction, prophets were no longer heard. In point of fact, what we know from the history of Jérémjá and other sources agrees with this: but the *perf.* מָצְאוּ must be taken as strictly narratory.

Ver. 11. *Daughter of my people* like daughter of Juda, daughter of Sion, *i.e.*, poetic name of the mother-city and so of the land.—Also the words, ver. 11 *c* and ver. 12 are only narratory. of how it was in the last most fearful months and days. And manifestly this extremest horror is only touched on here at the end.

Ver. 12. *b*. *they languished*, the children, as is clear from ver. 11.

Now wherewith conjure I thee? compare I thee—thou
daughter of Jerusalem?
what compare I to thee, to console thee,—maiden
daughter of Sion?
yet great as the sea is thy wound!—who will heal
thee?
Of false and insipid things—prophesied to thee thy
prophets,
uncovered not thy guilt—to make thee sound again,
prophesied to thee high sayings — of deceit and
seduction.
Riding by, men clapped their hands at thee—all, 15
hissed, shook their head,—at the daughter of Jerusalem;
" is that the city called—the crown of beauty, the
delight of all the earth?"
Spreading open their mouth at thee—all thy foes
hissed, gnashed with the teeth — said, "we have
destroyed!
that is truly the day that we hoped for—found—
saw!"
Thus Jahvé carried out in deeds—what He had determined,
fulfilled His word, long commanded—destroyed without
pity,
let the enemy rejoice over thee—raised thy oppressor's
horn.

4

Unweariedly cry to Jahvé, O wall of the daughter of Sion!

Ver. 13. Conjure, *i.e.*, by serious words, the poet would instruct or comfort Sion by comparison of similar calamities with her present condition; but immediately finds that there is nothing to compare with this condition of guilt and punishment; comp. iv. 6.

Ver. 14. The reading השיב שעת has the same sense which rightly understood it has everywhere, and which I.

now along time ago, further explained, comp. on B. Job, p. 309.

Ver. 15 c, from Ps. l. 2, and xlviii. 3, comp. above, Vol. I., 313, 222; but changed for כְּלִילַת מִכְלָל prop. *the city crowned with beauty*, according to Ez. xxvii. 3, comp. with xxviii. 12.

Ver. 17 c, according to 1 Sam. ii. 1.

Ver. 18. As the two first words in the connexion give no sense, לִבָּךְ

let streams like to the brook—run tears day and night!
be not numb,—let not the daughter of Thine eye rest!

Up,—cry by night at the beginning of the watches,
pour forth like water thy heart—before the face of the Lord,
lift to Him thy hands—for thy children's soul!
[who fainted in hunger at all street-corners].

20 " View, Jahvé, and behold—whom dost Thou so deal with?
shall women consume their body's fruit, the children of their care?
shall in the Lord's sanctuary—priest and prophet be destroyed?

Weltered on the ground without—boy and old man,
my maidens and youths—fallen by sword,
slain by Thee on the day of Thy wrath, slaughtered without pity!

To (Zu) me callest Thou as if it were a feast—my sojourners round about:
but none escaped, survived—on the day of Jahvé's wrath;
those I tended and brought up—my foe annihilated!"

עֲקִי must be read for it, "cry with thy heart" (as above, ver. 4 b), i.e., let the heart-cry resound, comp. Ps. lxxvii. 2, 3, where the סוּב is found again, just as in ver. 4 the much-used הִתְעַמֵּף. Perhaps that song is of the same poet. *Daughter of the eye, i.e.,* apple of the eye. The whole ver. 18 corresponds fully to ver. 19.

Ver. 19. The bracketed words would, if they proceed from the poet, form a fourth verse-member. Actually they point to related images of the poet, vv. 11, 12, iv. 1, and stand here, not unsuitably to the mere sense. But if this solitary violation of the law of these verses can hardly be thought original, then accidentally the poet would here for once neglect his own law.

Ver. 20, according to the LXX, פְּרִי בִטְנָם for the here too short פְּרִים.

Ver. 22. The very frequent phrase מָגוֹר מִסָּבִיב in Jérémjá, *horrors around!* (comp. above Ps. xxxi. 14) cannot be compared, because מְגוּרַי points to something else, and must be

SONGS OF THE DISPERSION. 115

CHAPTER III.

1.

Ah, I am the man who saw misery—through the rod of
His wrath! 1
Ah, He led and brought me—into gloom, not into light!
Against me He returns repeatedly—every day His hand,
Blighted my flesh and skin—broke my bones,
Built round about me—poison and trouble, 5
Brought me into darkness—like the dead of old,
Drove me within thick rails, made heavy my chains,
Depressed my prayer—although I lament and cry,
Drew hewn stones about my ways, destroyed my paths.
Even as a lurking bear is He to me, a lion in ambush, 10
Even as a leader astray, tearing in pieces and leaving
desolate,
Even an archer, setting me as a mark for the arrow.
Fixed He in my reins—His quiver's sons;
For all peoples I became a derision, their mocking-song
every day;
Full of bitterness He made me, drunk with worm-
wood; 15
Gave to my teeth gravel to crush, rolled me in ashes;

rather referred to the men named
in b and c. The word means *my
sojourners round about*, and by this are
certainly intended the inhabitants of
the defenceless country towns and
villages which are related to the
protecting chief city as *suburbs*,
בְּנִים (Metœkes, the LXX correctly
παροικίαι). Thus the whole verse
plainly alludes to a great occurrence in
those days of the siege: from the
country almost all fled into the capital
(the like took place under Titus) as if

there was to be held in it as, on other
occasions, a great feast: but alas! it
became in the end for her the great
feast of slaughter in the final conquest.
Thus the question is renewed whether
מִגּוּרַי does not signify the same in
Ps. lv. 16, comp. above, p. 257, Vol. I.
Vv. 6 sqq. much from the B. Job; ver. 6
literally as Ps. cxliii. 3; ver. 7 at the
end, as from Ps. lxxxviii. 9. *Sons of the
quiver*, ver. 13, arrows. On בְּנִי, ver.
14, see § 177 a.

Ver. 16. The בְּ of בֶּחָצָץ belongs
to the simple verb, גָּרַס, *crush*, which

like many verbs of the kind, *e.g.*, בָּרַשׁ,
i. 17, is connected either immediately,

8 *

Good I forgot utterly, prosperity was against me,
Gathering that my victory was at an end, my hope from
Jahvé.

2.

Hold before Thee my misery and sufferings, the worm-
wood, the venom!
20 Holds them before her, is bowed down—my soul.
Hold I rather *this* before me, *therefore* hope:
In Jahvé mercies endure, his compassion is never exhausted,
In the morning they are ever new, great is Thy
faithfulness;
In Jahvé my soul finds her portion! therefore I wait for
Him.
25 Jahvé is good to the waiter for Him, to the soul that
seeks Him.
Jahvé's salvation quietly to await, that is good,
Just and good is it for a man in his youth to bear a yoke;
Keeping silence, let him sit alone, if He has bowed him
with burdens,
Kiss rather the dust—perhaps there is yet hope.
30 Knocks let him receive on his cheeks, take fully the
reproach.

i.e., with the accusative, or more loosely with בְּ; it is properly He caused my teeth to crush stones. כפש is like *khafas*, bend, Hiph., cause one to bend, cast down, or rather roll himself.

Ver. 17. Here כפש must be subject, to, which תינח as third pers. *fem. sing.* belongs. זכר is, therefore, here intransitive. That in ver. 19, not God, but the first best hearer is addressed, is self-intelligible; the sharper is then the opposition of self-recollection, ver. 20. For here כשי is subject for the whole verse. In this and the following verse, the poet has, however, plainly Ps. xlii. 5, 6 before his eyes. The *this* and *therefore*, ver. 21, point to vv. 22, 23, hence כִּי, ver. 22.

Ver. 22. המנו must, either as a reading, or rather as a possible expression, be corrupted from תָּמוּ, § 84 v.—Ver. 24 *a* after Ps. xvi. 5.

Ver. 26. The ויחיל is here (§ 235 a) to be so taken, that יָחִיל, although with *t* remaining, is jussive. Good is it that one should wait, and that quietly, for Jahvé's salvation.

Ver. 28. *He*, Jahvé, according to vv. 25, 26.—Ver. 30 later, still further carried out as a picture, B. Jes. l. 6.

Look! not for ever does the Lord cast away!
Let Him cause grief,—so also pity according to His
fulness of grace,
Letteth mortals suffer, grieve,—not according to His
heart.

3.

Maiming, crushing under foot of all earth's prisoners,
Miscarriage of the man's right—before the face of the
Highest, 35
Misrepresentation of any man's cause—the Lord approves
not.

Never spake any, and that came to pass—which the Lord
had not commanded;
Not evil like good should—proceed from the mouth of the
Highest?
Nor should the living man sigh—only over his punish-
ments!

O try, search we our ways, return to Jahvé, 40
O lift we heart with hands—to the God in heaven!
O we transgressed, followed not—Thou pardonest not;
Round about Thou didst draw in anger, pursuing, slaying
without pity,
Round about Thee clouds, that no prayer pierces through;
Round about amongst peoples Thou makest us—refuse
and shame. 45

See! they open the mouth against us—all our enemies,
Snares and terror have we—deceit, wounds;

Vv. 34-36 prop. *to tread*, that one should tread under foot all prisoners, *i.e.*, that all prisoners be trodden down; *the Lord has not seen*, *i.e.*, determined and approved.

Ver. 39 prop. for what sighs the living man? (who therefore, as long as he lives, can better himself and do better than sigh) the man for his punishments? (for strictly taken he sighs more over his own transgressions, instead of doing away with these).

Ver. 43. After סכותה באף, this sentence is broken off, only to be completed in ver. 44. Prop., Thou madest a covering in anger—madest them as if intercepted by clouds from Thee.

Streams of water run from my eyes—for the wound of my
                                    people's daughter!
Tears without rest, without ceasing drips mine eye,
50 Tears—till Jahvé behold and see from heaven.
Tears storm my soul—for all the daughters of my city.

4.

Urge me in chase like birds—my causeless foes,
Underneath, in the pit, bound my life, rolled stones on me;
Upon my head waters flowed, I thought, "I am lost."
55 Unto Thee, Jahvé, I cry from the deepest pit;
Unheard be not my complaint! Thine ear is open to my cry;
Unto my call Thou art near;—sayest: fear not!
Verily Thou defendest my soul, Lord, redeemest my life;
Viewest, Jahvé, my oppression; O judge my cause!
Viewest all their vengeance, what they only think
60   of me;
Well hearest Thou their scorn, Jahvé, what they alone
                                    think against me,
What my adversaries speak, counsel—against me every day,
Where they stand and sit, behold! I am but their
                                    sing-song.
(Zealously) wilt Thou punish them, Jahvé, according to
                                    their handiwork!

Ver. 48 as ii. 11, iv. 10.
Ver. 51. עוללה comp. i. 12, 22, ii. 20, is here quite as the Lat. *afficit* meant in the bad sense; and -ל as iv. 5 (§ 277 c). The *daughters of my city* are the country towns (Ps. xlviii. 12), and what is here so briefly said is explained from ii. 22.
Ver. 53. צמת must here be identical with צמד, bind; comp. צפד, cleave, iv. 8. The words here and vv. 54, 55, from Pss. xl. 3, lxix. 2 sqq., with xlii. 8, xxxi. 23.
Ver. 56. If צוחתי may not be read for רוחתי, then רוחה must

be understood as a ventilation, *i.e.*, loud complaining; it is certain that it must signify as much as the immediately following more frequent word שועה which looks like a gloss.—On the many *precatives*, vv. 56-66 comp. above, i. 21; they pass desultorily, up to ver. 63, into the more restless *imper.*, till finally, vv. 64-66, restful expectation follows. Just so, with them concludes the following prayer, iv. 21, 22.
Ver. 63. Sit and stand, *i.e.*, live, act. —*Sing-song*, a word in Hebrew also intentionally thus lengthened, to designate mocking songs.

(Zealously) blind their heart, on them Thy curse! 65
Zealously pursue, destroy them—under Jahvé's heaven! *

CHAPTER IV.

1.

Ah, how common becomes gold, the best ore is changed, 1
sacred stones are cast away—at all corners of the
streets!
Burghers of Sion, the dearest and most esteemed for gold,
ah, how do they pass for earthen pitchers, work of
potter's hand!
Drawing out the breast, the she-wolves suckle their
young:
my people's daughter becomes—cruel like the ostriches
in the desert.
Even the suckling's tongue—clave for thirst to the palate,
children demanded bread; none brought it to them;
Forlorn sat in the streets—they who ate dainty bits, 5
those brought up in purple—embraced the dung.
Greater became the punishment of the daughter of my
people—than that of Sodom,
that as in a twinkling was overturned, whereon hands
did not rage.

Ver. 1. Apparently the lament begins with something foreign to this connexion; how common and base becomes everything in the world! Gold, best ore, sacred stones themselves (e g., those of the high-priestly attire) came to be regarded as in a world turned mad and raging, the commonest things! But how near this complaint lies nevertheless, is shown forthwith in ver. 2 ; ah, the noblest of Juda, who in the beginning of the second strophe, ver. 7, are further designated, - how were they treated as the commonest wares, as in a moment of rude horse-play broken in pieces! But the language passes thence, vv. 3, 4, 5, immediately to the sign of quite another picture from those and from still later days of horror,—of the staring obtuseness with which the besieged, under the prevalence of hunger, looked even upon the whimpering of children! So that it may be finally said, ver. 6, that Jerusalem is still more grievously fallen than Sodom.

Vv. 3-6. *My people's daughter*, the mother-city, as ii. 11, iii. 48, iv. 6. 10. The *ostriches* after Job xxxix. 13-16.

2.

Higher than snow beamed her princes, purer than milk
glittered in their body with pearls, with sapphire in
their shape;
Inkier than blackness is now their form, they are not
recognized without;
their skin clave to the bones, become dry as wood.
Judge them happier who by the sword—than those who
by hunger have fallen,
who melt away, pierced through—as by the dryness of
the field.
10 Know, they cooked their very children—the pitiful hands
of the women,
they became to them for food, because of the wound of
the daughter of my people.
Launched not forth Jahvé all His terror, poured out His
fiery anger,
and kindled in Sion a fire that consumes her foundations?

3.

Might they believe, kings of the earth—and all inhabitants
of the world,

Ver. 7. It seems that the poet is thinking of the royal and high-priestly stock. *Unrecognized*, so that they might be the more readily utterly despised, as here from the beginning onwards, vv. 1, 2, was described. For the whole second strophé is also filled, vv. 7-11, with the heartrending pictures of hunger; so that ver. 11 at the end forms only an equally general conclusion to that in the first strophé, ver. 6.

Ver. 9. תנובות appears to have arisen through change of sound from תלובות or תְּלָאָבוֹת, *dryness*. For if one would explain, with that reading, כְּמוֹ as *without* fruits of the earth (which however does not mean

from want of them), the necessary elucidation to *pierced through, melt away*, would be wanting. *Who pierced through, i.e.,* slain, died, as *melting away from the field's dryness*, emaciated by the sun's heat; but, alas! here hunger withers them up! This strong figure (comp. v. 10) thus expresses but the same as the above, ver. 8 b, and is drawn out by this. If כְּמוֹ could stand so readily before another proposition, it would so stand here.

Vv. 12, 13. None among the Gentiles, neither king nor others, had supposed that the sins of the prophets and the priests would bring the besieging Gentiles into the city, as came

SONGS OF THE DISPERSION. 121

that foe and oppressor would come—into Jerusalem's
  gates,
Now for her prophet's sins, her priest's iniquities,
who forgot the blood of the just—in her midst ?
O how they staggered blindly in the streets, spotted with
  blood,
so that their clothes—could not be touched !
Retire, unclean one! they cried; depart, depart, touch 15
  not !—yet they brawled, yet they staggered ;
said, " among the heathen—they shall sojourn no
  more !"
Scattered are they by Jahvé's glance, no more beheld :
the priests were not respected, old men not favoured.
Truly, our eyes languish—for our vain help,
in our waiting wait we—for the people that helps not ?

4.

Upon our steps they spy—we must not go to our markets ;

to pass. This is an important testimony on the opinion of the Gentiles of the prophets and priests of that time in Jerusalem.

Vv. 14-16 explain, ver. 13, further by bringing forward a striking fragment of the history of the last siege, which indeed we now find nowhere so definitely touched upon as here. We know from Hezeqiel's book the internal controversies of those years; a schism, brought on by the most considerable priests and prophets, must at that time have induced a blind confidence that the banished would soon return, *not longer sojourn among the Gentiles* (ver. 15 b), and would render the insurrection in Jerusalem victorious by their own rising and return. But the prophets and priests themselves so raged,—when they should have been collected and pure,—filled with delirious passion against their own fellow-citizens who would not believe in this, caused their adversaries to be slain, and were stained with blood, so that men must avoid and shun them as unclean; nevertheless, they go on in this way ; and therefore, in Jahvé's angry glance at such priests, the heathen were victorious, determined on destruction, and carried it out both on these madmen and on all other citizens. כִּי is here, and ii. 13, just as גַּם, yet, although no negative proposition precedes, § 354 a; אָמְרוּ stands often thus shortly, without *copula*, and as it elsewhere stands so alone; therefore here too בַּגּוֹיִם must not be connected with it. But the more emphatically ver. 17 now concludes with the glance at the foolish confidence of Egyptian help prevailing amongst those who had fled to Egypt; for certainly here by *the people that helps not* are meant, after Isa. xxx. 1-7, xxxi. 1-3, the Egyptians.

Ver. 18. In the beginning of the last strophe the glance at Egypt as it

near is our end, full our days—yea, our end comes.
Untiring, swifter than the eagles of heaven—were our pursuers,
followed us up on the mountains, lurked for us in the desert.
Verily, our own breath, Jahvé's Anointed, was snared in
20   their pits,
he in whose shadow we thought—to live among the peoples.—
Well! rejoice only in joy, daughter of Edom dwelling in the land of Uss!
to thee too will the cup come, wilt intoxicate, strip thyself!
To (Zu) its end is thy punishment come, daughter of Sion! not again He leads thee forth;
He visits thy punishment, daughter of Edom! discovers thy sins.

CHAPTER V.

1 Remember, Jahvé, what was done to us,—behold and see our shame!
Our inheritance is fallen to strangers, our houses to foreigners,
Orphaned were we without fathers, our mothers are as widows;

then was, continues: from mere fear of the Chaldæans, it had manifestly forbidden the fugitives at that time from trade and intercourse with Palestine; this appeared with justice the extremest prohibition that could be placed upon them. — But, ver. 19, the language returns suddenly thence to the pictures of the many unhappy attempts at flight before and after the siege, and finally casts, ver. 20, a glance at the king kept at that time captive in Babel, probably Jojakhin (*Gesch. des V. Isr.*, iv., p. 9).

All seems lost; yet, with the rising recollection of the present victory of the Idumeans (comp. the *Gesch.* iv. p. 105 sq.) in conclusion, vv. 21, 22, the Messianic hope again springs up. Elated as they at present are owing to the allotment to them by Nabukodrossor of a wide-territory, so that they now dwell far to the north east *in the land of Uss*, nevertheless the Messianic hope remains secure. The figure of the *cup*, after Hab. ii. 15, 16.

Ver. 3. *Fatherless orphans* because   without our legitimate king, ii. 9, iv. 20,

Our water we drank for money, our wood is on sale for
silver.
On the necks were we pursued; became weary, restless: 5
To Egypt we gave the hand, to Assyria, to eat our fill.
Our fathers sinned, are no more; *we* bear their iniquities;
slaves became lords over us: none frees us from their
hand,
With our soul we fetch our bread—before the sword of
the desert:
our skin is as the oven heated through—before the glowing
breath of hunger. 10
Women did they put to shame in Sion, maidens in the
cities of Juda;
princes were hanged up among them, the elders' countenance not respected;

and without the Theocracy; and as *father* cannot here hold good in the nearest sense, so further *our mothers*, i.e., communities and towns *are as widows*, as i. 1; the words immediately connected, ver. 4, allude to the dear *water* and *wood* in Egypt, necessaries which they had for nothing in Kanáan.

Vv. 5 sqq. By all these attempts at flight touched upon, iv. 19, of so many during and after the siege of Jerusalem, we have attained nothing but that we, *pursued on the necks* (so pursued that the pursuers were ever as it were on our necks) and deadly weary, must at the end be content to subject ourselves partly to the Egyptians, partly to the Assyrians, only in order to eat our fill, not utterly to faint (comp. the same otherwise expressed, i. 11, 19).

Vv. 7 sqq. What an ignominy, that we, atoning for our father's sins, must have for our lords only *slaves*, i.e., Egyptian and Chaldæan eunuchs (court officers)! Comp. the same in Qoh. x. 7, 16.—And nevertheless hear how in vv. 9 sqq. is further depicted—the horri-

ble want of all and the incessant hunger: we must wrest our bread from the desert and its robbers. A noteworthy indication that most of the fugitives in Egypt dwelt on the north-east frontier close to the desert, probably were even bound to dwell there. The עָרִיב connected with the *plur*. (§ 176 *b*).

Vv. 11 sqq. and vv. 12 sqq. now depict the way in which misery seizes on all conditions, ages, sexes; public dis-
honouring of the best women and public crucifixion of the noblest men; the strongest young men, like Samson, Judg. xvi. 21, forced like slaves to the mill-service, the younger as bearers subjected to the burden; neither popular assembly nor music more! (The בָּיִד ver. 12 is best taken locally).—
With this the language turns, vv. 15, 16, and vv. 17, 18, again more to general matters and back to its beginning; for *the fallen crown* can only figuratively signify the whole honourable status of the people, now lost. The connexion between vv. 17, 18 is quite as iv. 21, 22.

Young men they took for the mill, boys tottered under wood;
Elders keep holiday from the market, young men from their singing,
Our heart's joy ceases, into mourning is turned our dancing;   15
Our head's crown is fallen: woe to us that we sinned!
For this our heart became sick, for this our eyes darkened:
for the mount of Sion, that it is desolate, that in it the foxes stray.
Thou, Jahvé, art throned for ever: Thy seat is from generation to generation;
why wilt Thou forget us for ever, forsake for so long a time?   20
Turn us to Thee, Jahvé, that we return! renew our days like those of old!
Or wilt Thou utterly cast us away? be excessively wrath against us?

Ver. 22. On כי אם and the *inf. abs.* see § 356 b. Here again, vv. 19-22, is seen very plainly that two verses are always connected, and each twice two form a higher similarity: ver. 22 corresponds entirely to ver. 20. But the deep prayer for help to genuine repentance corresponds only to the sincere confession of sin made in ver. 16.

D. 71-80, Psalms LXXIII., LXXVII., XCIV.

The longer the sufferings and the whole perplexity of the time of the Exile lasted, the higher might rise the feelings of gloom and despondency of many even of the uncorrupted members of the people of God. But ·the more too might genuine fidelity and the wondrous power of the Messianic hope be brightened and strengthened during this long trial. And the three songs here placed together,—which, according to all signs, are from *one* poet—show to what extent both of those things came to pass, how greatly even among the best men despondency threatened to prevail, and how sore was their struggle against it. For this poet was most deeply affected in this way, by those sufferings, griefs and doubts; but the results and fruits were great in his experience in the end, after he had happily fought his way out of them. He found no rest until he had penetrated the very heart of those Divine secrets, and recognized with piercing glance that if only a true spiritual Israel—to which he himself will cleave with full heart—be distinguished in the Israel of the time: the old truths of the eternal deliverance of good men and the mere deceptive prosperity of the wicked retain their validity. Indeed, history itself ever teaches in the main that the end of unjust men is never to be envied. Having won this higher truth, feeling blessed joy in Jahvé, he can never again utterly despond, he fortifies himself repeatedly by prayer, and by recollection of the light of the old history, and becomes finally for the whole community the never-wearied, inspired singer of praise to Jahvé. Thus he is in this time, when the old power of song threatens more and more to become dormant, one of the last great and fine singers, still full of independent power and beneficent intensity,—like a softly refreshing evening glow after the bright beams of ancient Hebrew poetry.

From this same poet are also, according to all writers, the remaining songs from Pss. xcii.—c., which, however, as only falling in the following period, are not yet brought forward here. Throughout is exhibited in these twelve songs the same intensity and strength of joyous spirit, the same serenity, not admitting of disturbance under painful occurrences. The verse-structure is alike, the construction of the song throughout, short and poetically slight, especially for these times. The poet loves reminiscences of the more ancient history of the splendid times of Israel; but even here he is a genuine lyric poet, lxxvii. 14-21, xcv. 8-11, xcix. 6, 7. He is one of the first poets who again in these late times introduces the ancient abbreviated name of God, *Jah*, lxxvii. 12, xciv. 7,

12, comp. cxxii. 1, cxxx. 3, lxviii. 5, B. Jes. xxvi. 5 (without regard to places like cii. 18, when it is forthcoming only along with the הַלֵּל). It is peculiar to him to call Jahvé *our Creator*, our Shepherd, xcv. 6, 7, c. 3, lxxvii. 21, and to boast that He is now King, Ruler, xciii. 1, xcv. 3, xcvi. 10, xcviii. 6, xcix. 1, 4, comp. xlvii. 3, 7 sqq. (that is, because at that time the new community had again collected itself in greater power, and—its religion being more honoured—began to look upon Jahvé as sensibly ruling from its midst). Further, the strong figure is peculiar to him of the irrational cattle, lxxiii. 27, xcii. 7, xciv. 8, and the similarity in the use of the אָחַר is to be noted, lxxiii. 24, xciv. 15, of the חָשַׁב, lxxiii. 16, lxxvii. 6, of the מָרוֹם, lxxiii. 8, xcii. 9, xciii. 4, of the צוּרִי, lxxiii. 26, xcii. 9, xciv. 22, xcv. 1, חִצָּמִית, lxxiii. 27, xciv. 23, עֵדוּת, xciii. 5, xcix. 7, &c. With Ps. xlvii., lxvi., the here forthcoming songs of praise have much in common, as the frequent רָנַן, הָרִיעַ (where we hear, as in so many elsewhere, the echo of the mighty voice, Isa. xl.—lxvi. vibrate), while the similar הַלֵּל is most favoured only in still later songs: yet the above songs certainly fall in about the same times.

Ps. lxxiii. is entirely characterized by the outburst of the first violent reaction from those doubts, and fresh elevation to the pure truth. In the long and severe sufferings of the people the poet would have almost abandoned himself to the general despair had he not—after long tormenting himself in vain to solve the riddle of the time—finally (instructed probably by some unexpected occurrence, vv. 19, 27) penetrated to the truth; perceiving that according to the eternal mystery of the Divine government, all happiness of the wicked is but apparent, deceptive, quickly passing away, while for innocence and for Israel, so far as it is innocent, there certainly remains even in suffering and in death eternal comfort and inward blessedness. In like manner this enigma of the inequality of outward good is earlier solved by particular great poets, as, *e.g.*, in Ps. xlix.: but in this poet the truth under quite other times and conditions was bound to come to light in a new way and with peculiar force. And now, having endured the conflict, he feels himself, looking back on the sad time of doubt and of danger,—so singularly blessed and enlightened, that he feels urged to express his whole inner experience in the song, and thus this instructive song originates, in which in the godly Israel of that time a nobler and freer self-manifestation begins. Having placed in the very beginning, ver. 1, the supreme truth at which he had arrived, and this quite briefly, he describes in detail the long danger and distress in which he had been under the enigma of the time, until he made his way into the innermost seat of God, and firmly resolved never again so foolishly to doubt, vv. 2-22; and concludes, glancing into the future, with a few beautiful words of immovable fidelity to Him thus known, of most joyous confidence and enlightened hope, vv. 23-28.

The membering of this long song is only doubtful at first sight, on closer investigation is seen to be fixed and certain. For plainly four verses, with eight members of elegant structure in each case form a strophé, while ver. 1 sounds as a happy prelude, and the last strophé, with its five members, in like manner once more comprises the whole contents of the song, closing the whole with brevity and sharpness. Among the six strophés which make up the long body of the song between this prelude and epilogue, the third is extended to five verses and ten members; and this is plainly done only because it ought to give a longer rest in the very middle of the song. For as the first three strophés depict most vividly in long and difficult representation the despondency of that time from which the poet has scarcely as yet freed himself, with equal vividness the last three mark the picture that finally rose out of that despondency. And here only two great strophés might be distinguished, if the smaller measure out of which only the larger ones are developed were not plainly to be recognized.

1 *Good and only good is God to Israel,*
  to those of pure heart!

1. a.

But I—almost staggered my feet,
 my steps had all but slipped,
because I cast envy on the haughty,
 saw the prosperity of the wicked,
" they have no torments,
 well and fat is their body,
in folks' sufferings have no share;
5 are not punished with mankind.

b.

Therefore pride attires their neck,
 cruelty clothes them as an ornament,
their sin came forth from their fat inside,
 they swelled over with heart-images,
they scoff and speak wickedly of oppression,
 speak proudly down,
laying their mouth to heaven,
 while their tongue rages upon earth.

c.

10 Therefore He brings His people *so* far
 (and in full draughts it sups the water),
that it says: ' how knows it God,
 and is knowledge in the All-Highest?
Lo! these are the wicked,
 very long have the careless had the greatest power!
All in vain have I purified my heart,
 and in innocence washed my hands,
and yet remained chastised every day,
 my punishment comes every morning!' "

2. a.

15 When I thought to speak the like,
 I betrayed the manner of Thy sons;

and I purposed to know this,—
vain was it in my eyes:
till I went into God's holy places,
observed their end:
Upon slippery places Thou settest their lot,
hast caused them to fall into deceptions!

b.

O how have they become desolate in a moment,
ground up, consumed in terror!
like as a dream after awakening, 20
Lord, Thou despisest their image, rousing Thyself!—
When my heart is embittered,
I feel my reins as cut through:
I am stupid, without understanding;
like a beast was I before Thee!

c.

Yet I am truly ever with Thee!
hast seized my right hand,
wilt by Thy counsel guide me,
to receive honour lead me.
Whom have I in heaven? 25
and on earth I love naught beside Thee!
though my body and heart fade away:
my heart's rock, my good is ever God!

3.

For lo! they who hate Thee perish,
Thou destroyest every one who is unfaithful to Thee:
but—God's friendship is a good to me,
on the Lord Jahvé I place my trust,
to praise all Thy doings!

1. From vv. 4-14, the considerations which had tempted the poet to depression and to envy are plainly and fully set forth: the sight of the many sufferings of the faithful in the midst

of the wicked who remain in power and far from grief, vv. 4-5; and how thereby their own haughtiness in deeds and thoughts is raised to an extreme pitch, vv. 6-9,—as conversely, the despondency of Israel is increased, vv. 10-14. But it is very conceivable that the poet, according to the custom, often remarked above, of many poets of these centuries, here only repeats expressly what he had said still more explicitly in an earlier song.—Ver. 4. לְמוֹתָם is very suspicious; the sense cannot be: they have no torments *until* their death, because in that case a לָמוֹ is wanting; but the sense which would lie in the words, "their death has no torments," is unsuitable, because this can neither be said generally (in Job. xxi. 13 the connexion of the language is quite different), nor is death here spoken of, for this is to be spoken of in vv. 19 sqq. It seems therefore better to read לָמוֹ תָּם separately; תָּם may well, as seldom תָּמִים and תָּם, Job. xxi. 23 stand in the lower sense. Ver. 7. According to the Massôra the first member would mean: *their eye stares out of fatness* (fat countenance), in arrogance, comp. Job. xv. 27; but according to the second member the breaking out of arrogant thoughts and ill designs from the fat, loose, and stupid heart is spoken of; better therefore according to the LXX עֲוֺנֵמוֹ, comp. xvii. 10. But in that case the עָבַר *b* is best taken, as in Hab. i. 11, of the swelling-over and passing *into* evil thoughts, so that it is connected according to § 281 *b*. What presumptuous thoughts and plans which proceeded from them and still proceed—are here meant, can be more closely ascertained (were it not clear of itself) from Ps. xiv. 1-6. But the poet hastens here,—having hinted in the second strophé at the presumptuous thoughts of the heathen who put themselves in the place of the gods,—to subjoin to them in the third, those of Israel, as if thereby called forth, and totally opposite, vv. 10-14: and here is depicted from the first in the words *therefore He brings* (according to the K'tîb יָשִׁיב)—that is, God Himself (who however as in Job. xiii. 20 and other passages is in reverence not named),

His own *people back thither*, turning them aside from the direct way, so *that it thinks* what is further expressed in vv. 11-14. But in the middle—by the words *and water in fulness is sucked up by them*, v. 10 *b*—the ever increasing greed with which Israel absorbs words and thoughts of cowardice and despair, is compared to the eagerness with which one gulps down water in full draught. Comp. the like in Job. xv. 16, Prov. xxvi. 6; also other representations from the same source, Ps. lxxv. 9; especially similar is *Arabs: Fâkih.* p. 12, 6 v. and 24, 17 sqq. 46, 22 and *tshrab*, p. 118, 2. This second member, ver. 10, is merely expressive of a state, and הָלֹ־כֵּן is explained by וַיֹּאמְרוּ, ver. 11; so far comes (according to the (*l'ri*) or falls the people ever more greedily swallowing the poison of despair, that it says.

2. With ver. 15 the transition plainly comes; but great difficulty lies in כְּמוֹ. This only appears elsewhere as a preposition; and it is difficult to say what it should signify without complement, because the case stated in § 360 *a* is not relevant here. Assuming that the word was used here for the broken-off How—? the verse would bear the sense: *I thought to enumerate* or to explain the *how*—? that is, how it is possible that God acts so unrighteously, *lo, thus I should betray the race of Thy sons*, in not speaking as is to be expected from the truly faithful and pious in Israel,—placing myself out of their society, consequently becoming unfaithful to them,—and this at the bottom of my soul I did not desire, therefore fruitlessly seeking after the causes, as ver. 16 further explains. But in this case we should rather expect that the poet would here explain his peculiar thoughts, if he had them, and this he does not do. Again this sense of כְמוֹ would be in point of usage very doubtful, because the cases in § 299 *a* cannot be adduced here. Therefore כְּמוֹהֲגִיתִי might so then be united into one word: *if I thought to speak like that*—as is explained in vv. 10-14,—or if I thought to make speeches in like manner utterly despondent and injurious against God, *I should*

betray the manner of Thy sons, not acting as a true Israelite or son of God (Deut. xiv. 1) should do, becoming faithless to God, "thy sons" must be much more significant than "His people," (ver. 10); therefore I desired to guard myself against such wicked speeches; but the attempt to find the causes by personal reflection miscarried (ver. 16),—*until* I finally looking at the *end* of the wicked,—consequently at the same time following the Divine conduct, *penetrated into the sanctities* or *secrets* (mysteries, comp. on מִקְדָּשׁ the *Alterth.* p. 123) *of God*, was initiated into the Divine meaning. הנה may be again supplied as הִנֵּה before the *apodosis*, as though the hiatus in the present text had arisen only through the omission of the letters הנה before this הנה.—Not without reason does the poet place *the secrets* in the *plur.*: for more closely considered the three deeper points of knowledge belong here : (1) that a Divine punishment of all heathen wickedness is generally certain ; (2) that it will come in a season known to God; and (3) that it will come,—making the wicked previously secure, as by a Divine mockery, and the more harshly tearing away all delusions—pulling down those who from the beginning are placed only on slippery ground, as that assigned to them by the Divine allotment. This is indicated as briefly as possible at the end of the strophé, ver. 18 : *only in slipperinesses Thou settest for them*, determinest for them their portion, that they ever oscillate in danger ; *hast caused them to fall into deceptions*, to become as a booty ; מַשּׁוּאוֹת are self-deceptions, hence also haughtiness, transgression, lxxiv. 3, when the LXX gives correctly ὑπερηφανίαι. The same image of deception leads, ver. 20, to one related ; as one on awakening, reluctantly dismisses a dream-picture as a deception, by which one has been troubled,—so God,—when He at the right time rises for judgment (בָּעִיר for הָעִיר *inf. Hiph.*),—will dismiss the horrid, but vain and empty wicked ; comp. Isa. xxix. 8. But as the poet in the strophé, vv. 19-22, would further develop generally the whole thought only sketched in ver. 18, he immediately points here at the beginning of ver. 19, to a great event in the most recent time, which might substantiate those truths. We do not know indeed sufficiently from these very brief words what event he means : probably it was the fall of the house of Nabukodrossor during the continuance of the Chaldæan dominion. The words, ver. 19, cannot, according to their sense, be regarded as an anticipation like xxxvi. 13.— Ver. 24. The second member quite as Zech. ii. 12, like as ver. 13 is after xxvi. 6. Ver. 25 gives a fine description of how the poet has but one genuine eternal friend in heaven and on earth, who remains to him even if all his earthly good passes away, as xlix. 16 ; comp. the *Jahrbb.*, x., pp. 195 sqq.

3. At the last, vv. 27, 28, the same with renewed glance at the above instruction of the present, vv. 18-20; and the language bounds anew with higher joy in the feeling that there is no higher good for man than that of *being near to God* and experiencing His friendship. *Businesses* or *doings* for works, is an expression peculiar to this poet.

Ps. lxxvii. A fresh and sore trouble of the poet. Before he felt himself strong for the present composition, his spirit had in a night (vv. 3, 7) traversed all manner of diverse thoughts—those that cramped and those that exalted him ; and their play and alternation strongly beset him, until he came to tranquil, composed prayer. The mere thought of God and the present had only awoke sighing, vv. 2-4 ; the mere comparison too of the unhappy present with the past, vv. 4-7, led, in the first instance, only to all kinds of complaining questions, vv. 8-10 : only *the* thought that the same Jahvé who formerly wrought marvellous deliverance under Moses, still in like manner operates, resolved doubt and grief into solace and thanksgiving, vv. 11-13. Therefore while he now, after the recovery of blessed repose, would—praying and hoping in full confidence —indite a song, he again runs in thought in the most vivid manner over the whole course of those inconsolable and heavy thoughts, in the midst of which he desired to pray to God (vv. 2-5), from reflections and questionings (vv. 6-18) until the beginning of the true consolatory thoughts (vv. 11-13). It is as though he would suffer those gloomy thoughts once more to pass in all their vividness and in all their horror before his spirit,—that he may, because of their very disconsolateness, for ever renounce them, and only hold with the greater firmness to *the* thought at which in the end he arrived, and in which he now tunes, with the more purity, a hymn of praise to God and His wondrous deliverance according to the sacred history of Israel under Moses,—and finishes it in blessed calm, vv. 14-21. In this hymn, begun out of a full heart, all doubt and all unrest is removed, which held in fetters the sensitive spirit ; and the inspired true recollection of the immortal history of older days is here for the first time a means of serenest consolation.

This song, therefore, mirrors, on a small scale, the same alternation of considerations and of moods from which the B. Habaqquq (I., pp. 83, 84, *Dichter des A. B.*) is developed on a large scale. It falls of itself into two very diverse halves, because the loud resonance of the historical hymn of praise forms a quite peculiar song. In it there break forth only sparkling beams of reminiscence of the highest points of ancient history, similarly to Pss. cxiii., cxiv.; but it is plainly broken up into three small strophés, the middle one of which rises to the highest flight in contents and strain. Elsewhere the short verse-structure prevails in it; while in the main song the ordinary verse-structure carries on the movement first by seven lines (twice), then by six lines (twice), as befits (I., p. 152) a song beginning with lament. In the hymn of praise there are, on the other hand, six members (twice) and then five.

1 *a*.

2   " Loud to God, so will I cry,
        yea loud to God ; and He will hear me !"

In my day of oppression I sought the Lord,
  by night my hand was out-stretched, not weary,
  my soul would not be comforted :
" if I think of God, I must groan,
  I meditate—and feeble becomes my spirit !"

b.

Thou heldest my eyelids,
  I was perplexed, speaking nothing.
I bethought me of the days of old,   5
  the years of the eternities :
" I call to mind my song in the night,
  musing in my heart !"
and therefore my spirit inquired in quiet :

c.

" Will then the Lord only cast away for ever,
  and never more find favour ?
is then for ever His mercy lost,
  gone His promise for all times ?
hath God forgotten to be gracious,   10
  or in anger shut up His compassion ?"

d.

Then I thought : " it is my suffering
  but meanwhile the right hand of the Highest rules !
I will call to mind the histories of Jah ;
  yea, I will think of Thy wonders from the early
                                                time !
will indite concerning all Thy work,
  and on Thy deeds let me meditate."

2 a.

God ! in sanctity is Thy way ;
  who is a great God as God ?

Thou art that God who doeth wonders,
  madest known Thy might among peoples;
15 Thou didst redeem with the arm Thy people,
  Jakob's sons and Josef's.

b.

Waters saw Thee, O God, Waters saw Thee—they
  circle;
yea, sea's depths tremble;
clouds streamed over with water, loudly sounded the
  bright heights;
yea, Thine arrows went round;
loud Thy thunder becomes in the whirl, lightnings
  enlightened the world;
earth trembled and shook.

c.

20 Forth through the sea Thy way,
  Thy track through many waters,
  Thy steps were not known—
  Thou leddest Thy people like a flock
  by Moses and Ahron!

1. The LXX take here throughout the usual cohortative form as *imperf. præteriti* (see on lxxxviii. 16) according to which from vv. 2-13, all without distinction would be spoken in the simple style of narration. But the poet himself distinguishes between this cohortative form and the form of narration, so that his narrative is only carried on in the latter, but the former may very well pass as an immediately vivid word. Indeed, the poet begins, ver. 2, forthwith with the words wherewith he also in quiet meditation began the night at that time, and leads only with ver. 3 all into narrative, as upon that first beginning, ver. 1, soon more strong words followed, ver. 4, comp. xlii. 5.—He could not, then, in that

stormy night come to rest, ver. 5; and even when he afterwards plucked up heart, and thought he would—rather than remain in dull silence—sing and play, in recollection of the old days, vv. 6, 7, his word became at first a lament over the apparently eternal loss of the height and the promises of the ancient days, vv. 8-10. Nevertheless this historical recollection led at last readily to true consolation through the recollection that this wondrously-delivering God is still and ever the same, ver. 11 sqq. חַלּוֹת must be an *inf.* like חַנּוֹת, ver. 10 (comp. § 238 *c*) from חלל, be wounded, suffer; שְׁנוֹת, as accusative of time: the year long,—therefore while not an earthly king rules, but the right hand of Jahvé, ver. 6.

2. The hymn itself praises the wondrous power of Jahvé according to the history of Moses,—not to exhaust all that might be said of this, but bringing out the most important and most Divine features in higher flight,—hence also concluding appropriately with abruptness with the mention of Moses and Ahron. But the acmé of that Mosaic time and its wonders is the passage through the Red Sea, on the picture of which the poet therefore here lingers, describing how in this moment of most vivid commotion of heaven and earth, from below the mass of the flood trembled, ver. 17; while from above over the whole earth, the Divine majesty commanding, terrifying, and protecting, appeared in the storm, vv. 18, 19, till the earth trembling, yielded to the Divine Will, ver. 19 *b*. Thus He wondrously led His people, making a way for himself, which, so soon as the Divine majesty had passed by, immediately disappeared and became untraceable,—for Jahvé, indeed, as invisible and spiritual, cannot leave such outward traces behind as an earthly king may; in this the spiritual, the wonderful is shown,—that it invariably seizes on the spirit, and as it comes freely and in a moment, passes away without trace like the wind, only to be recognized in its effects and consequences. In vv. 17, 19, Hab. iii. 10, 11 is echoed. In the middle strophé, vv. 17-19—wherewith the matter, language,

and song rise to their highest,—the first member of each verse is expanded into a double member, and the whole movement becomes trochaic. The more finely does this disquiet fall suddenly in the last strophé again to rest, vv. 20, 21; but it must not be overlooked that all the words, ver. 20, only give propositions expressive of state, to the concluding proposition, ver. 21.

Ps. xciv. New occasion for complaint, new agitation. The heart of the poet, troubled by the sight of the wicked, first turns—complaining with great bitterness and praying to Jahvé as Avenger, vv. 1-7, but afterwards directs itself with serious denunciation and instruction against the wicked themselves and their false opinion, vv. 8-15; and finally returns with renewed serene consciousness and glorious hope, within itself, vv. 16-23. So clear is the abiding influence of the preceding songs in the bosom of the poet; and the most various interchange of thoughts takes with him the most symmetrical and restful form. As the second and third strophé are each constructed of eight verses, in the first one must have fallen away.

1.

1   O God of vengeance, Jahvé,
   O God of vengeances, brighten!
  Rise, Judge of the earth,
   give back recompense to the arrogant!
  How long shall wicked men, Jahvé,
   how long shall the wicked exult,
  shall they spout forth, speak pride,
   plume themselves—all evil-doers?
5   Thy people, Jahvé! they tread down,
   and deeply oppress Thine heritage,
  widow and stranger they murder
   and orphans they kill
  and yet say: "Jah sees it not,
   Jakob's God marks it not!"

2.

O observe nevertheless, ye most senseless among folk,
    and ye fools, when will ye have understanding?
how? He who plants the ear, should not He hear,
    or the former of the eye, should He not see?
He who chastises peoples, should he not punish,   10
    He who teaches knowledge to men?
Jahvé knows human thoughts,
    that they are but vain.—
O blessed the man whom Thou chastisest, Jah,
    and teachest him out of Thy direction;
to give him rest from the worst days,
    until a pit is dug for the wicked!
For Jahvé will not cast off His people,
    nor forsake His heritage:
but to the right shall judgment return,   15
    and Him all the upright in heart follow after!

3.

Who will hold ground for me against evil-doers,
    who will stand for me against malefactors?
Were Jahvé no help to me,
    perhaps my soul had already lain in the land of quiet!
When I think: "trembling is my foot,"
    Thy grace, Jahvé, supports me;
If my troublous musings increase in my bosom,
    Thy consolations sooth my soul;
is the throne of wilfulness allied to Thee,   20
    that invents mischief against right?—
They throng together against the soul of the righteous,
    innocent blood they condemn;
then Jahvé becomes my defence,
    my God the rock of my refuge,
and He requites to them their own misdeeds,
    for their evil He destroys them,
        destroys them Jahvé our God

Ver. 1. הוֹפִיעַ according to the connexion can be neither *perf.* nor *inf.*, but only *imperat.*: § 224 *b*, 1. L. 2 is present to the mind of the poet. The description, vv. 2-7, agrees almost verbally with lxxiii. 6-9. Ver. 10 : He who, through the spirit and through history, ever chastises and teaches men, shall He not hold just judgment? The nature of God and of man themselves refute the careless fools. Ver. 11 thus concludes: such foolish thoughts Jahvé, well knowing them, may long leave unpunished, because they are self-injurious and destructive. He is rather to be felicitated (vv. 12, 13) who is strengthened and encouraged in sore times by learning to know all the greatness of God, that he may at the right time see the greater salvation; for if, according to the ancient certainty that the true community is not forsaken (ver. 14 from 1 Sam. xii. 22, comp. Jer. xii. 7) there finally comes a more mighty revelation of salvation,—all the faithful follow after Him, the Redeemer, to enjoy His salvation, comp. lxxiii. 24. On ver. 16. comp. lxxiii. 25. Vv. 16-20 and 21-23 are to be connected.

E. 81, 82. Psalms LXXXII., XIV. (LIII.)

If in the dispersed and deeply depressed Israel such energies and truths were still stirring, she was bound in the course of the exile itself gradually to rise again to higher courage and to a freer prospect. And these two small but very noteworthy songs show how this new life,—towards the end of the exile, when Babel soon became degraded by internal corruption, and hastened to its fall—rises with wonderful power, and is directed outwards as a prophetic voice against Babel, and the kingdoms of the world at that time. They have indeed, like Pss. xci., cxxxviii., and several other late songs, a style elevated far above that of the last preceding songs. Pss. lxxxii., xiv., cxxxviii. have even one that is very concise, compressed and pregnant; but this is explained from the new elevation of the best spirits of these years, and short, winged expressions of new inspiration, pointed and bitter, small songs of the kind become henceforth for a time more frequent. For according to their contents these two songs certainly belong most correctly to the present place.

Ps. lxxxii. gives the irony which comes to the surface in Ps. lviii., in its finished form and executed in the cleverest style of representation, so that it produces and supports the whole song. While the poet sees the great satraps and governors of the earth to be entirely unworthy of the supreme dignity which they have enjoyed as gods and sons of gods,— that they discharge their sacred office in the most godless and wicked manner, and in incorrigible blindness and perversity fail to maintain the rest and order of the earth, but destroy it, —his spirit foresees clearly their certain and sudden fall by the agency of the true and supreme God. Yea, it is a peculiar delight to his acute spirit to contemplate for once the true God as Judge of these earthly gods and judges, and to follow out in thought how these are silent before the strict Judge of the world; and because they cannot defend themselves and approve themselves as gods,—must be given over to punishment like ordinary men. *This* is the bitterness and seriousness of the irony—that they who will to be and might be gods upon earth, are finally once for all judged by the supreme God, and then fall like ordinary men. Full of this truthful view, the poet introduces the supreme God on a solemn day dispensing justice in the midst of the gods,—denouncing indeed at the same time and reproving, but not immediately condemning, but freely allowing the defence, vv. 1-4. None however can defend himself, all are without understanding and blinded, confessing everything, ver. 5; therefore the punishment follows, determined in the above ironical turn of expression, vv. 6-7. But as this judgment and this punishment,— however truly and finely conceived and described,—are so far only in the imagination of the poet, not actual; at the end the poet is forced by calmer reflection, in a short after-address, to summon *that* God to judgment over the earth who rules all peoples without distinction, ver. 8. This supplement shows most plainly that the poet understands heathen greatness, and doubtless he lived in the midst of Gentiles, seeing close at hand the perversity of a great kingdom. Ez. xxviii. prophetically further develops the same thought in his manner.

According to the structure of the strophés, the whole contents, in this sharp and pointed discourse, are compressed as into *one* great strophé, starting from the smaller with eight elegant members, but this is shortened on the repetition to seven, and in the echoing address at the end to only two.

1   God stands in Divine assembly,
    judging in the midst of gods;
" How long will ye to judge—unrighteousness,
    and with the wicked—to be pleased ?
" Judge the bowed down, orphans,
    give justice to the sufferers and the poor,
" deliver the bowed down and helpless,
    from the hand of the wicked free them !"—

5   They have no understanding and no sense,
    in the darkness they walk;
    all the earth's foundations tremble.
" I thought, ye were gods,
    sons of the Highest, all of ye:
" but as men shall ye die,
    and at once, ye princes, fall !"—

    Up, God ! judge the earth !
    for Thou art of all peoples supreme Lord !

אל ver. 1, indicates merely the way and manner, in our mode of expression the adjective (§ 287 *f.*) Ver. 2. Note the sharp opposition; *judge—injustice*, instead of right, as in lviii. 2. Vv. 3-4, after Isa. i. 17, reproving, supplying the forgotten principle of right.—Ver. 5. The disorder and confusion, the trembling of all foundations of the earth, is justly deduced from want of understanding, but for this very reason judgment and punishment is now necessary; comp. xi. 3, lxxv. 4. Vv. 6-7 must be the words of the highest judge, although the peculiar irony in the sense of the poet strongly comes out. The אָדָם ver. 7 *a* leads readily of itself to the bye-sense which it has in xlix. 3, comp. Job xxxi. 33. The words כְּאַחַד הַשָּׂרִים *b* would on the other hand, according to this punctuation and accentuation, signify *like one of the princes*, *i.e.*, like an ordinary prince, a true Hebrew idiom, 2 Sam. ix. 11, Judg. xvi. 7, 11, 1 Kings xix. 2. But the opposition requires here not princes and gods, but mortal common men and gods. Therefore כְּאֶחָד must be expressed, a word which, in the signification *without distinction all at once*, is just now much in use, Isa. lxv. 25, Ezr. ii. 64, iii. 9, vi. 20, Eccles. xi. 16; earlier in a more complete form כְּאִישׁ אֶחָד Num. xiv. 15, which also reads in Ezr. iii. 1, Neh. viii. 1; quite correspondent is the Syr. expression. So is also הֲרִים quite as B. Jes. xxi. 5 in a prophetic piece of about the time.—*At once* shall they fall because this is the Messianic judgment.

Ps. xiv. (Ps. liii.) shows in style and sense the greatest resemblance to the preceding song,—so that probably the poet is the same. But if in the preceding only irony could predict the certain although possibly distant fall of the rulers of the kingdom of sin,—here a purely serious spirit expresses the equally near and certain overthrow of the whole corrupt world by the agency of Jahvé as highest Judge. And as everything is here more concrete, nearer, more strained and decided,—the poet must have written somewhat late, possibly a few years before Babel's fall. Babel,—not conquered, but utterly degenerate, and, according to inner truth, already condemned by God, rapidly advancing to its overthrow—is plainly before the eyes of the poet, as the centre of the world-dominion of that time; while he looks upon Israel as finally to be redeemed, comp. the same in a more strictly prophetic strain in Isa. xxi. 1-10. The poet then makes the drama pass before the imagination, as he has in spirit already beheld it brought on and complete,—in fugitive but grand pictures with most vivid truthfulness, vv. 1-6. Finally follows, as in the preceding song, upon the view thus pressed forward,—more calmly the wish for a speedy execution of that which is in itself certain, ver. 7. In the painting of the vision or the main part of the song, all is very select, the materials are artistically fitted together, and the end of the grand drama is set forth in its necessity in the most striking manner: scarcely can anything great and true be sketched with shorter, more telling touches. Exactly at the time when folly and sin through denial of God have reached their highest measure on earth, God comes to the assembly, vv. 1, 2. But a cry of indignation—when He finds everything corrupt, and nowhere salvation and soundness —over the incorrigible blindness of the tyrants who recklessly oppress Israel, escapes from the supreme Judge, vv. 3-4. He cannot suffer Israel, *i.e.*, the true community to perish; and immediately the just punishment falls, striking the cowardly without chance of escape.

The mode of structure of the strophés is similar to that of the preceding song, only still more fugitive and rapid. The strophé consists of only three verses, but each has three elegant members, and a half strophé after the second concludes the unique part of the song:

1   The fool said in his heart: "There is no God!"
       corruptly, horribly did they act,
          none was there who did good.

Jahvé from heaven looked upon the sons of men,
to see whether there was a man of understanding,
one who sought God ?—

All was astray, all together turned sour,
none who did good,
nay, not even one !
" are then all evil-doers without understanding,
who consumed my people, consumed like bread,
called not on Jahvé ?"—

There they quaked a quaking which was no quaking: 5
for God scattered their bones.
They missed their blow against the sufferer, because
God despised them !*
O that from Sion the deliverance of Israel might come !
when Jahvé turns His people's turning,
let Jakob be merry, Israel rejoice !

For כְּלִילָה, ver. 1 in Ps. liii., עָוֶל less suitably ; it arose from a cursory reading. *Soured*, ver. 3, corrupt, after Job xv. 16. How thoughtless they are is clear enough from the fact that they do naught but carouse and squander, even dissipating and bringing to naught whole peoples, even the spiritual people, Israel, simply for their own increase and sensuous comfort (as very similarly we read in B. Jer. l. 17, li. 34), without thinking of the true God or calling upon Him. *To eat bread*, *i.e.*, feast, comp. Loqmân, *Fab.* 5 and 29, with Rödiger's vocabulary thereto ; the transition of the *particip.* into the *verb fin.* : § 350 *b*. It is further stated in the *Theol. Stud. u. Krit.*, 1829, pp. 774-5, why, ver. 5, the readings of Ps. liii., are better, and

---

* Or, according to Ps. xiv. :
  There they quaked a quaking
    because God is in the generation of the just !
  Ye will see the blow against the sufferer to be vain,
    because Jahvé is His refuge !

how they may have arisen; but in Ps. xiv. some original ones have been retained. According to Ps. liii. the sense must be: so suddenly and in a moment bringing to naught, did the Divine punishment fall on them, they no sooner quaked than they were dashed to pieces, while the bones of the foe who attacked and besieged thee (Israel! comp. § 252 a),—now slain,—were scattered, as on the battle-field the bones of the vanquished, about which none takes further trouble. (In this case we must assume that the image is borrowed from the siege of Jerusalem by Sanherib's army). Thou, Israel! mightest justly show scorn because the God whom they despised, ver. 1, has much more despised them. Much weaker and tamer is everything in Ps. xiv., in which they only quake because they feel that in Israel, as they had not believed, there is a mighty avenging God. But it must not fail to be recognized that חָנָךְ here gives an image of besieging which is not prepared by the preceding, and in itself is difficult to understand, but the thou *didst despise* would stand here very abruptly. But if the arrangement of words was originally

פִּזַּר עַצְמוֹתָיִךְ . . . .
עֲצַת עָנִי הֵבִ

we can readily see how (1) on the concurrent writing of the two members עֲצַת might have been dropped after עַצְמֹתָם, and (2) חֲנָךְ may have arisen from עָנִי. But in that case, for הֱבִישׁ תָה we must read הֱבִישׁוּ, which also better suits תְּבִישׁוּ, and the whole is thus consistently brought into its original state: their attack upon the *sufferer*, *i.e.*, on Israel was, according to ver. 4, entirely to consume him. עֵצָה is an accusative (§ 281 c) to be taken with הֵבִישׁ, *blush*, which, according to the other reading, must give to this the active signification *put to shame, scoff*, which, indeed, would be still more easily intelligible if, with a slight alteration, הֱבִישֻׁתַם with the suff. might be read.

From *Sion*, ver. 7, because in exile, especially towards the end, under the generally rising hope, the high regard for the ancient sacred place, as the seat of Divine influence on Israel's behalf, remained in force, Isa. xl.—xlii. The poet did not however himself live there, but probably in Babylonia.

But how far then from fruitless inwardly, for the disposition and state of the heart, the exile had been, is shown by nothing more plainly than by the songs which in the great turning period of all affairs of the time arose from purely personal excitations. For they show already the germ of new life, as if Israel had again become worthy through an inward change and invigoration of external redemption and deliverance. The heart once so faint, almost prostrate beneath sufferings and grief, has learnt to overcome the sorrows of the world,—amidst the constant pressure of dangers, scoffs and persecutions, readily finding and ever anew, rest and solace in Jahvé. Distorted proud thoughts and claims, such as, *e.g.*, might readily arise out of the Messianic expectations, are recognized in their erring character, and are incessantly repressed, every passion is subdued; pure hope and energy, the new re-born man appears in new glory; and while thus a spirit become restful and clear, prepared on all sides, meets the external world and its changes, it gazes towards the unfolding of the nearest future, and the manifestation of the salvation inwardly now again apprehended, and confident in God. And this, although with the glow of longing desire, yet with collectedness and composure. Not only so: but the limits of time are enlarged, and of the hope of salvation in it—even into infinity. For he who actually beholds and hopes for the pure object out of his own strength, becomes sure of it for all eternity. Hardly can the hope and the attention be more fiery and full of longing, yet at the same time more resigned through higher considerations than here, indeed more humble; and where the inner salvation is now so clear and firm, there—it is observed—the external can no longer be distant. But as this is a hope ever on the stretch, ever waiting, observant of all signs and readily excitable, the feeling gushes forth most freely and beautifully in a number of small fugitive songs, as each rude or gentle fluctuation of the time touches a new side of the easily agitated mind, while they all in harmony permit only the governing mood of the poet's soul to be perfectly audible and distinct. They are the few strong pulse-beats of a moment of great expectations; and with each, the decision, the victory moves nearer. Thus a series of five songs are

83-87. Pss. cxx., cxxi., cxxiii., cxxx., cxxxi.,

which are derived without difficulty from the same poet (although Ps. cxx. does not present itself as the first song of a poet), and express the deepest thoughts in winged words; each complete and noble by itself, and yet only perfectly clear in connexion with its sisters. In Ps. cxx. we see the poet forced to tarry in the midst of unpeaceable rude men, who vex and torment him keenly with deceitful and malicious speeches, with quarrels and slanders, so that he, who in his inspiration feels the necessity to speak loudly and openly, though injuriously to none, can never find rest and peace. And thus fallen into distress and oppression, he calls here, according to wonted custom, on Jahvé as Deliverer, vv. 1-2; proceeding with threats, when he calls to mind how sharply the Just One would punish malicious slander, vv. 3-4; but again forthwith sinking to gentle repose and contemplation, vv. 5-7.

On the style of the *short-songs* which from this point occur in greater number, and consistently spring from the high excitement and haste of these times, comp. I. *Dichter des A.B.*, pp. 33-4. Each song bursts forth as in *one* strophé alone, being constructed chiefly out of the four-membered double-verse of elegant style, mostly breaking in the middle into two halves, often with a short echo. But none of the short-songs of our poet is without any division, nor even the very short Ps. cxxxiii.

To Jahvé in my distress 1
    I call and He hears me.
O Jahvé, deliver my soul from lying lips,
    from the treacherous tongue!—

How will He punish thee and how chastise thee,
    Thou deceitful tongue,
ye sharp murdering arrows
    together with broom-coals!—

O woe to me that I am a guest of Méshek, 5
    sojourn among Qedar's tents!
enough has my soul already dwelt
    among haters of peace;
I—even when I speak peace,
    they are for war!

Ver. 1 spoken out of experience, as introduction to the prayer, ver. 2. But that the language then turns immediately, vv. 3, 4—with sharp menace of Divine judgment—boldly against the persecutors, is clear from the phrase יִתֵּן וְיֹסִיף, which is most readily understood as a slight change from the well-known threatening oath, 1 Sam. iii. 17. But in such strong passages we must not overlook the fact that even verbally punishment is not wished against men as such, but only against sin. But if the treacherous tongue embraces a multitude of sharply hitting, deeply wounding and stinging words, it is plain of itself how, ver. 4, sharp arrows of a murderer (גִּבּוֹר in the bad sense as tyrant, cruel man) and coals of broom (*i.e.*, the most glowing, burning longest and deepest, because the broom-coals *aljaddu Hamâsu*, p. 443, 9, retain fire very long, Burckhardt's *Syr.*, p. 1073, Petermann's *Reisen*, ii. 89, 134) may be compared to the deceitful tongue; comp. lix. 8, lvii. 5; Prov. xxv. 22. Much is taken word for word from lii. 2-6.—Since the mountains and peoples of

Méshek lie in the extreme North (Gen. x. 2), but the seats of the Qedarenes in Arabia, it is easy to see that the two peoples, ver. 6, are named only by way of example for the rudest foreign peoples; where the poet actually dwelt we do not learn from this, though such may not be his intention. *My soul*, ver. 6, because here the innermost feeling, pleasure, or pain of the soul, is concerned. שָׁלוֹם might (§ 296 *b*) be taken: *I am peace*, nothing but peace: *yet if I speak*, etc. But the whole series of words *a*, is better taken as an individual proposition so constructed in deeper excitement, § 362 *b*.

Ps. cxxi. Reflections, in a new moment, of disquiet and disturbance. As the longing and the need to look around for help becomes heard, ver. 1, the consciousness is again immediately clear as to whence the true help comes, ver. 2; again the former arises, more mildly, on the consideration: Jahvé will not weary of helping? ver. 3, and immediately the higher consciousness is anew invigorated, conquering even the lightest doubt, and is unfolded, assuring the soul of rest and solace for all time, vv. 4-8. Comp. Ps. xci., only that we here see still the violent fluctuation and agitation of the mind, which again seeks and finds rest.

1   I lift my eyes to the mountains,
        whence will my help come?
     My help comes from Jahvé,
        the Creator of heaven and of earth.—
     He will not suffer Thy foot to stagger,
        Thy warder surely slumbers not?
     —O no, he slumbers not and sleeps not,
        The warder of Israel!

5   Jahvé is Thy warder,
        Jahvé Thy shadow on the right hand!
     by day the sun will not scorch thee,
        and not the moon in the night:

· Jahvé will protect thee from all evil,
will protect thy soul;
Jahvé will protect thy coming and thy going
henceforth and even to eternity!

To the mountains, ver. 1, is not so much merely round about in the distance, to see whether from the distance in any direction help may come, but points away to Palestine, and is thus most appropriate in the mouth of distant ones speaking of it, as Nah. ii. 1, and often in Hezeqiel. How greatly the view and the hope are widened, is clear from the mighty names and ideas of Jahvé, vv. 2, 4: the world-Creator is also the Warder of Israel, who can never suffer the true community to perish, comp. Isa. xl.—xlvi. אל, ver. 3, is a question about what in personal opinion is impossible: *doch nicht?* as I hope and think, that it will not and cannot be; as also μή is used. *At the right*, at the same time, withal, ver. 5, comp. xvi. 8, cx. 5; *thy going and thy coming*, i.e., thy activity, influence upon earth. That even the moon on a bright night may injure him who sleeps without proper protection, is a general opinion in the East (also in Central America), and quite possible, owing to the cool nights, comp. Sur. 113, 3; Carne, *Leben u. Sitten im Morgenl.*, translated by Lindau, Th. 1., p. 73 (1827); *Ausland*, 1834, 18 Oct., p. 1161, 1840 June, p. 630; Sellberg's *Reise nach Java* (1846), pp. 85 sq., Wellsted's *Reisen nach der Stadt der Chalifen* (translated by Pforzheim, 1844), p. 64.

Ps. cxxiii. Still continues sore vexation and manifold suffering, as severe chastisement from Jahvé; He must be supplicated anew. But as the slave fixedly looks to the hand of his lord as communicating hints and commands, so the faithful long, with jealous watchfulness and tension wait for Jahvé's hint; and what can this hint, if given be now, except the sign that finally the hour of salvation comes, that grace finally takes its course? for the spring of compassion in Him is inexhaustible.—That this image gives too slavish a sense, cannot be said; but it is new and probably first struck the Hebrews in the exile. But as the poet feels strength and light only in the community, and neither wishes nor can wish to be redeemed for himself alone, the *sing.* gradually passes over, and rightly, into the *plur.*

1   To Thee I raise my eyes,
      who art throned in the heavens!
    yea as to their lord's hand slaves look,
      as a female slave looks to her mistress' hand,
    so look we to Jahvé our God,
      till that He be gracious to us!
    Be gracious, Jahvé, to us, be gracious to us,
      for we are sated enough with contempt:
    enough has our soul been sated
      with the scoff of the careless, with the contempt of
          the proud!

Only between ver. 2 and 3 a small pause, while vv. 3, 4 first explain with the prayer also the cause of the longing waiting. On the article in הַלְּעַג, comp. § 290 *d*, and how because of this article added with emphasis to the first nomen, לְ stands in preference, in lighter style, the second time before גַּאֲיוֹנִים (K'tib) § 292 *a*.

Ps. cxxx. Because anew grief must call to Jahvé out of deepest sufferings, the consciousness only indicated in the preceding song comes clearly out, that the Divine forgiveness for the old transgressions and aberrations of Israel must at last come, for the furtherance of Divine fear (religion) upon earth; because genuine fear of God is demanded not only by the revelation of His power, but at times still more by that of His goodness and compassion; and the time was incontestably one of those. In the second half, vv. 5-8, calm hope returns on such considerations, and to this the poet exhorts not merely himself but also, vv. 7, 8, all Israel. For always more plainly appears how the poet finds his whole weal and woe in the community alone.

    Out of the deep chasm I call on Thee, Jahvé!   1
    Lord, hear my crying, be Thine ears attentive
        to my loud supplication!
    If Thou keepest sins, Jah,
        O Lord, who will stand?
    rather Thou hast indeed forgiveness,
        that Thou mayest be feared!—

    I wait on Jahvé, my soul waits,   5
        and on His word I hope;
    my soul upon Jahvé, more
        than watchers for the morning, watchers for the
            morning.

    O wait, Israel, on Jahvé!
        for Jahvé has grace, and much redemption hath He;
    and *He* will redeem Israel
        from all his sins!

Ver. 3: *Keepest* sins, lettest them not out of sight, overlookest, forgivest not; *Jah,* later frequent abbreviation of Jahvé, comp. p. 125. *His word,* ver. 5, the eternal word of God through all time, that of salvation, of redemption, almost entirely as lvi. 5, 11; *the soul waits,* ver. 5, as is completed in ver. 6, on Thee and Thy salvation still more longingly and watchfully than watchers for the morning that releases them from their hard position.

Ps. cxxxi.—spoken a short time after the preceding—finally makes known the completest and most collected resignation, as the poet, subduing the storm of all passions, renouncing all excessively proud and great expectations,—now like a contented child, resting in the bosom of God, freely and joyously looks toward the future; quiet and modest, but with infinitely joyous certainty, expecting not so much his salvation only as that of Israel, and exhorting Israel to be trustful, waiting with such a mind and disposition. Nothing can be finer and more striking than the description here sketched with most child-like feeling of the new birth to a fresh life; nothing more noble and decisive than this new birth itself,—certain and bearing within itself the pledge of a better future, as it here appears with full power and certainty; nothing more compensatory than this utter renunciation of one's own external welfare, this utter resolution of one's own wishes into the wish for the weal of the community. He who was found thus disposed on the external redemption from exile, was certainly prepared for and capable of enjoying the salvation.—The members are here formed involuntarily otherwise, — longer, more extended, calmer. Only in the echo again the ordinary measure.

1   Jahvé ! not proud is my heart, not high my eyes,
       nor do I walk in a way too high and too wonderful,
    certainly, I have smoothed and quieted my soul;
       like a child weaned from his mother,
    So lies in me my soul weaned.—

    O wait, Israel, on Jahvé,
       henceforth and to eternity !

I walk not in that too high and wonderful for me, namely, too proud thoughts and deeds corresponding to them, *e.g.*, if the poet had desired to bring about the Messianic salvation by force, deceived by fanaticism; comp. what Jer. xlv. 5 proposed. *Smoothed* the soul, which earlier was like a strong sea; and *quieted* as the weaned child lies quite quietly and still on the same bosom which earlier roused most violently all its impetuous desire; so the soul of the poet now calmly rests with his wishes in God, without being further irritated and too violently carried away by these.

IV.

SONGS OF RESTORED JERUSALEM.

According to all above said, the final deliverance came to those who were truly the noblest and most capable portion of Israel, when they had been inwardly prepared and fitted, born anew to the new life, and worthy of the great salvation. But although the deliverance itself did not come unexpectedly, yet the peculiar historical mode of the deliverance might create surprise, and carry away and influence the multitude. With the actual deliverance, the return from the forced banishment, the new building of Jerusalem and the temple, the new establishment of the community and some kind of state, the loudest joy resounds; the merriest jubilation, long silenced, breaks out most impetuously, partly from the feeling of individuals, partly from the sensibilities of the whole community, both in winged delicate songs of the moment, and in more artistic and longer pictures. After long errors and sufferings, finally with the deliverance, a crisis, a turning had come, in which Israel had become conscious, as the basis and beginning of the true community, of its indestructible duration, its peculiar position on earth, its destiny to bring all Gentiles to Jahvé,—and all this with a most vivid power and certainty earlier unknown. And thus, next to the prophetic words of that time, the songs breathe peculiar lofty power and inspiration, infinite confidence and hope, bold views of all times, relations and kingdoms of the world, and the certainty of final victory over all Gentiles. There are also many keen glances and subtle observations in regard to the depths of the human spirit and of morality. With this turn of thought Israel obtains a powerful advance, and makes a strong movement, soaring towards Christianity. And therefore these songs are full of new spirit and impetus, pervaded by the certainty of high truths, obtained through the fire of trial, and not to be lost. The firmness and higher confidence at this time gained never ceases; a fresh circle of understanding and steadfastness was seen by Israel to be placed around its old rock-firm stock, which could defy all future storms.

For certainly there soon again came sufferings, trials, and sore dangers, fresh disasters and perplexity. For had all possible profit been drawn from that moment of first fresh inspiration and elevation: there must have proceeded from it in Israel a new shape of everything, a new law adapted to the altered times and necessities. But the time for rising above Moses was not yet come, because the precisely opposite danger, that of the over-estimation and confused reverence for the old and popular, was not yet recognized, on the contrary had grown up anew, was far therefore from being overcome. The complete conquest of the heathen effects then in the first instance only a closer cohesion in the nationality, now become victorious and glorified, though earlier often despised, rejected and misunderstood. Sion and the Temple are again to rise in greater glory, the old sanctuary is again to become the place of union of the fearers of Jahvé, the ancient written law is to serve as the basis of living. But thereby the principle of nationality is too highly prized, the heathen, whom it was desired to attract, are repelled, jealousy and discords, yea, schism and war between the new Israel and the Gentiles are the more called forth, because the ancient popular enmities again revived, and the heathen rulers became embittered against a people which boasts of a world-dominion. Through the consequences of this narrow troubled adhesion to the popular principle, Israel, which had advanced by so mighty a step, retreated with one foot. In the confusion beginning and increasing, a mass of new plaintive songs and lament streams from the bosom of many poets. The long duration of these heavy uncertainties and sufferings, the ever-increasing limitation and narrowness, and gradually also the too anxious reverence for the written law so depress the spirit, that after the first noble songs, there are many feeble and nerveless ones amongst those that follow, and the ancient power of the song is lost in softness and diffuseness. The poets in part themselves feel this, and content themselves with imitation and repetition of older songs.

Yet this period possesses again a peculiar advantage in the fact that in it joy and sorrow, contemplation and hope are so general and equal, that the individual ever passes away in the general, and we now see the community more than the poet. Already in the songs of the second age this closer fellowship of the like-minded and this turning to the multitude began: now all is still more definitive, because the exile has produced so sharp a separation, and especially because only the faithful assembled themselves into a new community under the still remaining restrictions of these times.

The light which earlier shone in a few great spirits, is now divided among the multitude, and enlightens and consoles many; the poetic power which at first is cumulative in David, is only now distributed a thousandfold among many, and more in the most numerous band of poets and friends of songs. This is fine, and nothing better can be desired, the very number of the songs is valuable. And as now the more firmly constituted community prevails over the individual, and he only feels himself strong in the former, only seeks to operate upon it, and as moreover no great blessing soon remained to the people but its Temple and its religion: the Temple-poesy only now comes into full bloom, and there arises a number of festive songs for the needs of the community. Again, didactic poetry now greatly improves upon the beginnings of an earlier time; that which is too peculiar and

personal more and more passes away in most of the songs.
Finally, there prevails in very many songs the high regard for
antiquity, the advantages of which were only now generally
prized, and in the memory of which the later [writers] found
their pride, indeed the best elements of their own life. In
this way Antiquity comes to a close.

1. THE FIRST TIMES OF THE DELIVERANCE.

A. *In the voices of Individuals.*

88-97. Pss. CXXII., CXXIV.—CXXIX., CXXXIII sq., LXXXVII.

These ten songs belong, according to all traces, to *one* poet,
—the same who sang the five last explained. We see everywhere the same highly inspired, yet collected and acquiescent
soul, which had longed for the newly germinating salvation of
Israel before the deliverance, and now follows after it with
most intense love and sympathy; and now again seized and
filled by every noble thought, which is awakened by this
higher time, expresses it in a short original song. He appears
after the return from exile to have dwelt not in Jerusalem
itself, but rather as an agriculturalist in a country-town of
Galilee, and to have gone at times thence to the capital and the
temple in course of re-erection; this plainly follows from
Ps. cxxii., comp. the (with the exception of Amos) unusually
frequent and singular images of agriculture, cxxvi. 4-6, cxxix.
3-8. But only his external salvation is altered by the deliverance; inwardly he is in these ten songs quite the same as in
those five. Throughout we find an extraordinary breadth and
elevation of the thoughts, partly in words which are echoed in
many late songs, as the *henceforth and for ever*, cxxi. 8, cxxv.
2, cxxxi. 3 (cxxxiii. 3, cxxviii. 5), the name *Creator of heaven
and of earth*, cxxi. 2, cxxiv. 8, cxxxiv. 3, which later so often
recurs. In thought and in word he is full of *peace*, cxx. 6, 7,
cxxii. 6-9, cxxv. 5, cxxviii. 6, of *blessing*, cxxviii. 5, cxxix. 8,

cxxxiii. 3, cxxxiv., of *waking*, cxxi. 3-5, cxxx. 6, cxxvii. 1 (cxxxiv. 1). In expression again there are several noteworthy features, as רַבָּה, *enough*, cxx. 6, cxxiii. 4, cxxix. 1, 2 (cxxiii. 3), the shortened יָהּ for *Jahvé*, cxxii. 4, cxxx. 3, comp. above, p. 125; and the colour of the language departs with him as with many writers of the time of the exile and immediately after him, strongly from the genuine old Hebrew; but takes a form in his case in this direction quite peculiar, comp. the constant שֶׁ, § 181 *b*, קָדְקָה, cxxix. 6, בְּרוֹב, lxxxvii. 6, modes of writing like שָׁנָא, cxxvii. 2 (§ 173 *b*).—The result is that the whole collection of the *pilgrim-songs*, Pss. cxx.—cxxxiv., with exception of the entirely different Ps. cxxxii., presents itself as proceeding from the like source, comp. further Vol. I., p. 15.

Ps. cxxiv. and Ps. cxxix. express with fine intensity the fresh feeling of that time—how that the community, not by its outward power, but only through the spiritual blessings living and ever operating in her, or through her fellowship with Jahvé, could be saved. Both are arranged as songs to be sung by the community (probably according to the type of Ps. cxviii.); and Ps. cxxiv. casts simply a glance upon the just fled past, vv. 1-5, with short thanksgiving and hope, vv. 6-9.

    Had not Jahvé been with us,   1
        let Israel say,
    had not Jahvé been with us
        when men rose up against us;
    yea, then had they swallowed us up living,
        when their wrath was kindled against us;
    yea, then had the water streamed over us,
        the brook had gone over our life;   5
    they had gone over our life
        those over-boiling floods!—

Blessed be Jahvé,
   that He gave us not for a spoil to their teeth!
our life—like a bird it escaped from the hunter's toils,
   the net brake,—and we escaped!
Our help is in Jahvé's Name,
   Creator of heaven and of earth!

לוּלֵי־שׁ, prop., if it had not been Jahvé whom we had; on vv. 4, 5, comp. above Ps. xl. and Ps. lxix.

Ps. cxxix. brings out—after the experience that Israel although of old and deeply bowed down, is nevertheless invincible by Jahvé's help—more plainly the hope thence arising for all the future; with rare images borrowed from agriculture. Invincible is Israel, vv. 1-2, through the righteous Jahvé, that is, who suddenly destroyed the base oppression of the tyrants, vv. 3-4; therefore the cruel tyrants will never attain their purpose against Him, but themselves wither away like the most transient, useless and most wretched grass, vv. 5-8.

1   Much have I been oppressed since my youth
      let Israel say,
   much have I been oppressed since my youth,
      —nevertheless they have not prevailed against me!
   On my back ploughers ploughed me,
      drew their furrows long:
   Jahvé is righteous;
      cut away the cord of the wicked!

5   Full of shame shall they retreat backwards,
      all who hate Sion,
   become like to the grass of the roofs,
      that before it blooms withers away,
   wherewith his hand a reaper never fills
      nor his arm a binder of sheaves,

~where they who pass by never said :
"Jahvé's blessing upon you !
we bless you in Jahvé's name !"

On ver. 3, comp. Isa. li. 23 ; they cut through my back not slightly, but drawing as it were long furrows upon it ; לְ is accordingly to be understood, if מַעֲנוֹת after the K'tib is taken as *plur.*,—as Aram. sign of the accusative (see on lxix. 6) But as the ploughman, so soon as the cord which binds the oxen to the plough is cut through, cannot proceed cruelly to tear up the earth : even so God suddenly cut off from the tyrants the means of their cruelty, יבשו ויסבו, after xl. 15. The second picture of agriculture, elicited by the first, gives the meaning of the most transient, and at the same time useless, unpleasant thing,—while the faithful bloom and profit, blessed by all, like a rich and joyous cornfield; for the greeting of passers-by, see Ruth ii. 4. שלף, *draw out*, push blossoms and fruit, where plants are spoken of; correctly the Targ.

Pss. cxxv., cxxvi.—The just founded and still very weak structure of the new Jerusalem had soon to contend again (about 530-520) with many evils, enmities, and seductions from without at the hands of heathendom, as the power in the world at that time,—besides internal division, scarcity, etc., so that the building of the temple came to a stand, and the whole state of the city became doubtful. Comp. Haggai and Zacharja. Yet the poet is too full of pure hope and high confidence in Jahvé and the true Israel, to admit of despondency in his repeated supplication, even under the increasing danger. Ps. cxxv breathes the boldest confidence, so that the poet feels himself urged first to express this in its height for all times and for the present, vv. 1-3, whereupon prayer then obtains free course, vv. 4, 5.

    They who trust in Jahvé,—   1
        are like the Sion's mount that never wavers,

for ever remains inhabited :
Jerusalem—round about hath it mountains,
and Jahvé is round about His people,
henceforth and unto eternity.
For the rod of the wicked will not rest on the lot of the
righteous,
that the righteous may not stretch their hands in
unrighteousness !—
O Jahvé, do good to the good
and to those who are honest in their heart !
5   But they who turn aside to their crookedness,
may Jahvé cause them to depart with evil-doers !
Salvation upon Israel !

As Sion, in itself very strong and protected by its surroundings, also according to history ever again inhabited, gives the eternal image of constancy, so also are those surrounded and guarded by Jahvé and His sanctuary (in the same Sion) firm and unshaken, for all times as in the present danger. For the rod, the rule of the wicked, which now sorely weighs upon the lot, the Divine portion, the property (Ps. xvi.) of the just, *i.e.*, on the promised land (lxi. 6), will not ever rest upon it. And for this reason, the poet thinks, that the excessive distress and the fear of the oppressions of mighty men (*e.g.*, of the Samaritans at that time powerful in Palestine and the Persian magnates supporting these) may not seduce the new builders to anything inconsistent with the stricter religion, comp. xix. 14 above, Vol. 1., p. 103. Only nothing half-hearted, nothing dishonest and incompatible with strict conscience ! no yielding in matters of religion from human fear and human complaisance ! This was the feeling of those first founders of the new Jerusalem, and the conclusion, vv. 4, 5, agrees well with the sharp opposition between the honest in their own heart, and those secretly meditating departures and concessions, of whom there must at that time have been a considerable number in Jerusalem, who, the poet justly so far desires may be punished, even as evil-doers=ignorant heathen.

Ps. cxxvi. first leads memory, amidst enduring sufferings, to the surprisingly joyous and beautiful time of the first deliverance, vv. 1-3; in order then the more urgently, yet in full hope, to pray for the mitigation of the present sufferings, vv. 5-6; as if the poet desired to conjure up again the joyous time of the beginning of the present conditions.

> When Jahvé restored again Sion,   1
>   we were like dreamers;
> then our mouth was filled with laughter,
>   and our tongue with jubilation;
> then said they among the heathen:
>   " great things hath Jahvé done to these!"
> Jahvé had done great things among us,
>   we were full of joy.—
>
> O restore us again, Jahvé,
>   like water-beds in the South land!
> They thus sow in tears,—   5
>   in rejoicing they reap;
> he goes forth indeed and weeps who bears the seed-cast;
>   but come, come home in rejoicing will he
> who bears his sheaves!

Ver. 4. The expression, שוב may be intended to say only the same as ver. 1, comp. above, p. 113: thus only is understood the image of the *water-beds in the South land*. The forest-brooks in the South land, *i.e.*, in Southern Juda are at times utterly dried up and desert; but just as an extraordinary rich rain from above may restore them to general refreshment and joy, so mayest Thou restore us who languish in misery!— And in vv. 5, 6 a corresponding hope comes in: if it is a

11 *

general expectation and experience that out of sorrow and humility joy and exaltation germinate, that the countryman sowing in bitterest distress reaps in joy (certainly the new building had known this experience at that time, comp. lxvii. 7, lxxxv. 13 with Hagg. i. 10, ii. 19) so will also Sion, now founded in trouble and tears, as if sown abroad, have yet a fair future. For not *that which* is sown and reaped, is here set forth as different, which would be incorrect; but only the manner and feelings *at* the sowing and reaping. The two sentences with *inf. absol.* form thereby a very strong opposition, § 280 *b*, only that in the first proposition the *inf. absol.* is carried on by a new verb, § 312 *c*.

Pss. cxxvii., cxxviii., cxxxiii.—As at that time community and house were founded anew, yea were restored with new love and high zeal, there stream over these relations from time to time short winged songs from the poet's mouth, while each small song skilfully marks a fine self-included picture, full of speaking truth. Ps. cxxvii.: human haste and industry by themselves,—especially such as would force everything in its anxiety and onesidedness—succeeds neither in the great nor the small human societies, nor by any means furthers the prosperity and building up of the house (the family); but all blessings come to the man who toils in hope and believes, as free gifts from God; and this is peculiarly manifest from the fairest of these gifts and the best ornament of the house,—a band of strong sons, serving as a guard to the house.—This and the following song may well be conceived and designated as *Table-songs*.

The two halves of the song have here the finest symmetry; each has seven members.

1 If Jahvé builds not the house
    the builders have had vain toil therein;
   if Jahvé guards not the city,
    the guard has watched in vain.

' Vain is it for you to rise early,
to sit late, eating the bread of sorrow :
thus giveth He it sleeping to His beloved !— '

See, Jahvé's heritage are sons,
His reward the fruit of the body;
as arrows in the hero's hand,
so are the sons of youth.
Hail to the man who hath his quiver full of them :   5
never will they be ashamed
when they speak with enemies at the gate !

The *particip.* ver. 2 *a* and *b* standing in a dependent half-proposition, which in itself might pass for a static proposition, according to Hebrew and Aramæic usage, is possible also in Greek.—שֵׁנָא, *sleep*, ver. 2 *c* is subordinated (§ 299 *d*) ; but the use of the כִּן seems here to be harsh. It lies at hand to suppose that the different, apparently irreconcilable elements, are thereby stated as alike, in respect to something higher; as by the German *gleichwohl*, ὅμως, *tamen*, comp. *tam*, as Hos. xi. 2 and יַחַד, ver. 7 : ye may trouble yourselves never so much ; nevertheless God gives (what He gives) to His beloved in sleep, therefore unexpectedly and surprisingly as to a dreamer, but yet only to *His beloved*. Meanwhile it is sufficient to hold to the nearest signification : *thus*, namely, as was expressed in ver. 1, and is immediately further proved in vv. 3 sqq., *Himself caring*, Himself watching, comp. cxxviii. 4, whereby the sense is substantiated, comp. also on Ps. lxi. 9, lxiii. 3, 5, above Vol. I., p. 273. But this *thus* becomes most plain, if the head of the house, who sings this song sitting at table with his family, indicates by the word the children sitting by him. That from ver. 3 onwards simply a weighty example and a proof of this general truth follows, is evident also from the indicatory " see !" *Reward*, namely, Jahvé's again, even as His heritage, the good to be given only by Him. That on the dismemberment of families, strong sons availed as the strongest protection of the house and the ageing parents, is clear from Gen. iv. 1, and many other passages; the whole phraseology also of ver. 5 c is derived from Gen. xxii. 17, xxiv. 60; only that instead of the older, harsher words, softer and milder ones are selected; comp. also the Beduin phraseology, DMGZ, 1851, p. 7.—The image of the arrows in the same application, Ham. p. 384 ult.

Ps. cxxviii. congratulates, quite in the sense and the examples of the preceding song, but in new pleasing pictures, the actual honourer of Jahvé as in manifold ways blessed, and also as happy in his domestic life, not living in vain; a fine completion of the preceding song. Finally, vv. 5-6, the language, passing over into generalities, finishes with a manifold word of blessing.

1 Blessed every fearer of Jahvé,
    who goes in His ways !
The toil of thy hands—yea, Thou shalt enjoy it:
    blessed thou and prosperous !
Thou spouse like a fruitful vine
    in the inner rooms of the house !
thy sons like young olive-trees
    round about thy table ;
see, that *thus* is the man blessed
    who fears Jahvé.

5 May Jahvé bless thee out of Sion,
    and look on the prosperity of Jerusalem
all the days of thy life !
And behold sons of thy sons !
    Peace be upon Israel !

כִּי ver. 2, in exclamation, § 330 *b*, just so cxviii. 10-12. We feel with what dread the poet looks back in thought upon the previous perplexed and insecure times, when in manifold moral confusion every possession had become insecure. The inner rooms, ver. 3, as the worthy scene of the wife's activity Ver. 6 *b* as cxxv. 5 *c*.

Ps. cxxxiii. signalizes a fine laudation of brotherly concord with the rich blessing attached to it. Although the praise holds good of every house: yet the poet certainly proceeded from a higher point of view. The fresh settlement of several tribes in Canaan, the image of those united in love to Jahvé and Sion, and through such concord blessed, is plainly present to his mind, as also the recollection of the sorrows which finally arose through disunion; and the conclusion, when the poet hastens to Sion, further confirms this. The song then proceeds, similarly to the two preceding, from the domestic relation, but conducts the thought immediately into the related but much higher sphere of the national.

> Behold, how pleasant and how fair   1
>   is it that brothers should live well together!
> As the best oil, that upon the head,
>   running upon the beard, Ahron's beard,
> that runs upon the seam of his garments.
> As Hermon's dew, running on Sion's mountains!
>   Jahvé appointed thither the blessing,
> life for evermore!

On גַם ver. 1, see § 352 *b*, it merely strengthens further the notion of the יַחַד. The blessing of unity, because it descends upon all, even the more insignificant in the mass, softly and refreshingly, is compared by the poet very aptly first to the most costly oil of anointing which runs down from the head, over the lower parts, over the long beard even to the seam of the garments, pervading all with a sweet perfume; and then still more effectively to the dew which descends from the highest and most snowy mountains of Canaan in the North on the lower and dry ones, e.g., Sion. But because the poet has, in the application of the whole truth, peculiarly Jerusalem and the Temple in his eye, the thought compels him to connect the two pictures with something more closely related to these; therefore, ver. 2, Ahron, i.e., the High-priest, is mentioned, and ver. 3, Sion, which is moistened and refreshed not merely by earthly, but (in correspondence with the image) also by heavenly dew, and refreshed for ever (the conclusion, ver. 3 c, like cxxxi. 3.). Thus with b the thought is expanded: how unobtrusively is Sion named, and yet is it not here the last goal of all discourse, for a dew quite other than the common is, according to the Divine Will, to flow down upon her!*

Ps. cxxxiv. is a small Temple-song, which exhorts the priests and Levites to be alert and faithful in the nightly temple-service, vv. 1-2; and so, in the unceasing service of the sanctuary, the poet hopes for himself some blessing from the rich spring of blessing, ver. 3. Since the poet in ver. 3 seems to speak to himself in opposition to the Levites, and to think from his own stand-point of all of his kind (somewhat as cxxviii. 2-6), it follows,—as can be readily observed in other respects—that he was a layman. Further, we see that at that time the priestly service at the holy place had scarcely been again appointed, Ezra iii. 8, 9.

> Now then, bless Jahvé, all ye servants of Jahvé,
>   who stand in the house of Jahvé by night;
> lift your hand to the sanctuary,
>   bless Jahvé!—

---

* It is therefore equally incorrect to place the Hermon of this song nearer in the direction of Jerusalem, or even by Jericho (Ritter's E. B., xv. 403), and to compare ציון with שׂאו, Deut. iv. 48, as John Wilson (Lands of the Bible, II., p. 187) does.

Jahvé will bless thee out of Sion,
the Creator of heaven and of earth !

Ps. cxxii. is probably later than those just explained, at least it appears entirely like a recollection of earlier times. An Israelite in the country, probably aged and unable to join in pilgrimages, but still of cheerful strong spirit, rejoices concerning those who take pleasure in the journey to Jerusalem, ver. 1, recalls fondly his own sojourn in the gradually restored city of ancient sanctity and dignity, vv. 2-5, and wishes for her a comprehensive well-being resting on a manifold basis, vv. 6-9.

I rejoice at those who say to me : 1
" we journey home to Jahvé's house !"
Yea, our feet stood
in thy gates, Jerusalem.
O Jerusalem, renewed like
a city firmly shut within itself ;
whither tribes went, tribes of Jahvé after the law for
Israel,
to praise Jahvé's name ;
for there were set thrones for judgment, 5
thrones of David's house !

Wish the weal of Jerusalem ;
happy be thy tents !
Peace be in thy defences,
prosperity in thy palaces !
because of my friends and brothers
will I wish thee well ;
because of the house of Jahvé our God
will I entreat prosperity for thee !

Gates, ver. 2, as cxxvii. 5. Vv. 4, 5 must refer to the old and glorious time when (as the Pentateuch prescribes in certain places) all tribes journeyed to Sion as the place of the sanctuary, of the supreme judgment and oracle, of the kingdom. Solely because of these sacred recollections Sion stands so high among later worshippers. יָדְוּת subordinated, to describe the measure, the mode and the circumstances, § 229 d. חִיל, ver. 7, probably as xlviii. 14, because here merely the city is spoken of. *Wish thee well,* ver. 8, properly *speak peace of thee,* even so speak of thee that I wish thee peace and say שָׁלוֹם לָךְ! But because in the whole song only the city and its restored external weal is spoken of, for אֹהֲבָיִךְ *who love thee,* ver. 6, אָהֳלָיִךְ, *thy tents,* is a better reading, comp. cxviii. 15, and on the idiom, Job xii. 6.*

Ps. lxxxvii., probably also by the same poet, is an utterance of all the grand views and expectations of that time concerning the higher dignity and destiny of Sion in the whole world-history; the sight of the new temple-building might readily prompt the poet to so inspired a song. For at that time there appeared along with the immortal religion of Jahvé, its ancient seat Sion, in the splendour of eternally firm, immovable foundation; and the reflection of all splendour and glory of the former fell upon this wondrously restored holy city. As the hope of a general conversion of the heathen was at that time so powerfully aroused, it appeared that Sion must become the spiritual metropolis of all peoples,—so that everywhere on earth, even amongst the peoples at present most hostilely disposed, persons would be found who, as the worshippers of Jahvé, had in Sion their higher fatherland. And since with this worship yearly journeys and longer sojourn of the many pilgrims coming from all distant lands was connected,—how great, it seemed, must the confluence of all outward splendour and glory and joy to Sion become! Such expectations, as they had often been announced by prophets of the time, appear also for once here

---

* That copy 1 actually so reads, I did not know when I made the remark in the *Jahrbb.*, v., pp. 176 sq.

poetically, in the moment of a most joyous mood—sketched with equal brevity and rapidity, power and beauty. But the poet does not conceal the fact, ver. 3, that his words in great part were only called forth by preceding lofty prophetic ones, comp. Ps. xii., Vol. I., p. 197. That the song only takes its start from the new Sion, is also clear from the omission of Assyria with Babel, ver. 4.

The short song best gives the type of a strophé remains simply, for the section after ver. 2 makes little-incision.

(Jahvé's is for ever Sion,   1
   of His) foundation the city on holy mountains :
Jahvé loves the gates of Sion
   more than all the seats of Jakob.
Most glorious things are spoken of thee,
   O thou city of God ! *
" Rahab, Babel I boast as my confessors,
   see Peléschet, Tyrus with Küsch
   " ' He was born there !' "

And of Sion men will say :   5
   " ' man for man was born in her,
   and He will hold her fast, the Highest !' "
Jahvé will reckon in the book of the peoples :
   " ' he was born there !' " *
Singers also and Temple-dancers,
   all my arts are in Thee !"

The present beginning, ver. 1, is too short and obscure even for this winged song : neither as exclamation are the words clear, nor can they in this song of very small verse-members be attached to the following verse, so that here the second member should begin with שׁעֲרֵי ; I conjecture that עִיר has fallen out, because of the similar שִׁיר in the superscription, and also a whole verse-member before it, possibly צִיּוֹן לְיִי לְעוֹלָם. On מְדֻבָּר, ver. 3, comp. § 295 b; that the poet has the material for vv. 4-7 from prophets, he himself says, ver. 3; from prophetic phraseology, too, the "I" of God, vv. 4, 7, is retained. *Ráhab* is a poetic name, unknown in the Pentateuch, for Egypt, which is derived from an Egyptian name (*Rif.* see Burckhardt's *Nubia*, p. 457, *Arabic Proverbs*, No. 139), but only received its full meaning through the mythology therewith connected, of *Rahab*, as a monster (see on Job ix. 13) =crocodile; as מָצוֹר (place of oppression), is a Hebrew poetic transformation of מִצְרַיִם. Among Philistines, Tyrians, Kushites, will ever be found this and that man of whom it is said, "he was born there," *i.e.*, is enrolled in the birth-lists there, or is there, in Sion, citizen, member of the second mother-city; while it is said of Sion, in her are man for man, all these immensely numerous foreigners and Israelites, born for the second time; yea, finally, if Jahvé, at the day of the last judgment makes up the roll of all peoples of the earth (comp. lxix. 29), He will miss among no people citizens of Sion. The Greeks would here speak of the Delphic *Proxenia*, comp. the *Gött. Nachrichten*, 1864, p. 169. From these customs at the great sanctuaries of antiquity at least the figures are here borrowed, although the last sense of the song, as Messianic, goes far beyond it. Further, an addition like אֵם, *mother-city*, before מַעְיָן, ver. 5, would well suit the sense; but it probably came into the LXX only through correct explanation. Ver. 5 *b* from Ps. xlviii. 9, xlvi. 5.—With great brevity, it is observed, ver. 7, as if incidentally, quite at the end, that there is no longer a want of the necessary living attire of the sanctuary, so to speak,—that there already are singers, dancers, and other artists of the kind who, according to ancient custom, belong to a sanctuary. By חֹלְלִים is most correctly understood not *flute-players*, from חָלִיל, *flute*, because these (I., p. 217) were not used in the Temple-service, but *dancers* (*Alterth*, p. 327). Only the word מַעְיָנָי is here obscure: this must mean (as in Aq. Syr.) *my springs*, as if the sense were: the springs of my fatness, of well-being are inexhaustibly in Thee; but this spiritual sense does not lie in the connexion. The LXX (κατοικια) read מָעוֹנִי, which would be in the sacred sense (1 Sam. ii. 29, 32): *all my sacred huts*, *e.g.*, the hut of singers, flute-players, and so many other artists employed at the sanctuary (as with us the *bau-hütte* (building-board), *i.e.*, the guild of architects is spoken of); for the arts served at that time specially sacred purposes alone, and at the sanctuary there was the only confluence of them; but probably each kind of artists had a special dwelling at the Temple. The word still remains in this connexion too obscure, if the translation *crafts* is not given. The following hypothesis seems best: עוּן, *'ain, chn*, Arab. and Syr. is *help* and *profit*, מָעוֹן, either *refuge*, place of help, or something useful, *fit for use*, hence an *art*. How wide a signification this word once had, is still shown by the Arabic *m'inch*, and *má'nan*, Sur. 107, 7.

THE SONG OF ANOTHER POET.

98. PSALM CXXXVII.

pours forth likewise, but in quite another manner, the first fresh sensations after the deliverance and return: on the one side new inspiration for Jahvé and His community, the highest feeling of delight in again possessing the fatherland, and the free exercise of precious worship and joyous praise of Jahvé, tenderest love to the finally again acquired Jerusalem; but on the other side still the most grievous and indignant recollection of the scorn and cruelty experienced shortly before and during the exile. In the presence of these violences, the released faithful, still contending with so much hardship, and not seeing, as had been expected, Babel and the rest of the most vicious heathen fully subdued,—can scarcely as yet come to rest and full content, especially at the first melancholy sight of the ruins of the holy city. It is this bitter recollection which particularly distinguishes this poet. Meanwhile, amidst these mingled feelings which move his breast, the most mighty feeling is that of infinite joy and pleasure in Jerusalem (and its spiritual blessings) which now may again be freely expressed in song. In Babylonia, indeed, this pleasure was in many ways affected and chilled, especially by the scornful demands of such conquerors to hear the sacred songs in praise of Jahvé and Sion from the mouth of the conquered (and to make merry over them), vv. 1-3. But how should they desecrate the holy songs before the ears of the scorners? for Jerusalem was and is to them ever the dearest good, vv. 4-6: O that those who destroyed Jerusalem, still lying in melancholy ruins,. and scoffed at Jahvé, might suffer the merited punishment. Edóm, which had enticed the Chaldæans to the destruction and had helped it on (comp. B. Obadja, Jer. xlix. 7, Lam. iv. 21, Ez. xxv. and xxxv.); and still more Babel! vv. 7-9. Since Babel was under Darius 516 B.C. in quite another condition than under Cyrus, we see thence clearly that this song must fall between 536-516.

The fluctuating feelings of the song are gathered into the highest uniformity in their expression: each of the three strophés of the song has three verses with seven members.

1.

1 By Babel's streams, there we sat, yea wept
    when we thought of Sion;
on the willows in the land
    we hung up our harps:
for there our conquerors demanded hymn and song,
    our taskmasters' joy:
"sing us of Sion's songs!"

2.

O how should we sing the song of Jahvé
    in the strange land?—

O, if I forget thee, Jerusalem, 5
  let my right hand forget herself ;
  let my tongue cleave to my palate,
    if I remember thee not,
    if I set not Jerusalem—above the crown of my joy!

3.

Remember, Jahvé, Edóm's sons on that day of Jerusalem !
  they who said : " make bare, make bare ·
    to the ground in her !"—
Daughter of Babel thou devastator !
  hail to him who requites thee—thy deed done to us
                                           by thee ;
  hail to him who takes and dashes
    thy children against the rock-wall !

Babylonia has many streams (comp. Tuch, *De Nino urbe*, p. 33) ; but because here the times of recollection of Sion, and harps brought with them, and left silent in their despoilment, are mentioned, we must think of gatherings held in the open air ; as *e.g.*, at the memorial feast of the destruction of Jerusalem, Zach. vii. 1, 2, comp. the *Gesch. des V. Isr.*, vi., pp. 375 sqq., 448. Here, too, the *willows*, ver. 2 (comp. *arab* in the *Journ. As.*, 1853, I., pp. 495 f.), lead us to think of such shady places by the streams.—תּוֹלָל, ver. 3, is either shortened from תְּהוֹלָל, prop., he who has become raging, then as substantive, the madman, as מְהוֹלָל, cii. 9, or since this on many grounds is difficult, comes from תָּל = שָׁל, prop. *draw*, hence also *draw out*, pillage ; the ancients mostly here translate "robbers," which according to Isa. xvii. 14, xlii. 22, 24, would not be unsuitable ; yet with שׁוֹבֵינוּ *a*, the signification *slave-leaders* would still better agree, if *atal*, Arab.=*akad*, Qam., may be compared.—Vv. 5, 6 ; if I ever forget Sion and that which befits her, I will rather forget myself, let my right hand in the point of acting forget her duty and renounce the service, the tongue especially if it would speak, let it stick fast. As שָׁכַח is prop. intransitive: be forgetful, in the moment of need be confused and too weak, it might be said quite shortly: my right hand be oblivious, forget and confuse itself, as quite in this way B. Jes. xlix. 15; comp. the like, *Hamâsa*, p. 69, ver. 1, and above, Ps. lxxvi. 6.—שְׁדוּדָה, ver. 8 might be passive: those (now) to be laid waste, the devastation of which is sincerely to be hoped (§ 168 *b*); meanwhile it suits the whole much better that thereby the whole condition of the punishable city should be shortly designated, in accordance with which שְׁדוּדָה is to be read, or at least as shortened from this שְׁדוּדָה according to the formation, § 152 *b*. *Dash in pieces*, ver. 9, according to ancient war-customs among rude Northern peoples, Hos. x. 14, xiv. 1, Jer. xiii. 16.

B. *In voices of the Community and Individuals.*

99-102. Pss. cxv., cxvi., cxviii., cxxxviii.

These four distinguished songs, again, present themselves in style, verse-structure, contents and spirit, as proceeding from *one* poet. In the language there is much that is similar and rare, as the extraordinary preference for כִּי,—cxv. 2, cxvi. 4, 14, 16, 18, cxviii. 2, 25, the continuation of a thought in each second member, cxv. 9-11, cxviii. 1-4, 10-12, cxxxviii. 4, 5, the mention of the חסד and אמת from the very beginning cxv. 1, cxxxviii. 2, &c. In Ps. cxvi. there are indeed strong Aramaisms impressed on the style; but in this merely personal song they are more tolerable than in the three others which were manifestly from the first designed for public use. The verse is in the three first songs throughout of elegant brevity, the language fugitive, but fine and rich in thought. The whole tone is sublime and powerful as we expect from that great time. Perhaps according to Ps. cxxxviii., Zerubabel is the poet.

Ps. cxviii., which finely sets forth the freshest sensations of the time in brief and powerful language, is, it is highly probable, that memorable song which the just-returned community carolled at the first feast of tabernacles in Jerusalem, when first a simple altar was erected at the holy place, Ezr. iii. 4 (not at the feast meant in Neh. viii. 17). That it was originally composed for this particular feast and no other, *e.g.*, the Pascha, is clear from the fact that it is mainly a thanksgiving and sacrificial song, without alluding to the peculiar occurrences of antiquity which we should expect in a pascha-song; and the mention of the *tents*, ver. 15, leads to the time when the people dwelt as in huts or tents. It is a noble thank-song for the last great deliverance of Israel, drawn from the boldest and clearest consciousness of the dignity and destiny of Israel, afresh so grandly preserved, with the prayer for further peace, which was so necessary to the new settlement, ver. 25. And since the song was destined for the full temple-service of praise, it is divided into alternate hymns; but in the hymn of the congregation, as the longest and most important part, the longer execution is suitably assigned to a choir-leader, who with joyous hymn of praise explains the high sense of the great deliverance through Jahvé, vv. 15-18, and the wish presently to render the thanksgiving by sacrifice in the name of the whole people, vv. 19-23. That which follows after the words of the high-priest receiving the prayer and the sacrifice with blessings, the choir-leader and choir are to sing at the end of the sacrificial function. The clear alternation of the language leads to all these assumptions; comp. Ps. cxv. and the remarks, I., p. 194, *Dichter des A. B.*

The main song, vv. 5-23, is manifestly broken up into four strophés, each uniformly of five verses and ten members. If the second has a member more, and the third only four verses but nine members, this cannot do away with the obvious law of the structure. Certainly the three first of these strophés form according to the thoughts a higher unity,—the first with loud jubilations starting with the glance at Jahvé, the second with that at the heathen, the third with that at Israel. With the close of this proper song of praise the train arrives at the gate, and the praise passes over into wishes, ver. 19-23. Thus the third strophé as the provisionally concluding one, might be somewhat shorter.

(Choir.)

1   Thank Jahvé, because He is good,
  because His grace is for ever!
 therefore let Israel speak :
  because His grace is for ever ;
 therefore let Ahron's house speak :
  because His grace is for ever ;
 therefore let all fearers of Jahvé speak :
  because His grace is for ever !

(Choir-leader.)

1.

5 Out of distress I cried to Jah :
  with deliverance Jah heard me ;
 Jahvé is mine, I fear not ;
  what shall men do to me ?
 I have Jahvé among my helpers ;
  so shall I calmly behold my haters !
 but better is it to hope in Jahvé
  than to trust in men ;
 but better is it to hope in Jahvé
  than to trust in mighty ones.

2.

10 The heathen all surrounded me :
  through Jahvé's name yea! I ward them off!
 surrounded, yea encircled me :
  through Jahvé's name yea! I ward them off!

surrounded me like bees,
  are quenched like fire of thorns;
through Jahvé's name yea! I ward them off.—
Thou indeed didst thrust me that I might fall;
  but Jahvé helped me up;
my praise and song is Jah!
  for He became salvation to me!

3.

Hark! jubilation and victory 15
  in the tents of the righteous:
  the right hand of Jahvé puts forth power!
the right hand of Jahvé is highly exalted,
  the right hand of Jahvé puts forth power.
I shall not die, but live,
  ever tell the deeds of Jah;
Jah has indeed sorely chastised me;
  but not given me up to death.

4.

Open to me the gates of gracious-right,
  that I may go in and thank Jah!
Jahvé's is this gate: 20
  Righteous men go in;
I will thank Thee that Thou hearest me,
  and hast become to me salvation!
The stone, rejected by the master-builders,
  has now become the corner-stone.
by Jahvé's power this came to pass;
  that appears to us wonderful.

(The Congregation.)
This is the day which God has made:
  exult we and rejoice in Him!

25 O give us, Jahvé! give us help!
    O Jahvé! give us, we pray, prosperity!

(High-Priest.)
Blessed be he who comes in Jahvé's name!
we then bless you out of Jahvé's house!
God is Jahvé; and He gave us light:
    bind then the feast with cords,
    to the altar's horns!

(Choir-leader.)
My God art Thou: I thank Thee,
my God, I exalt Thee!

(Choir.)
Thank Jahvé, because He is good,
because His grace is for ever.

Ver. 1.—A saying of older date, here and in many still later songs, just as in Jer. xxxiii. 11, taken from a standing temple-word; its beginnings, see in lii. 11. This saying all in the congregation are now to repeat, so that it three times resounds, vv. 2-4. *The fearers of Jahvé* must, because they are distinguished from Israel and the priests, be necessarily the proselytes of that time who attached themselves more closely to Israel (Isa. xiv. 1, 2); so in cxv. 9-13, cxxxv. 19-20, and the σεβόμενοι τὸν Θεόν in the New Testament; otherwise when they stand alone and in general, Ps. xxii. 24 sqq.—Ver. 10. כי appears here in a position like cxxviii. 2; אמילם, *I make that they give way*, lxx. correctly ἠμυνάμην αὐτούς. —Ver. 12: *like bees*, *i.e.*, wild ones, Ex. xxiii. 28; but the sting of their persecuting wrath was destroyed as quickly as thorn-stalks burn in the fire, Eccles. vii. 6. Ver. 14 and 28 from Ex. xv. 2, 1.—The sense of ver. 19 is quite as that in the hymn, B. Jes. xxvi. 2. Ver. 22, the proverbial phrase is clear enough from vv. 10-18, 21: the small, contemptible Israel which the heathen had already utterly rejected and desired to destroy as useless, has become nevertheless the foundation and corner-stone of the building of the true kingdom of God, yea, is now recognized and prized as such. The poet may have Isa. xxviii. 16 before his mind.—*This is the day*, etc., ver. 24 can only be said of a feast-day, fixed and constant by ancient sanctity. Ver. 29: *bind the feast, i.e.*, the festive sacrifice (Ex. xxiii. 18, Mal. ii 3) with *cords*, that it may not escape during the sacred function, and so lift it up till it comes *to the horns of the altar*, above on the altar. Comp. the like in the *Vishnu-Pur.*, p. 31, 9; 60, 11.

Ps. cxv. is a new Temple-song, to be sung alternately by congregation and priest. Its contents are properly only a further development of the short prayer for help, cxviii. 25. We know that the new community had from the very beginning a hard situation, due to the envy of neighbours. Thus the congregation here prays for Divine help; but not for their own sake, a human frail community, but for the sake of Divine truth and religion they pray for victory and honour; because heathenism, as it is here depicted in all its folly in strong colours, cannot subsist upon the earth; and only in so far can the priest promise blessing from Jahvé to the suppliants.

The main-song, vv. 1-11, breaks up into three strophés each of four verses, also quite similarly to Ps. cxviii., so that the first glances at Jahvé, the second at the idols, the third at Israel. If the first has only seven members, that can only be accidental here.

(The Congregation.)

1.

Not to us, O Jahvé, not to us,   1
    but to Thy name give honour
for Thy grace and truth's sake!
why should Gentiles say:
    " where then is their God ?"

for our God is in the heaven,
 all that He wills, He executes.

2.

Their images—are silver and gold,
 work of men's hands;
have mouth—and speak not,
 have eyes—and see not;
have ears—and hear not,
 have noses—and smell not;
their hands—nevertheless they feel not,
 their feet—nevertheless they walk not,
and they sound not with their throat.

3.

Like them be their makers,
 every one who trusts in them!
Israel, trust in Jahvé!
 their help and their shield is He;
Ahron's house, trust in Jahvé!
 their help and their shield is He!
Ye fearers of Jahvé trust in Jahvé!
 their help and their shield is He.

(High Priest.)

Jahvé has been mindful of us; will bless,
 bless will He Israel's house,
  bless Ahron's house,
 bless will He Jahvé's fearers,
  both the small and the great.
Jahvé will increase you,
 you and your sons;
be blessed of Jahvé,
 the Creator of heaven and of earth!

(The Congregation.)
The heaven is for Jahvé heaven,
but the earth He gave to the children of men;
the dead praise not Jah,
none who go into stillness:
but we—we bless Jah,
henceforth even unto eternity!

Ver. 3 is a proposition of state § 341 a. The counterpart of the heavenly = spiritual, living God follows, vv. 4-7, in a long description which, because of its sharpness, serves always as a pattern to later writers. In other respects, the sense was already given in Isa. xl.—xlviii. Ver. 15 after cxxxiv. 3, ver. 18 after cxxi. 8. *The earth he has given to men*, ver. 16, that they may know and praise him upon it; and this will we do, so long as it is day; ver. 17 after vi. 6, xciv. 17.

A peculiar phenomenon in these two songs is the recurrence three or four times of the same second verse-member as a half return-verse, cxviii. 1-4, 10-12, cxv. 9-11. According to what has been explained concerning this (I., pp. 199 sqq., *Dichter des A. B*), it cannot be doubted that it was always only a pithy saying, to be intoned by the whole congregation or by stronger voices, which formed this refrain. Hence also is explained how in cxv. 9-11 the whole tenor of the language in the half recurrent verse may be quite different, even though the subject is the same.—Still further is this extended through the whole song, Ps. cxxxvi.

In conjunction with this elevation of the time in public matters, the purely personal feelings of expository songs also breathe a perfectly peculiar lofty, joyous spirit, as if at that time every man among the people had felt lifted above himself. Pss. cxvi. and cxxxviii. show this; they belong to the finest monuments of this period.—In Ps. cxvi. we see a poet in misfortune and confinement (vv. 10, 16) far from Jerusalem and the already renewed temple, vv. 17-19. But praying for grace and deliverance he is in such wise impressed by the feeling of great Divine benefits in the past, that his suppliant song becomes more like a thank-song, full of high faith and noble spirit. According to custom, the poet prays to Him whose help he knows, vv. 1-6; may even now rest return in faith on Him, who has delivered out of greater dangers! Vv. 7-10; He, who alone is to be trusted, whose inexhaustible grace is only worthily praised by serene acceptance of His benefits and loud praise,—He is indeed willingly the Redeemer of His godly ones, vv. 11-15. In this sense, therefore, with this hope and these promises, the now necessary prayer at last pours forth, vv. 16-19.—Rarely do prayer and thanks to God meet with such wonderful intensity as in this noble song; Ps. xl. remains, precisely in respect of this intensity and this glorious interfusion of all feelings, even the most opposite, far behind this song. In this sacred glow simply a clear stream of thanksgiving might be found, were not other reasons adverse to this.

The structure of this song appears not thoroughly clear. But as vv. 7-10 and vv. 16-19 manifestly form two self-included and mutually correspondent strophés, each of nine verse-members, we expect also in the two others a similar relation. After ver. 11 the language manifestly sounds very abrupt and incomplete, so that we may conjecture that three members have fallen away, and the first strophé in the two great halves of the song probably consisted of 13 members. The relation then of the two double strophés is similar to that, *e.g.*, in Hizqia's song,' I. pp. 161 sqq. *Dichter des A. B.*—The division of the song into two in the LXX (before ver. 10) is groundless.

1 *a*.

1   I am glad that Jahvé hears
        the loud words of my supplication;

He verily bent to me His ear,
  and as long as I live, I will call.
Death-nets have surrounded me,
  pains of hell seized me,
    distress I meet and trouble :
I call on Jahvé's name,
  " O deliver, I pray, Jahvé, my soul !"
" gracious is Jahvé and righteous,
    pitiful our God ;
Jahvé protects the inexperienced ;" 5
  wretched was I—and He helps me !

1 b.

O soul, return to Thy rest,
  for Jahvé hath done well to thee !
Verily thou hast freed my soul from death,
  my eyes from tears,
    from stumbling my foot :
I will walk before God
  in the lands of the living.
I have *faith*, when I say : 10
  " unhappy was I, greatly."

2 a.

Indeed in my distress I have bethought myself
  that all men lie.

* * *

How shall I thank Jahvé
  for all the good that He has done me ?—
The cup of salvation I take
  and call on Jahvé's name,
my vows I pay to Jahvé,
  yea, before all His people !
In Jahvé's eyes is dear 15
  death for His saints.

2 b.

O Jahvé! truly thy slave am I,
I am thy slave, son of Thy maid:
Thou loosest my fetters!
To Thee will I offer sacrifices of thanksgiving,
calling upon Jahvé's name;
pay my vows to Jahvé
O truly! before all His people—
in the courts of the house of Jahvé,
in the midst of thee, Jerusalem!

Ver. 3 is a protasis to ver. 4, not according to its tenor, but to that of the second proposition (§ 357 b); the images from xviii. 5. But the apodosis thus begun in ver. 4 is—according to its most powerful sense—first completed ver. 6 b,—the words vv. 5, 6 a only repeating something which in such cases the poet spoke before God.—Vv. 8, 9, 14. Plainly recollections from lvi. 12; like cxviii. 6, from lvi. 12. In the probation of the exile he has learned to believe on Jahvé, experiencing how vain it is to trust in men and not in Jahvé, even if *all* men stood on the one side, on the other Jahvé alone, ver. 10.—Ver. 11 from xxxi. 23. The best thanks are according to ver. 13,—serenely taking the cup of manifold salvation (xvi. 5) to praise the dispenser. On ver. 15 comp. lxxii. 14.—פְּתָהּ, ver. 16, can only as *precative* express certain hope, § 223 a. The אַרְצוֹת חיים, ver. 9, is (§ 270 c) formed from אֶרֶץ ח.

Ps. cxxxviii. now presents itself as the thank-song promised in the preceding song, and is perfectly similar to it in thought, only the style is more elaborate. After the first outburst of thanks, vv. 1-3, follows a demand upon all kings of the earth along with the poet himself to know and praise God, as if one spake thus out of their midst, vv. 4-6; finally confidence and prayer for the future, vv. 7, 8.

The verse-structure is manifestly governed by the predominance of long lines, such being peculiarly adapted for a thank-song. The three strophés into which the song is thus divided, have each 6 to 7 members. But the poet of Pss. cxviii., cxv., is disclosed by the fact also that in the first strophé he begins with Jahvé, but in the second proceeds to think of the heathen, only that he as prince here immediately speaks of their princes. Looking at the lofty character of the thoughts, and the proud tenor of the whole song, we might possibly think if not of David, yet of one of the earlier kings of Juda as the poet, did not the glance at the actual conversion of the heathen princes and other traces in the style and stamp of the language lead us only to think of Zerubabel. Then the historical matter which lies at the basis of these two songs, may very well be found in the relations touched on in the B. Zakh. iii., iv.

1.

Thank I Thee with my whole heart,   1
   in the sight of God I play to Thee!
worship at Thy holy Temple and thank Thy name
   because of Thy grace and faithfulness,
     that Thou over all Thy name hast glorified Thy word.
When I cried, Thou didst hear me,
   makest me proud in my strong soul.

2.

Let all earth's kings thank Thee, O Jahvé,
   that they heard thy mouth's words!
let them sing of Jahvé's ways,   5
   that very great is Jahvé's power!
for exalted is Jahvé, beholding the lowly,
   but the proud He knows from afar.

3.

If I go amidst distress, Thou wilt revive me,
   against the wrath of foes lift up Thine hand,

and help me with Thy right hand!
Jahvé will work for me;
Jahvé, Thy grace is eternal!
Thy handiwork—O leave it not!

In the sight of God, ver. 1, *i.e.,* immediately at the Temple, as the similar phrase, Gen. iv. 14, 16. The words כָּל אִמְרֵי פִּי כִּי שָׁמַעְתָּ *that Thou didst hear all the words of my mouth,* which the LXX have at the end of ver. 1, would in themselves well suit the connexion, because they only prepare for the last number of ver. 2. Ver. 2: *over all Thy name,* over all that was hitherto known and promised of Jahvé; for the name expresses the known attributes. The words בנפשׁי עז, ver. 3, are best connected as a subordinate proposition of state, *so that in my soul is strength,* spirit! (otherwise than lxxi. 7.) The כִּי must (vv. 4 and 5) introduce the contents of the song of praise to be sung by the king: for (ver. 6) through Jahvé's doctrine they learn to know and repent their perverse pride. Here plainly Isa. lvii. 15 sounds through; and the regard to the heathen kingdom and kings to be converted pervades many oracles of the time, comp. also xlvii. 10, lxviii. 33, but nowhere in such a way as here. Ver. 7 c as xvii. 13, 14, lx. 7. —Ver. 8 again after lvii. 3. The מעשׂי may (§ 213 e) be the singular number, and this better suits according to Ps. xc. 17.

We place here the eight songs

(103-111) Pss. xcii., xciii., xcv.—c.,

which we ascribe to the poet more closely described above, pp. 124 sqq., and which manifestly all belong to the first years after the new foundation of Jerusalem; but we expect already from Pss. lxxvii., xciv., the noble way in which this poet, freed from his earlier doubts, will thank God.

Ps. xcii. is spoken by the poet, after full triumph over the nearest dangers of that time, in pure joy and gratitude, sharing the new prosperity of the whole people and in the sound of the temple-poetry,—yet simply from his own heart. It has three progressive strophés: the first merely introduces the song, vv. 2-4, the second gives the praise of Jahvé's operation in the present, clear only to the faithful, vv. 5-9, the third still more eloquently depicts the victory of the just on the overthrow of the wicked,—growing high like the palm, because he stands founded in the sanctuary, and increases by holiness, ever serene, mighty, and prepared for the praise of Jahvé, vv. 10-16.

According to I. p. 194, *Dichter des A. B.*, the ancient style of a song of joy once more here recurs, with strophés of increasing length.

1.

Beautiful is it to thank Jahvé,   2
    and to play to Thy name, Highest!
early to tell of Thy grace,
    and by night Thy faithfulness;
to the ten-stringed, to the harp,
    to the artistic play with the cither!

2.

For glad in Thy work, Jahvé, Thou madest me,   5
    over Thy handiworks I rejoice.
How great are, O Jahvé, Thy deeds,
    unfathomable Thy plans!
unreason understands not,
    and the fool comprehends this not.
If the wicked were green as the grass,
    and all evil-doers blossomed—
it was to be destroyed utterly.
But Thou art exalted for ever, Jahvé!

3.

For see, Thine enemies, Jahvé,   10
    for see, Thine enemies perish;

all evil-doers are scattered:
and like buffaloes Thou didst raise high my horn,
   fresh oil I drop;
calmly looked mine eye upon my lyers-in-wait,
   mine ear heard of wicked adversaries.
15 The righteous like the palm-tree is verdant,
   grows like cedars on Lebanon;
well planted in Jahvé's house,
   in the courts of our God flourishing,
they will still sprout in age,
   be fresh and full of sap:
to praise Jahvé that he is upright,
   He my rock in whom there is no unrighteousness!

Ver. 2 is as cxlvii. 1, cxxxv. 3, a transformation of the saying, cxviii. 1. Ver. 8 quite as lxxiii. 19, xciv. 13. Vv. 13-16 after lii. 10, 11, comp. with Klausen's *Æneas und die Penaten*, II. p. 644. The conclusion, ver. 16, strong as the conclusion Ps. lxx. iii.

But higher does the poet's thank-song rise in the following seven pieces in praise of Jahvé in the whole community and on its behalf; and the words of jubilation which sounded first in the mouth of the Great Unknown, B. Jes. xl.—lxvi. here now find their nearest and loudest echo in the mouth of the great new community. It now appeared as if Jahvé for the first time, sublime and manifested as was desired, again ruled from out of Sion for the spread of the true religion; and the new community could, after the old jubilee songs, sing truly *new* songs of thanksgiving, xcvi. 1, xcviii. 1, comp. xl. 4, Isa. xlii. 10, Pss. ciii. 5, cxliv. 9, cxlix. 1, xxxiii. 3.—We see here in the first instance three songs of praise on the thus founded, thus ever enduring rule of Jahvé; the two first turn in the last strophé to exultation. Ps. xciii. is the shortest and finest: it breaks like most of these songs into three winged strophés, but nowhere are they so winged as here. Each contains only two verses but each with three members, the last only one verse. In the first are now found only five members, but probably one has here fallen out, just as the LXX omit ver. 3 c.

1.

Jahvé rules, adorned with majesty,   1
   might-adorned,—girded, Jahvé :
   and the world without trembling stands fast.
Of old Thy throne is firm:
   Thou art from eternity.

2.

High raised floods, Jahvé !
   high the floods their voices ;
   high their roaring raise the floods:
more than many waters' voices,
   more magnificent than sea-breakers,
   in the height is Jahvé magnificent.

3.

Right faithful are Thy testimonies ;   5
   thy house holiness becometh,
   Jahvé, for endless time !

Ver. 4 c alludes to the thunder, which in the height still more sublimely sounds than the most stormy roaring upon earth : so does God quell the unrest here below. So after xlvi. 4, lxxvi. 9.—Ver. 5. *Testimonies* are sacred assurances, oracles and laws, like those in the Pentateuch.

In Ps. xcvii. the primary thought falls into four similar strophés, each of three ordinary verses, while the language becomes only somewhat more excited in the beginning of the third and fourth, vv. 7, 8, 10. For the historical reason of the joy comes out more strongly with each of the three first strophés; but while the third at the beginning turns vivaciously towards the heathen, the language in the last collects itself the more into simple exhortation to Israel.

1.

1 Jahvé rules! the earth exults,
  many coasts rejoice!
clouds are about him and rain-darkess,
  right and truth his throne's foundation.
Before him goes fire,
  scorching His oppressors round about.

2.

His flashes lightened through the land :
  seeing it the earth trembled;
5 mountains melted like wax before Jahvé,
  before the Lord of the whole earth;
the heaven makes known His right,
  That all peoples see his splendour!

3.

" Let all image-worshippers blush, who boasted of idols!
  do homage to Him, all ye gods!"
Hearing this Sion rejoices, Jordan's daughters exult,
  —because of Thy judgments, Jahvé!
For Thou, Jahvé, art higher than all the earth,
  greatly exalted above all gods.

4.

10 Jahvé's friends, hate evil!
  He keeps the souls of His beloved, will snatch them
      from the wicked's hand.
Light is scattered for the pious,
  joy for the heart-upright;
rejoice, ye righteous, in Jahvé,
  thank His holy fame!

Ver. 1 from Isa. xlii. 10, 12, li. 5. Vv. 2, 3, 6 from l. 3-6., Ver. 8 from xlviii. 12. Ver. 9 as xlvii. 10. Ver. 4 as lxxvii. 19. Particularly noteworthy in ver. 7 is the connexion of the thought, B. Jes. xliv. 9-11 and Ps. xxix. 1, 2, as if the time had now come when both the idol-worshippers are ashamed and the highest angels themselves must most deeply do homage to God; because He at once on both sides preserved in the highest degree His truth. Such heavenly words sounded long ago: the more intensely does the congregation now rejoice, ver. 8.

Ps. xcix. praises the power before which again all must bow, —the justice and the revelation of Jahvé—in three strophés, in such a way that at the end of each the exhortation to praise recurs, and each ends with a holy! Each contains with this conclusion six, but the last twice as many members. Comp. I., p. 199, *Dichter des A. B.*, and above, p. 18. Pre-eminently important is here only the glance at the exalted ancient foundations of the community,—which fills the last large doubled strophé.

1.

Jahvé rules : peoples tremble ; |
    He who is throned on Cherubs : the earth trembles.
Jahvé is great in Sion,
    lofty *He* over all the peoples.—
Praise be to Thy name, great and sublime :
    holy is He !

2.

And to the fame of the king who loveth right !
    Thou hast founded equity ;
    right and truth in Jakob *Thou* protectest !—
Highly exalt Jahvé our God,   5
    do homage at the footstool of His feet :
    holy is He !

3.

Moses, Ahron were priests to Him,
    Samuel, callers upon His name:
    they cried to Jahvé and *He* heard;
spake in pillar of cloud to them,
    His testimonies they kept,
    and the ordinance which He gave them;
Jahvé, our God, Thou heardest them,
    wert to them a pardoning God,
    and an avenger of their deeds!—
Highly exalt Jahvé, our God,
    do homage to His holy mountain:
    holy in truth is Jahvé our God!

The beginning of ver. 4 is, in spite of the new strophé,—for the strophés are very small in their structure—interwoven with the end of the preceding, comp. lxxx. 15, 16, Rev. xix. 3. Ver. 2 after lxxvi. 2. Ver. 5 *b* after Isa. lxvi. 1.

Pss. xcvi. and xcviii. are most general songs of praise to Jahvé, the wondrous Saviour in the past, the mighty Ruler in the present, the great universal Judge in the future, to whose praise Israel, the heathen, the whole world are summoned. Thus in a twofold point of view three strophés, since the wondrous past must refer peculiarly to Israel, the present also to the other peoples, the future to the whole world.—The build of the strophés is plainly founded uniformly on four verses, for ver. 13 is better broken up into two. The words, vv. 5, 6 are however probably inserted here from another similar song.

1.

1   Sing to Jahvé a new song!
    sing to Jahvé all the earth!
  sing to Jahvé, bless His name!
    gladly tell day by day His salvation!

among the heathen relate His splendour,
  among all the peoples His wonders!
For very great and sublime is Jahvé,
  fearful above all gods He.
[For the peoples' gods are all idols!   5
  but Jahvé the heaven's Creator;
splendour and pomp is before Him,
  power and beauty in His sanctuary].

2.

Give to Jahvé, ye hosts of the heathen,
  give to Jahvé honour and praise!
give to Jahvé His name's honour,
  take sacrifices, come to His courts!
do homage to Jahvé in holy attire,
  tremble before Him, all the earth!
say among the heathen: Jahvé rules,   10
  and the world stands without trembling;
He will judge peoples equitably!

3.

Let the heaven rejoice and the earth exult,
  sea roar and its fulness!
field makes merry and all that is in it,
  all forest trees then jubilate
before Jahvé, that He comes,
  that He comes to judge the earth,
to judge according to right the world,
  peoples according to His truth!

The אף is, ver. 13, explained of the future world-judgment.
At the foundation of the whole song lie very strongly Ps. xxix.
and Isa. xl. sqq. Ver. 10 as xciii. 1; the strong figures ver. 12,
as also xcviii. 8 from B. Jes. lv. 12.

13 *

Ps. xcviii. presents itself merely as a shorter alternative of the former; the strophés are here simplified to three verses.

1.

1   Sing to Jahvé a new song, because he did wonders,
       His right hand and His holy arm helped Him!
    Jahvé has made known His salvation,
       clearly before the Gentiles revealed His right;
    thought of His grace and truth for Israel;
       all earth's bounds saw our God's salvation.

2.

    Exult before Jahvé, all the earth!
       break out into jubilation and play,
5   play to Jahvé, with the cither,
       with the cither and loud play!
    with trumpets, with sound of horns,
       exult before the King Jahvé!

3.

    Roar sea and its fulness,
       land and they that dwell therein,
    clap streams with the hand,
       mountains rejoice together
    before Jahvé, that He comes to judge the earth,
       to judge according to right the world,
          peoples according to equity!

On vv. 3, 4 comp. above on Ps. xcvi. 12, 13.

To exhortation which in Pss. xcvii. and xcix. was only briefly united with the thanks, Ps. xcv. now turns with peculiar preference. The song calls for thanks to Jahvé as the only Creator of all in the world, vv. 1-6, as the Trainer and Preserver of Israel, vv. 7-11; this last however only if Israel itself is willing and inclined, not again falling into the old errors,—but in that case immediately and instantaneously; hence with ver. 7 quick turn to exhortation from the old sacred history.—The song has manifestly only two strophés, each constructed of six verses; precisely where the language leads to the Ancient History, it is frequently suddenly broken, because its fulness is too great, and the history is known as a whole (comp. lxxvii. 21, lxxxi. 17, cxiv. 8). But in ver. 7 c a verse-member is plainly wanting.

1.

Let us jubilate to Jahvé, 1
 exult to the rock of our salvation;
offer thanks before His countenance,
 exult with hymns to Him!
A great God is Jahvé indeed,
 a great King over all gods!
He, in whose hand are the earth's foundations,
 whose are the mountains' sunny summits;
His is the sea, by *Him* created, 5
 His hands formed the dry land.
Come, do we homage in humility,
 bow we before Jahvé, our Creator!

2.

For *He* alone is our God,
 we people of His pasture, flock of His hands,—
to-day, if ye hearken to His voice;
 " have not a hard heart, as at Meriba,
 as on the day of Massa in the desert,
there where your fathers tempted me,
 proved me, saw also my deeds!
Forty years was the race adverse to me, 10
 I thought: " people of erring heart are they,
 and they know not my ways."
When I swore in my anger:
 " they shall not come to my rest!"

Ver. 4, תּוֹעֲפוֹת prop. shining point, sunny height, from יפע=יעף, glitter, Job xxii. 26, Num. xxiii. 22 (where it signifies *beams*, *i.e.*, horns) ; LXX according to the sense correctly ὕψη. Vv. 8-11 according to Ex. xvii., Num. xi., xii., xx. *Saw also my doing*, that is how He gave to them—to show His power and the folly of their doubt—what they prayed for, but at the same time also the punishment deserved, comp. lxxviii. 18-31.

Ps. c. is finally a sort of brief, pithy abstract from the mass of these noble, thank and victory songs of that time, the more serviceable for the ordinary Temple-song.—But here too are separated two small strophés,—the first praising God as the Creator of the community, the second as the ever gracious One.

1.

1   Shout aloud to Jahvé, all the earth !
    serve in joy Jahvé,
        come before Him with jubilation !
    Know, that Jahvé alone is God,
        He has made us, His we are,
        we His people and flock of His pasture !

2.

    Come with thanks to His gates,
        hence with praise to his courts !
    thank Him ! bless His Name !
5   for the Lord is good, eternal His grace,
        His faithfulness to all ages !

Verse 3. לֹא other mode of writing for לוֹ, although LXX; Syr., have thereby been led astray ; the sense as xcv. 7 in the same poet.

112-115. PSALMS LXVI.—LXVIII., XLVII.

are Temple-songs which we bring together here since they

stand somewhat closely together in the second Psalm-book, and belong to these times.

Ps. lxvii. is the carrying-out of the primæval priestly blessing, Num. vi. 24 sqq., in the form which now seemed the most suitable. It becomes the blessing which the congregation in the Temple speaks concerning itself, or rather which a priest, including himself, speaks concerning it. But the retouching bears the traces of the exalted time in which it arose: as in many of the songs and oracles (Isa. xl.-lxvi.) of this time, the look and the wish passes from Israel to *all* peoples, that all through the Divine judgment may come to knowledge, as though that were the first consequence of the blessing upon Israél. From the close, ver. 7, it is further clear that such high wishes were formed precisely in a time when the new settlement was snatched from imminent distress by an unexpectedly rich harvest, (therefore plainly enough at the time of Haggai, see above on Ps. cxxvi.) and this first blessing might serve as pledge for the further greater ones.

Two strophés may be distinguished in the song, although the second, just as in Ps. c., is shorter. As the first concludes with the summons to the peoples, the second begins therewith, but only through the glance at the immediate condition of Israel to return to the beginning.

1.

God be gracious to us,   2
    cause His countenance to shine among us!   *
that men upon earth may know Thy way,
    among all peoples thy deliverance!—
Let peoples thank Thee, O God!
    Let all the peoples thank Thee,
nations rejoice and jubilate,   5
    that Thou judgest peoples equitably,
nations—on earth dost lead them!   *

2.

Let peoples thank Thee, O God,
   all the peoples thank Thee!—
Earth gives already her fruit:
   God, our God, bless us!
yea, let God bless us,
   that all earth's bounds may fear him!

Ver. 5 sounds quite as xcvi. 11-13, xcviii. 9, and yet in the stamp of the speech somewhat differently.

Through all Temple-songs of the time a threefold feeling in reciprocal union runs, that of deliverance and power alone through Jahvé who glorifies Sion, that of the dominion of Jahvé from out of Sion over all lands and peoples, and that of the necessity that finally all must come to the pure knowledge and reverence of Him; they are joyous outbursts of the serene, far forth-looking mood in those days of the temple in the renewal of its youth,—a manifold and loud echo of the great prophetic voice, Jes. xl.-lxvi. But the greatest, most splendid and artistic song among them is Ps. lxviii., ascending to all indications composed for the consecration of the new temple, and probably at that time publicly sung. It is entirely in the style of a song not flowing from a momentary mood and inspiration, but with design and much art composed for a certain object. This object is the praise of Jahvé, as the only mighty, eternal leader and redeemer of Israel as well as of all just kingdoms of the earth that fear Him,—Who now in splendour has journeyed to Sion through the (Babylonian) desert, and takes His seat in His Temple, His firm seat as Ruler of the whole earth, to whom all kingdoms of the earth shall do homage to their own salvation. While the poet would sing this praise not alone for himself and in his own name, but would cause all priests and laymen present at the joyous feast of the dedication of the Temple according to their different orders to take part in it, the entire large song is divided into suitable sections and alternate hymns. As middle place appears the hymn of the Israelites going up to the Temple, of the people or the laymen in four strophés, probably in the progress of the train from the four lay-tribes, Benjamin, Juda, Zebulon and Naftali, present according to ver. 28,—to be sung in order, vv. 8-24; introduction and conclusion form five other strophés, two somewhat shorter at the beginning, vv. 2-7, and three at the end, vv. 25-36, which therefore the divisions of the priests sojourning at the temple and introducing and concluding the feast, were to sing. The external uniformity of this division into strophés is clear from the fact that a series of four verses here appears as the ground-measure of a strophé; but this is represented in so manifold a way that (1) the number of the members in the four strophés of the main song as of a song of joy is extended from 8 to 10; (2) each of the three strophés of the more prophetic concluding song is built up on the other hand of 9 members, but (3) the two of the introductory priests' song limit the measure to three verses from a false division of the verse. That the laity sing vv. 8-24, which give a complete and rounded whole in themselves, is clear from the "us" vv. 20, 21, while the priests address Israel as a people, ver. 36; the words ver. 2, are (Num. x. 35) priestly.

But most plainly this division is deduced from the contents of the whole song and its parts. For the opening, proceeding from the Divine destruction of the wicked (Babylonians) just experienced, especially summons to the praise of Jahvé as the gracious Redeemer of the forsaken and *captive*, as if now, as formerly in Moses' time, Jahvé had become the Redeemer of the people and was advancing once more through the desert to Palestine as His seat with noblest victory, vv. 2-7. Now follows as the main part the praise of Jahvé as of the only mighty and helpful one, who has finally taken his seat in Sion, protecting for eternal times from this centre His people, vv. 8-24; and thus in the first three strophés the three—in this sense—greatest and most noteworthy incidents of the ancient history are brought out. In the first the march of Israel from Egypt to Palestine and the training of the people under Moses and Josúa, in the second the time of the long struggles for the permanent possession of Kanáan under the Judges, in the third—and this is the outcome of all—the choice of Sion to be the holy seat under David is sung. To this the fourth and last subjoins the recent features of that period,— how Jahvé, thus mightily ruling from out of Sion, and even saving from *death*, abides also for all the future. The three closing strophés again to be sung by the priests, give partly retrospective, partly prospective glances: the first looking back on the splendid march accomplished, and appropriately celebrating it; the second supplicatory to Jahvé, and anticipating that also among the Gentiles the Temple and the religion of Jahvé will be highly esteemed, the third finally summoning all kingdoms of the earth to praise Jahvé who rules from out of Israel. Introduction and conclusion therefore contain peculiarly prophetic demands and anticipations, the middle piece the proper hymn of praise.

But it is as if the poet felt himself incapable of producing so high a song out of his own strength; for the finest and most powerful passages in it are like a garland from older songs, which we find partly elsewhere in the Old Testament, and partly must assume to have once existed. The whole is rather finely composed of a series of older brilliant passages than a new work and a firmly-jointed structure; and as many older passages are very abrupt (probably as known to the singers), the explanation is often difficult. Where however the co-operation of the poet—easily recognizable—is found, then we see everywhere this later time shine forth plainly in the thoughts (vv. 5, 7, 21, 33) and in the language. Therefore whoever considers this twofold content and then the whole style of the song, will not probably come to the opinion that the song springs from the time of the first dedication of the

Temple under Solomon, or was earlier composed than the building of the second Temple. It is also historically noteworthy that in ver. 28 only four lay-tribes are named as going to the Temple,—and this has no sense for Solomon's time; and we learn thence that already about the year 516 B.C., not merely Benjamin and Juda, but also Zebulon and Naftali, *i.e.*, inhabitants of Northern Palestine or of Galilee betook themselves to the Temple on Sion.*

I. 1.

When God arises, His enemies vanish,   2
    His haters flee before Him,
Like as smoke is blown away, blown away,
    like as wax melts before the fire,
    wicked men perish before God;
and just men joyously exult before God,
    leap in fulness of joy.

2.

Sing to God, play to His name,   5
    make way for Him journeying through the desert,
    named Jah; and exult before Him!
Him, the Father of the orphans and Judge of widows,
    God in His holy home;
God brings again the dispersed to their home,
    sets prisoners free for happiness and weal,
    causes the perverse to dwell only in dryness.

II. 1.

God, when Thou didst go before Thy people,
    when Thou didst march through the desert,

---

* Comp. on the true sense and the period of this song the *Jahrbb. der Bibl. Wiss.*, iv., pp. 52 sqq., v., pp. 172 sqq.

earth rose, heavens dripped before God,
 this Sinai before God, Israel's God.—
10 With rain of blessing, God, Thou besprinklest their
             heritage,
 and the wearied—Thou hast refreshed it;
Thy stock settled firmly in it,
 prepared for the sufferer, God, through Thy goodness!

2.

The Lord gives a hymn of victory,
 there is a great host of messengers of victory;
the kings of the host flee, flee,
 and the housewife divides booty:
" If ye rest thus between hurdles,
 doves' wings are covered with silver,
 and their pinions with green gold-shimmer:
15 Yet when the Highest scatters kings,
 It snows therein on Ssalmon!"

3.

" A mountain of God is Basan's mountain,
 a high mountain is Basan's mountain;"
why then leer ye high mountains
 at that mountain, by God desired as a seat:
yet Jahvé will for ever inhabit it!—
" See, chariots of God, twenty thousand, but thousand,
 the Lord therein, Sinai in holiness!
Thou wentest to the height, leddest captives,
 receivedst gifts at men's hands;
 perverse ones also must rest with Jah God!"

4.

20 Blessed be the Lord: from day to day
 He helps us to bear,—the God of our deliverance,
the God Who is our God to show help;
 and Jahvé the Lord—has for death ways of escape.—

Yea, God will dash in pieces the head of his foes,
  the crown of him who walks in his sins :
the Lord spake : " from Basan I fetch again,
  I fetch him again from the sea's depths,
that thy foot may shine in blood,
  thy dogs' tongues be refreshed on the foes !"

III. 1.

Men have seen thy trains, God,   25
  my God's and King's trains of holy kind.
In front went singers, after players on stringed instru-
                                                    ments,
    between maidens with the drums ;
in full choirs blessed God
    the Lord, they from Israel's spring ;
There was Benjamin the little as their leader,
  Juda's princes, their strong band,
  Zebulon's princes, Naftali's princes.

2.

O ordain Thy splendour, O God !
    make splendid, God, what Thou hast prepared for
                                                    us !
because of Thy Temple at Jerusalem
    may kings bring homage to Thee !   30
Chide the wildness of the reed, the herd of bulls, with the
                                                    calf-peoples,
    that they may haste with silver bars !
  scatter the people that do love war !
that nobles may come out of Egypt,
    Kûsh in haste lift his hand to God !

3.

Ye, kingdoms of the earth, sing to God,
    play to the Lord,   *

> to Him who passes through heaven, heaven of old,
> —see, He sounds with His voice, a mighty voice!—
> 35 give God praise, whose glory rules over Israel,
> and whose power is in the bright height!—
> Sublimely rules God from out Thy sanctuaries!
> Israel's God—He lends power and strength to the people;
> blessed be God!

I. Vv. 2-4. Further development of the old, certainly genuine Mosaic song, Num. x. 35, so that then in a second strophé, vv. 5-7, the proper summons to singing follows, comp. I., p. 192, *Dichter des A. B.* On ver. 2 *a* comp. § 357 *b*; on the image תִּנְדֹּף see § 240 *c*; the following תִּנְדֹּף cannot well be taken as the second person: *Thou* scatterest (them); since the address to God is nowhere found in the whole of the first strophé, and the supply of the object is here harsh; but then there remains nothing but to take עָשָׁן here (174 *c*) as *fem.* (against the general usage), and נָדַף as blow away, put to flight. Ver. 5: to Him advancing victoriously through the wastes, as He did in Moses' time, and now again marching from Babel (Isa. xxxv., xl. 3) opens the way, receives him on the victorious march to Sion with triumph,—Him who both protects from out of Sion all the forsaken (orphans and widows, ver. 6, comp. x. 14), and as has been just shown, redeems the crushed and the prisoners from exile. כּוֹשָׁרָה seems to be only a later word, comp. (Joh. בַּיְתָה: *He causes to dwell* individuals, isolated ones, who are therefore without house, bringing them again *home*.

II., 1. O how grand is the sacred past of this *home* of Jahvé! Its beginning, vv. 8-11, was due to nothing less than that wondrous time of the formation of the community under Moses himself! But that violent storm, in which Jahvé appearing on Sinai and ready to lead Israel further, shook the earth (vv. 8, 9, from Judg. v. 4-6, comp. Ex. xix.), became at the same time a refreshing rain and blessing for Kanáan, the land wherein Israel was to dwell. It is as if Kanáan, only after it became the seat of Jahvé, became also the fully rich, blessed land, appropriated to Israel as Jahvé's people. For the beneficial influence of higher insight passes over to that which is external, and a land, so soon as that influence appears, becomes a truly flourishing and blessed one. נִחַלְתָּ, ver. 10, is, against the accents, most readily taken with the first member, so that תָּכִין, "besprinkle," as words of refreshing, stands with a double object, § 283 b. כּוֹנֵן, *set up, enliven*, forms a word-play with הָכִין, *prepare*, as lxv. 10; but this stands here relatively, *which* land *Thou preparest*, closing with the review of all that has been said.

2. But what a new view is given, vv. 12-15, on the glance at the many changing conflicts in the time of the Judges; for the permanent settlement of Kanáan was only brought about by repeated victories over the enemy down to Davîd's time. But the first thing heard is: "The Lord gives אֹמֶר, *victory!*" (this word here in the same signification as in Hab. iii. 9, comp. ver. 8): and this *joyous message* is heard from *women* who in great number like an army meet with singing the heroes returned from the battle, 1 Sam. xviii. 6, xxi. 12, xxix. 5, Ex. xv. 20, 21; and divide the booty at the feasts of victory, Judg. v. 11. Vv. 14, 15, must now by way of example, select such words out of the old songs of victory: unquestionably they are from old songs. The words are indeed because broken from their context, very harsh; yet there appears to be plainly an opposition of sense between vv. 14 and 15; if ye (Israelitish men, for the women are singing) *rest between the folds, i.e.,* carelessly stretched out on grassy pleasant places by the water (Judg. v. 16, Gen. xlix. 14), therefore if ye have peace as at this very time after the close of a war,—*the wings of the doves are covered over* (נֶחְפָּה, fem. of the part. for כְּנָפֵי may be connected with the *fem. sing.*, § 317 a), *with silver, and their pinions with the most green-*

shimmering gold,—but they are only this through the sunshine,—therefore *so appears* most delightfully *the sun;* but *if God scatters kings*, in the sore battle, *it snows in it* (the same land) *darkness*, the same God sends dark snow (and hail) for the destruction of the foes who assail that which is sacred, Job xxxviii. 22, 23, as has been seen shortly before. Therefore the same wondrous land now shows the scene of the sweetest rest and of the serenest heaven, now, if the destruction of the wicked is in hand, that of the most gloomy and wrathful. בְּצַלְמוֹן only is difficult; this, Judg. ix. 48, appears as the name of a mountain in Efráim, and according to this passage it might appear to be the snowiest mountain in Kanáan. But the word might perhaps also signify "in the darkness," *talmon*, Arab., comp. צַלְמוּת; and in any case that mountain takes its name from the darkness. But if we reflect that the word most safely denotes that mountain, and further that this need not be precisely the snowiest if it only lay in a position to serve readily as an example of all, we do best to keep to this, and the more because we are thus brought into the very heart of the places where the great feasts of victory were chiefly held in the time of the Judges; comp. the *Gött. Gel. Anz.*, 1865, pp. 1671 sqq. And thus we have here a proverbial phrase from the midst of the time of the Judges.

3. Thus there naturally follows that sublime period under David when Sion, this in itself far from lofty mountain became, nevertheless, the most sacred and thereby the highest of all; and this is unquestionably depicted in words from songs out of that time—and therefore in all probability actual songs of David—in unusually lofty style. The high, snowy-topped Basan has by nature great advantages, and a right to be called God's mountain. Also (*Gesch. des V. Isr.*, i., pp. 497 sqq., ii., pp. 555 sqq.) it unquestionably was once held by the people Israel to be a holy mountain: but God can highly exalt that which in itself appears small and contemptible, through

the spirit and the spiritual. So Sion is now exalted above all other mountains, comp. above Ps. xlviii., and still further wrought out below, lxxviii. 69. Thus follows, vv. 18, 19, the description of the splendid train of the Holy One to Sion from out the old Sinai; while with the Highest and Holiest all the inferior spirits, the hosts of angels, marched to Sion (for where the highest good is, are also the particular inferior ones, Gen. xxviii. 10), Deut. xxxiii. 2, and at the same time casting down all that is hostile (as this was eminently seen in David's time), like a great king on his victorious march, and high in the battle-chariot (Hab. iii. 8), making captive among those that resist, receiving homage among the submissive (comp. in like manner vv. 30, 31). How this is to be historically understood, is explained in the *Alterth.*, pp. 328 sqq. That *the height* to which Jahvé in warlike train *ascended* is Sion (as similarly *e.g.*, xvii. 23) is understood of itself from the connexion. But if this was the issue of the great movement of that time, the general proposition finally is only thereby confirmed, that *also rebellious ones* nevertheless finally dwell *with God* in peace, must be reconciled to Him, and as it were dwell together with Him (lxxvi. 11) comp. § 237 c, 282 a, as the Kanaanites now peacefully dwelling as servants of the sanctuary at Sion testify.

4. That now in the beginning of the last strophe, vv. 20-24, the destruction and rebuilding of the Temple was to be announced in bald words, cannot be asserted: but the poet indicates all clearly enough when he says that God *forever* (not merely in the olden time) bears Israel (לְ עָמַס is bear *for* one, lighten his burden, the opposite of עַל '), ver. 20, as He even has ways of escape *from death*, gives Israel the means to flee from death, in which only the deliverance from exile can lie, ver. 21; and that He will finally fatally strike the still powerful tyrants, vv. 22-24. Instead of mourning over the troubled and intermediate time it is therefore rather befitting *to bless God* as that wondrously helping God; for הָאֵל is, ver. 20 and

ver. 21 to be taken according to *Lehrb.*, p. 680, *note.* The words, vv. 23, 24, are probably from an older song : should the mighty wicked ones conceal themselves in flight on all sides before the punishment,—and that as deeply as possible, in the East on the heights of Basan, in the West in the depths of the sea,—nevertheless Jahvé will bring them back to punishment, as in Am. ix. 2, 3; to bloody punishment, according to the experience of that time (as especially in later times when Israel had suffered such bloody retribution, the like is very sharply and pointedly taken, Isa. lxiii. 1-6). מָחַץ, ver. 24 is here *lighten, flash* (term from a violent shock, comp. *makhadd* and חָמֵץ, *red:* the tongue even of thy dogs (comp. 1 Kings xxi. 23 ; 2 Kings ix. 36) gleams *from the foes*, more definitely *from him*, his blood. That the last is somewhat awkward is easily to be felt; but the present text admits of nothing else. For תִּמְחַץ which is not found elsewhere in this sense, and which stands just before, ver. 22, in its ordinary significations, תִּרְחַץ might readily be conjectured from passages like lviii. 11, if the second member were not opposed to this, where however it is better to read בְּנִצְחוֹ : *the tongue of moist splendour*, Isa. lxiii. 3.

III. 1. The first strophé of the after-song, vv. 25-28, aptly throws a glance back upon the solemn march of the representatives of the four tribes: before these went the singers and musicians, and led by these they sounded the preceding hymn in full chorus (xxvi. 12). Thus בָּרְכוּ, *they blessed God*, those *from Israel's spring*, those of the stock of Israel who are then forthwith more definitely named, ver. 28. The figure of the *spring* as the remote last issue of the widely diffused descendants only further in Isa. xlviii. 1; li. 1. Benjamin, the smallest, goes here, as similarly in Deut. xxxiii. 12, merely for honour's sake in front, because Jerusalem lay in its district. But Juda remains the strong band, yielding the most and bravest men. On the Northern tribes, comp. the *Gesch. des V. Isr.*, Vols. iii. and iv. of the third edition.

2. How small indeed is the present beginning of the now

again dedicated Temple; this view leads to the wish, vv. 29-32: for the connexion of the whole requires all this to be taken as a wish to God, that He will show His glory also from this Temple, to glorify the new-made state (עִיר as active verb) that He will receive homage from the Gentiles, partly slowly, partly in haste arriving, that He will scatter the rude delighters in war. Hence we must read for אֱלֹהֶיךָ according to LXX, Syr., and several Codd., אֱלֹחִים, and ver. 29 צַוֵּה xliv. 5, ver. 31 בְּזֻר in the imperative. עַל, ver. 30, of the Temple which stands out above Jerusalem, as Syr. correctly. The wild reed-beast—(the lion or tiger, i.e., the great king) which with the drove of bulls (mighty ones, princes) and the calves i.e., weaker powers of the people is to hasten forward to offer his homage in silver bars, but because it is so slow in doing this must first be seriously censured and taught,—is certainly a circumlocution for the Persian kingdom at that time delighting in war, whose symbol is the Euphrates and the Tigris, rivers whose reedy banks lions love to haunt. So earlier the crocodile is a figure for Egypt and the Egyptian king, Ez. xxix. 3; Ps. lxxiv. 13, 14, and so now Assyria (Persia) might readily be termed a lion, with which then in descending relation, bulls (princes, magnates) and calves (peoples) are connected, and to all of which then according to old custom, ver. 32, Egypt and Kûsch are placed in opposition. Thus Syria and Egypt are mentioned together about the same time and in a like sense, B. Jes. xxvii. 1, figuratively, and ver. 13 literally. But for מִתְרַפֵּס necessarily הִתְרַפֵּס must be read, both because of the generation and of the summons. On רְצֵי כָסֶף as *silver bars*, comp. Dickinson in the *Numismatic Chronicle*, 1862, p. 130.

3. But still more purely, vv. 33-35, does the Messianic hope and exhortation to all kingdoms of the world without exception break through, as if the glance must finally without respect to the distress of the present embrace the whole future with full courage; ver. 35 from Deut. xxxiii. 28, 29. For *now*

—as finally in ver. 36 is added after the glance back at Israel, —the full theocracy is restored; and with this the end of the threefold song recurs to its first beginning. But Messianic hopes of the final punishment of all Gentiles lay already in vv. 23, 24.

More simply, independently and finally do the same contents lie in the short bounding song, Ps. xlvii. In rejoicing over the advance of Jahvé to the (new) Temple, and His rule from thence for the conversion of the heathen, it calls upon all the peoples to praise the God of Israel, vv. 2-5, who is now again universally honoured in Sion, vv. 6-9; and about whose sanctuary princes of the people assembled at its dedication, ver. 10. In other respects the song stands between Pss. xlvi. and xlviii., because these songs were again at that time studied for the sake of their similar contents.

1.

2   All ye peoples, clap the hand,
        exult to God in loud jubilation!
    Jahvé is truly a sublime Potentate,
        a great king over all the earth;
    subjects the peoples to us,
5   nations to our feet;
    chooses our heritage for us,
        Jacob's pride, beloved by Him.   *

2.

God went up in a noise of jubilation,
    Jahvé with sound of horns:
play to God, play,
    play to our king, play!
king of the whole earth is God:
    play a fine song!
Ruler was God over the Heathen,
    God now is throned upon His holy seat.

3.

Princes of the peoples have assembled   10
  before the God of Abraham;
God's truly are the shields of the earth:
  greatly is He exalted!

On such figures as יָדִּבְ, ver. 4, comp. § 343 b. Our *heritage, the pride of Jakob* is the holy land, as lxi. 6.—The *going up*, ver. 6, quite as in lxviii. 16.—Ver. 10. Comp. Isa. xiv. 1; certainly there might assemble in Jerusalem, particularly at the dedication of the Temple some princes, like Zerubabel, emissaries of the Persian empire; only we know the history of the time too little. Read עָם with LXX, Syr. For *away to the people* עָם cannot well signify, § 281 d; and elsewhere nothing more suitable is to be found. *Shields* = defenders, princes, Hos. iv. 18.

More like a mere echo of the high thoughts of that time sounds finally, Ps. lxvi. 1-12, a similar Temple-song, which calls upon all peoples to honour Jahvé, vv. 1-4, to consider His works and power, who in the Egyptian times wondrously delivered Israel, vv. 5-7, to praise Him who had just again taken Israel out of the sorest life-danger, vv. 8-12. Peculiarly is it clear from the last strophé that the exile was at that time not yet very remote.

1.

Shout to God, all the earth!   1
sing the honour of His name,
  do honour to His praise!
say to God: "how sublime Thy deeds!
  to Thee, Almighty, Thy foes offer adulation;
"all peoples do homage to Thee, play to Thee,
  play to Thy name!" *

2.

5 Come and see the works of God,
      His doing is fearful to the sons of men!
   the sea has He changed into dry land,
      through the flood they went on foot:
   there we rejoiced in Him!
   He rules by His own power for ever;
      upon the peoples His eyes look
   the rebellious—shall not pride themselves! *

3.

   Bless, peoples, our God,
      cause loud praise to sound to Him!
   to Him who set our soul in life
      let not our foot stagger!
10 For Thou, God, hast proved us,
      like silver hast sharply purified us;
   hast led us into captivity,
      laid a heavy burden on our hips;
   didst cause men to go over our head,
      into the fire, the water we came:
   and yet didst lead us forth to freedom!

Ver. 3 a from Ps. xviii. 45. On ver. 6 c comp. cxxxii. 6. Ver. 7 c sounds strongly like the conclusion of lxviii. 7 and 19. —Ver. 9 b comp. cxxi. 3. Ver. 10 after B. Jes. xlviii. 10, ver. 12 a after B. Jes. li. 23 b, after B. Jes. xliii. 2; in c רִוָיָה is to be read. On vv. 13-20, see above Vol. I., pp. 195 sq.

2. Enduring Sentiments.

But if the question is further (and this ever remains the main matter) what influence every unexpected revolution and every high joy of that time exercised upon the permanent sentiments of men, in this new period, we come upon

116-117. PSALMS XCI., CXXXIX.

two extremely noteworthy songs, which plainly show the abiding effect of that great time upon the inward life, on the state of mind. Ps. xci., whose penetrating, lofty style and mood likewise leads to this time, is simply a very serene inspired utterance of confidence in Jahvé; without special external occasion and impulse it is the free outburst of a lofty mood (somewhat as Ps. ci.). The whole heart of the poet is so deeply suffused with the consciousness that nothing in the world can harm him beneath Jahvé's care, and that he remaining true to Him ever finds in Him the loving Protector, that his own spirit becomes to Him the surest and most eloquent oracle of these truths. He may well have earlier heard similar words of Jahvé, uplifting and comforting from prophets. But the personal feeling and thought then only becomes full truth, if it sounds back as from without with proper force, and has been formed in the thinker who starts from his own personality, into Divine words and commands to Him; in short if his own spirit becomes his genuine and clear oracle. On this restful and blessed height we behold the poet; the Divine consciousness, ripened by inner and outer experiences, bursts forth in the moment of consecration in a firm form; and one of the finest songs arises from this human feeling and thought entirely glorified into the Divine. Having scarcely begun to speak out of his own experience, vv. 1, 2, the higher certainty and the oracular tone forthwith overpowers him, vv. 3-8; and while, collecting himself during a short pause, he has scarcely returned to the beginning and his own style (ver. 9 in the middle) immediately the same oracular tone breaks in again, giving utterance most decisively towards the end. Further there is no division in the song except in ver. 9, where the same thought, after a short time, rises anew in other figures; the whole song expresses only *one* experience, without stronger forward movement in strophés. But all is rounded off in the highest repose to two strophés, each with eight verses and seventeen members, all with the exception of ver. 7a of common length.

The historical situation cannot be more exactly inferred from the song,—so general is the tenor of the thought, because the song plainly proceeds from restful contemplation after a great deliverance, while the poet glances over the eternal foundation of the Divine grace,—past and future alike. From ver. 1 it only follows that the poet thus sang at the Temple; perhaps we have here again the poet of Pss. cxvi., cxxxviii.

1.

1   He who sits in the protection of the Highest,
         sojourns in the shadow of the Mightiest:
     I name Jahvé my refuge, firm fortress,
         my God whom I trust.
     " For He will deliver thee from hunters' nets,
         from the plague of affliction;
     will with his pinions lend thee protection,
         beneath his wings wilt Thou flee:
     shield and harness His faithfulness is,
     Wilt not tremble before the horror of night,
         before the arrow which flies by day,
     from the plague which glides in darkness,
         from the blow which rages at noon;
     though a thousand fall at thy side and ten thousand at
                                          Thy right hand:
     to thee it will not reach;
     only with Thine eyes Thou wilt behold it,
     and see the recompense of the wicked!

2.

     For *Thou* art, O Jahvé, my refuge:
         " hast chosen the Highest for Thy protection;
10   evil will not befall thee,
         misfortune will not approach Thy tent;

but His angels He will appoint thee,
   to protect thee on every way,
on their hands they will bear thee,
   that thy foot stumble not at the stone;
wilt tread on lion and adder,
   tread down young lion and dragon.
For on me he hangs; therefore I deliver him,
   protect him because He knows my name;
If he calls me, I hear him, 15
   with him am I in distress
will set him free and honour him,
refresh him with long life,
   and cause him to behold my salvation."

The person at first described more remotely as a ward of Jahvé, dwelling at the sanctuary in Sion happily and safely, is, as ver. 2 immediately explains, the poet himself; and thus in the relative clause the third person may stand by the first (or second) as Job xii. 4. It might indeed be supposed that for אֹמֵר it is better to read אָמַר so that the words run, "He who sits, *says* to Jahvé," etc. But from this song presents itself as by no means a word designed from the first for every one. It is too plainly an outburst of the most personal experience of a man high placed in the world, such as we may suppose Zerubabel to have been. Elsewhere there is present to the poet's mind in vv. 1, 3, 4, plainly lvii. 2, in ver. 9 perhaps xc. 1.—Ver. 3. The hunter's nets (properly bird-catcher's) is plainly a figure for death, according to xviii. 6; but the *arrow* and the *blow*, vv. 5, 6, designate in this connexion certainly dark modes of death, invisibly hastening on, by contagion, or lightning or the simoon, xi. 6. At no time and from no deadliest danger shall thou be bound to tremble.—Ver. 8: only see with eyes; not with pain oneself experience; and indeed see the punishment of the wicked.—Ver. 11. Comp. Gen. xxiv. 7.—Ver. 16 shows by the conclusion that the poet lived in a time when the ancient salvation, as David more nearly saw it, was entirely lost, and a new and great one must be hoped for, namely the Messianic, as according to all traces the noblest men of the time longed for it.

Ps. cxxxix. in like manner carries us into a movement when a poet feels himself entirely in God and God in him. But in quite another way. For while he has turned his attention to one of the greatest and most infinite but most mysterious of wonders,—that of the inner spiritual connexion of man with God, and his mind has become open and free for this side; he is struck to the depths of his soul by the truth that the human spirit (in all its remaining dignity and greatness) still as derived, proceeding from God, is ever held and upborne in the Divine, that God can never escape nor in any way withdraw from it, but God everywhere, in knowledge, in space, in time anticipates and accompanies him. With the clearness of this thought there opens an infinite self-contemplation in God, a serious trial and justification of the mind and the whole life. It is, *e.g.*, actually *thus*—that man cannot escape God and His probation; and how should he who has learned this, actually dare to desire to escape Him, and not rather entirely suffuse himself and his spirit in Him, so holding himself ready every moment for the strictest kind of examination?—As now the poet has thus found himself consciously in God, indulges in such thoughts about Him with endless refreshment and content (vv. 17, 18), and the further he reflects on the wonder, the greater and more divine he finds it: he here pours forth in the song the deepest contemplations and most noble inward experiences, as well as the purest love to the God he knows, revelling in soft tender description of the inexhaustible contents, only becoming at the end somewhat more excited and stormy. For as restful contemplation must predominate in him who in himself has found the infinite treasure, there comes out in the main portion of the song, vv. 1-18, only the inner side of the thought,—how the poet feels himself entirely seized and held by God inwardly and outwardly, vv. 1-6, because he even if he desired, cannot escape Him, vv. 7-12, because indeed God from the first anticipates man, vv. 13-18: three uniform strophés according to the three movements of the thought here possible from the *personal* deepest experience far away in the first instance, into the whole sphere of *space*, then into the *temporal* infinitude of the world. Only at the end, vv. 19-24, a further more brief glance outward, where the poet so greatly misses such height and purity of sentiment that he, carried away by the force of momentary noble agitation, desires the overthrow of all the wicked, but not otherwise than by God himself; he himself will at least keep his mind free from their vanity and wickedness, even purifying himself and longing for Divine probation, with which words, vv. 23, 24 the thought again returns in restful composure to its beginning. So deeply feels the poet the infinite nobleness of the sentiment to which he has risen, and which he will not have torn from him at any cost, that his heart, overflowing with this and revelling in it, can in such a moment turn to the resistance from without with nothing but horror; and he does not at once,—as many others in the Old Testament sing and moan,—advancing further, take up the thought more with a view to influence didactically the wicked and thus conquer the external foes.

Precisely the deepest intensity of the mightiest feeling of the immediate—the new thought seizing upon the heart with such power that occupied with it, it can scarcely look beyond, and the entirely free and unforced, sincere, penetrating, genuinely creative description along with novelty of thought, of this ebullient blessed inward state : constitutes the peculiarity and the beauty of this song,—unique in its kind. From this poet,—judging also by the style of the language,— we probably possess nothing further in the Psalter; according to time it appears less recent than the preceding.

Each of the four strophes is rounded off in six verses, with members of the ordinary character, but here and there surging up to a greater height and rising to a threefold sound. Nothing is more gentle than ver. 1.

1.

1   Jahvé, Thou hast searched and known me!
      Yea *Thou* knowest my sitting and rising,
        notest my thought already afar,
      hast already viewed my going and lying down,
        art entrusted with all my ways.
      Yea, the word is not upon my tongue—
        lo, Jahvé, already Thou knowest it altogether,
5   before and behind hast Thou beset me
        and on me laid Thine hand.
      All too wonderful is the knowledge for me,
        too exalted, am no match for it!

2.

      Whither shall I go from Thy spirit:
        whither flee from Thy glance?
      If I go up to heaven—there art Thou,
        if I should take hell for my bed—there art Thou!
      Were I to raise wings of the dawn,
        settle at the sea's end :
10   there also would Thy hand lead me,
        and Thy right hand hold me!
      Were I to think : " but darkness will cover me,
        night be the light round about me ; "
      darkness even would be to Thee not too dark,
        night like day would shine,
        dark, bright, would be alike!

3.

      For *Thou* hast made my veins,
        didst weave me in my mother's body :

praise to Thee that amazingly wonderful I became;
    wonderful are Thy works,
—my soul knows it well!
My bones were not concealed from Thee,   15
    as I was wrought in secret,
    in the earth's depths was embroidered:
my mass Thine eyes saw,
    and in *Thy* book they were all written
—already formed those days when there was none
                                among them.—
But how heavy lie on me Thy thoughts, God;
    how numberless their multitude!
If I counted them—they would be more than sand,
    I awake—and am still with Thee!—

4.

Would'st Thou but slay the wicked, O God!
    and ye bloody men—depart from me!
who speak of Thee only for shame,   20
    sinfully repeat Thy testimonies!
Should I not hate Thy haters, Jahvé,
    and loathe Thy adversaries?
—With fullest hate I hate them,
    have become my enemies!—
God! search me, and know my heart,
    prove me and know my dreams!
and see whether there be a vain way in me,
    and lead me in the eternal way!

1. The words, vv. 2-5, give the proof of what is said in ver. 1, even more closely, but with an advance in the proof. Not only all conceivable deeds, vv. 2-3,—the very words of men are known to God beforehand, ver. 4. In this ver. 4 the last member is very shortly added, as generally in this song the most figurative and lightest language predominates: but the sense is plainly *the word is not upon my tongue*, it is, although

in the thought, not yet upon my tongue, *Thou already knowest it altogether;* hence the "*lo !*" pointing to a state, and the *perf.* For he who feels God near on all sides, behind and before, as above and below, and by Him in every moment held andb eset, as was described in ver. 5,—he must also know that he can think and do nothing without God. The K'tib פִּלְאִיָה, ver. 6, is explanatory and correct.

2. The figure, ver. 9, is apt when we reflect that the light of the dawn from the east in a moment hastens to the extremest sea = the west. In ver. 8 all conceivable space being comprised in its four possibilities,—the last named west and the hell touched upon ver. 8, lead finally to the last thought, ver. 11, the possibility which appears easier than the former, *but at least* (אַךְ) shut oneself into outermost darkness, so that eternal night surrounds man instead of light; to which figure, however, יְשׁוּפֵנִי (LXX, καταπατήσει, Vulg. *conculcabit* after the Aramaic שׁוּף) so little suits that the correct reading rather appears to be יְשׂוּפֵּנִי from סָךְ = שָׂךְ, *cover*, as יָשׂוּר, for יָשֹׁר, xci. 6.

3. The wondrous formation of man before birth is, vv. 13-15, described somewhat as in Job x. 9-11. But the poet must here from the first in conformity with the connexion of the thoughts bring out the thought that God has also made his reins or feelings, so that He can never be strange to them; and then that he was formed in the most secret concealed corner in such a way, so concealed as in the depths of the earth (as generally the earth's and the mother's womb bear much resemblance, Job i. 21, comp. Sur. xl. 69, and the *djanyan* 'Amr's Moall. v. 14. 20), but yet clear and plain before God. And since the foresight of God does not begin with His defined boundary, but ever embraces all things, in ver. 16 finally appears the last that the human spirit can here in poetic boldness grandly conceive, from the standpoint of the personal consciousness,—that before birth all days were written in the divine book (lvi. 9, lxix. 29) as if they were already there and ready when as yet none of them existed. The וְלֹא (K'tib) introduces a proposi-

tion of state, § 341 a: *the days which were* creatively predetermined, while not yet *one among them existed*. The language is here strained quite unusually by the thought of that which is most wonderful; and the unusual brevity of the expression is connected with this. That the article before הַיּוֹם and the relative word before יֻצָּרוּ may be wanting is self-intelligible; on the אֶשֶׁר, *how*, comp. § 333 a. The conclusion, vv. 17, 18, almost like that in the Gospel of John. With such endless flow do these divine thoughts come in upon the poet, as in strongest currents, that he must now hasten to break them off in the song, as he would never get out of them, and their number is so infinite that he would seek in vain to count them, and sum them up as it were in firm masses. The יָקַר must be taken in its first signification as *be heavy*: so overpowering is to the godly man the stream of these divine thoughts that they present themselves to him as to our poet, ver. 18 b and ver. 23 b, as sweet dreams, similarly as in the 4 B. Ezra every longer interview with God and Uriel becomes a dream. But even if he would as now get free from such infinite sweet dreams, and actually *feels* as if *awoke* from them, as even now, he feels himself ever still *with Him*, a last and highest wonder! The words as the thought itself resemble that in Ps. lxxiii. 24 b, despite all difference in the first beginning of the contemplation. Further, comp. the *Jahrbb. des Bibl. W.*, v., p. 177. But the first strophé, ver. 6, the poet had also closed in a similar way, only that he speaks here more strongly because more creatively. Of the four members of these two verses, 2 and 3 correspond to one another, 1 and 4; but it is not necessary to assume after the fourth member where the awakening is spoken of, that this must be an early morning song.

4. by עָרֶיךָ as "Thy cities," the oath by holy cities must be thought of; but we know only Sion, and such an oath is too unworthy to suit here, where Ex. xx. 7, is alluded to. It might then stand for צָרֶיךָ, "Thy foes" (for precisely in this song ע is preferred instead of צ, vv. 2, 17, in רֵעַ, comp. רָצָה,

ver. 3 in רבע), so that the reference might be completed from the foregoing verse; falsely express (Thee) as "Thy foes;" if with many copies עֲדֶיךָ (or עֵדֹתֶיךָ, as in many later songs?) were not easiest to read, comp. B. (Roman 50) 16. But plainly hypocrites and seeming holy ones form the opposition in the poet's heart, accordingly עֲבֵי, ver. 24, as = עָמָל, אָיֶן is to be understood, as also here the opposition of the *eternal* = divine way teaches.

3. New Dangers and Complaints.—New Light.

If the Psalter closed here, we might readily suppose that that fair elevation of the first times after the deliverance had been of long untroubled duration; the close of the Psalter, one of the most instructive books for history of the Old Testament, would in that case appear entirely satisfying, and we should hardly expect anything higher.—In fact, the enduring effect of that elevation for the community is unmistakable; it looks more freely and widely upon the kingdoms of the world, and connects itself closely and inseparably with the ancient religion. The new settlement in Jerusalem becomes gradually firmer, more developed, the popular element again becomes collected and strengthened; even the language becomes again predominantly purer and more antique than it had been in many of the preceding songs. But in this repose there germinate unobserved new dangerous doubts, which supply proof that the ancient community had not yet learnt all its concealed errors and dangers, and therefore could not endure on this position. That very idea on which now, in the new foundation of the people all turns,—that of the community,—of Israel, has still much that is obscure, for few as yet comprehend what the poet of Ps. lxxiii. 1 had already said. Shall the old Israel again arise with all its promises, with Palestine as axis? Partly in victory, partly in the pressure of the time it seems so; becomes even in part necessary, because the old nationality is on the one side again too keenly disputed, on the other has not yet found its full goal. For the Messianic expectations were still unfulfilled, the ancient law had not yet been again fully restored, the old literature not collected. The national element then is for a time again fixed in the new community, so far as possible; the old promises remain and increase. But while Israel was to wait for this happiness, there come, in spite of its fidelity to the old religion, the times, ever becoming more oppressive, of the satrap-rule. The heathen, the wicked rule and destroy, Israel sees for herself no happiness, no hope! Here a new and hard enigma was presented; for in earlier times the unhappiness of the people never co-existed with such strict adherence to the ancient religion. But as the songs

118-125 PSALMS XLIV., LXXIV., LXXIX., LXXX.; CXXXII., LXXXIX.; LX., LXXXV.,

show, the greater dangers and more serious trials which were called forth by the development of the new state, did not long endure. Precisely when the new state was restored by the zeal of Zerubabel and of the High-priest Josúa, and in a manner established, when its citizens had attached themselves with one mind and with strictness to the ancient religion as it was understood at that time; in brief, when the time had finally come when the true Israel dwelling in Sion seemed bound to expect all Divine blessings: the new community seems to experience the most visible signs of the Divine displeasure. All Gentiles rise against her for a war of destruction, conquer Jerusalem and the Temple, treat the people and the religion with equal severity and baseness. Had indeed the higher spiritual idea of Israel which germinates in Ps. lxxiii. sqq., already penetrated more deeply and universally, such external misfortune would not have been received with such despair. But the conception of a spiritual Israel passes away again under the tendency of these times more and more, while the national, the tenacious adherence to the old and the more external faith is maintained; and as the people in this point of view is conscious of no guilt against Jahvé its God, the unexpected trouble is so severe, the humiliation and sorrow so deep. The elevation and inspiration from the first times after the exile,—yea, almost the recollection threatens to pass away (although according to Ps. lxxxv. men still thought of it) : and pre-eminently the recollections introduced with glowing features into the sacred books of the old lofty times under Moses and David still warm and strengthen the people. But the present state corresponds so little to these; hence the almost boundless dejection of the spirit, the oppressed prayer and lament, the great difficulty—never before so universally felt by the whole people—of finding solace and rest. In short, we see here on a small scale the same conflict of opposing thoughts and endeavours, from which the second Jerusalem—precisely as its development became more fixed—can never be free, and which carried to their height in the times lying beyond the Old Testament, bring about its overthrow.

Meanwhile it is more difficult to state the precise time in which these songs fall. For on the one hand the historical information concerning the new Jerusalem, especially from this to the previous period, flows in a very scant and troubled stream. And again, in all these songs the foes are notably not named exactly, and in particular, perhaps because they, unlike the later Ps. lxxxiii., were not written under merely threatened, but actual subjugation, when it was neither advisable nor necessary to give the names. If we ask, following all possible traces and evidence, *when* the Temple in Jerusalem was thus treated by heathen? it is certain on the one side that we may not think of an earlier conquest, of the Chaldean therefore, because at that time the community was not so united and incorruptibly true to the ancient religion as it here throughout appears. Comp. only the Lamentations above, pp. 99 sq., and the books of Jeremja, from which further, these songs borrow. That here already Jeremja's writings, the series of songs named, pp. 44 and 124, and similar such late writings are made use of, is a further reason against the origin of these songs in the time of the first Temple. But on the other side there as little lies a tenable reason for going down to the Makkabean times,—times which nowhere here clearly and certainly appear, which on the contrary are depicted in the B. of Daniel as times of internal religious division and strong defection, while these songs throughout presuppose the most unanimous, flourishing condition of religion in Jerusalem; not to speak of the insurmountable difficulties which in that case the whole history of the literature and the Canon would present, and which this is not the place further to set forth, comp. *e.g.*, Vol. I., pp. 4 sqq. Hence I was of opinion thirty years ago that the songs belonged to the times of the later Persian dominion, of which and its public discords because of the Temple we know something, comp. the *Gesch. des V. Isr.*, iv., pp. 263 sqq. of the third edition. But in 1851 I showed that we come here rather to the times towards the end of the sixth and the beginning of the fifth century, and this is anew elucidated in the last edition of that vol. of the *History*, pp. 155 sqq. Only thus do these songs fit into the series of all the preceding and following.

Further. Strictly considered, only the seven songs besides Ps. cxxxii., belong entirely to the above-described state of things in Jerusalem. But these seven songs show so complete a likeness in the language and colour of the style, that one might feel tempted to derive them from the same poet, were not the conclusion to be drawn from particular traces that at least Ps. lxxxix. must be from another poet than the others.

The four first songs are according to all tokens designed for congregational songs, but along with all likeness of their object are very different in art and tenor. Ps. xli. is the clearest and completest song of these. As those sufferings were inexplicable to the people according to the old faith, at first the vivid recollection of the eternal relation between God

15 *

and Israel appears, according to which Israel praises Him as the ancient and eternal giver of victory to the people, who can only be strong and mighty through Him, vv. 2-9; then the present weakness and degradation of the people—incomprehensible after such antecedents—is depicted with deep lamentation, vv. 10-17; and finally with the sincerest assurance and, as it were, conjuration that the community feels itself guiltless and faithful only to the true God, prayer for final pity, vv. 18-27. Scarcely in the first part, ver. 5, does prayer once break through.

Of the three strophés each is arranged with eight verses, but the last is extended by two more.

1.

2   O God! with our ears have we heard,
        our fathers have told us
        the work wrought by thee in their days
        days of the olden time:
    Thou, thine own hand, didst drive peoples out and didst
                              plant *them*,
        didst injure tribes and spreadest *them* out;
    for not through *their* sword did they inherit the land,
        and not *their* arm helped them,
    no, Thy right hand, Thy arm and the light of Thy
                                glance,
        because thou lovedst them.

5   *Thou* art my king, God?
        appoint all deliverance of Jakob!
    through Thee we thrust down our oppressors,
        through Thy name we tread on adversaries;
    for not in my bow do I trust,
        my sword never helps me,
    no, Thou didst help us before our oppressors
        and our haters Thou didst put to shame,
    of God we sang praise every day,
        and glorify Thy name for ever!

2.

And yet Thou hast rejected and put us to shame,   10
   and goest not forth in our armies,
makest us to yield before oppressors,
   and our haters drove their spoil,
givest us up like the flock to destruction,
   and hast scattered us among peoples,
sellest Thy people for a mock-price,
   and went not high with their prices;
makest us the scorn of our neighbours,
   a scoff and disgrace to those round about us,
makest us a bye-word among peoples   15
   and a shaking of the head among nations;
daily my shame is before me,
   disgrace has covered my face
before the loud scorner and slanderer,
before foe and thirster for revenge!

3.

All this fell upon us though we forget not Thee
   and have not denied Thy covenant,
for our heart is not turned back
   nor did our step decline from Thy path,
that Thou didst crush us in the desert,   20
   and didst cover us with death's night!
Never, never did we forget the name of our God,
   spread out our hands to a strange God
(would not God search this out,
   for He knows the heart's secresies?):
but for Thee we are continually put to death,
   esteemed as a flock for slaughter!
Awake! why sleepest Thou, Lord,
   wake up, reject not for ever!

> Why hidest Thou Thy countenance,
>   forgettest our sufferings, our oppression?
> for into the dust sinks our soul,
>   to earth our body cleaves:
> rise to help us,
>   redeem us for the sake of Thy grace.

On שְׁלֹה, ver. 3, comp. lxxx. 12. Ver. 13 properly: *for a trifling price* (*unpreis*) so low and contemptible, not sparing blood as dear, lxxii. 14, but giving it up very cheaply, yea for nothing; because no use and gain at all is seen from the many sacrifices which the enemy so readily overpowers. The figure from Jer. xv. 13: but an ancient poet would not have carried out this figure so far. Ver. 20. בִּמְקוֹם *instead* (Hos. ii. 1) might signify: thou didst strike us *instead* of wild beasts, as if we deserved as beasts of prey the highest punishment; or *Thou—as* beasts of prey, fearfully as beasts of prey crush. Both,—especially the last—are harsh; rather does the poet take the *place of wild beasts* for = desert, desolation, so that the following member may speak of darkness; for manifestly the figure is borrowed from Jer. ix. 10, x. 22, as ver. 15 from Jer. xviii. 16, and much else of the kind in these four songs. Ver. 21 must contain an oath; because ver. 22 most solemnly appeals to the Divine knowledge. *For Thee*, i.e., for Thy sake, ver. 23, quite as lxix. 8; but in other respects ver. 16 is from lxix. 8, li. 5, xxxviii. 18, but somewhat otherwise applied.

Ps. lxxiv. most deeply and unhappily laments, because the unhappiness has reached its furthest point. From the very first there gushes forth most mournfully the prayer for remembrance of the community now in the innermost sanctuary destroyed, vv. 1-9, and after that, upon new complaint, the whole greatness of God has been sung with praise and invocation, vv. 10-17, most urgently does the prayer as it were calling forth the feeling of God's honour, for the aversion of scorn and misery, recur, vv. 18-23. The language too is bent and with difficulty collects itself, like the whole state of that time. But the build of the three strophés still contains something of the old manner of a song of lament; they become always shorter, from 20 to 16 and further to 12 members.

1.

Why, O God, hast Thou cast off for ever, 1
   and smokes Thy anger against Thy pasture-flock?
think of the community which Thou hast long obtained,
   hast redeemed for the stock of Thy heritage,
     the mount Sion on which Thou didst take Thy
                                  dwelling!
lift Thy steps against eternal evil-doers:
   all in the Temple the enemy injured!
Thy oppressors roared in the midst of the festive house,
   set for signs their ensigns;
It seems as if men raised 5
   in the forest's thicket axes,
and now with hatchet and hammers
   broke down together its carved work;
into fire cast they Thy sanctuary,
   desecrated to the earth Thy name's seat,
thought in themselves: "dislodge we them together!"
   burned all the houses of God in the land;
we see no longer our signs,
   prophets are no more,
   and have none who knew "how long?"

2.

How long, God, shall the oppressor scoff, 10
   the enemy for ever proscribe Thy name?
why then withdrawest Thou Thy hand and right hand?
   out from Thy bosom, destroy!

for God is nevertheless my King from olden times,
 who gives help in the midst of the land.
Thou hast by Thy might divided the sea,
 broken dragons' heads upon the waters,
Thou has dashed in pieces the heads of the monster,
 didst give it for food to a people of savages,
15 Thou hast divided spring and brook,
 Thou hast dried streams of eternal flood;
Thine is the day—and Thine the night,
 Thou hast appointed light and sun,
Thou didst place firmly all earth's bounds,
 summer and winter—Thou hast formed them!

3.

Remember this: the enemy scorns Jahvé,
 and foolish people despise Thy name;
give not to the wild life the soul of Thy turtle-dove,
 the life of Thy poor forget not for ever!
20 O look upon the Covenant:
 how full the earth's asylums are—of dwellings of cruelty!
let not the bowed-down return ashamed,
 let the poor and helpless praise Thy name!
Up, God, O conduct Thy cause,
 think of Thy scorn by fools continually!
forget not the voice of Thy oppressors,
 the adversaries' noise ever arising!

Pasture-flock plainly here and lxxix. 13, after xcv. 6, 7, c. 3. On ver. 3 comp. lxxiii. 18. Ver. 4, comp. ver. 9, shews that the enemy, after seizing the Temple, set up instead of the genuine Israelitish signs, *c.g.*, Cherubim, their heathen ones; the former they struck down and burnt; but further, despite all the bitter complaints of these songs, their rage did not go. The *suff. fem.* in מֹעֲדֵי, ver. 6, must refer to the readily recognizable "Sion." The words, vv. 13, 14, yield instead in, the first place only a decorated form of Ex. xiv. sqq., and B. Jes. li. 9, 10, for Egypt or Pharao and his princes in this time are readily compared with crocodiles (see above on lxviii. 31): but (1) allusion is made to the old legends of these monsters of the early world which appeared to have returned in Pharao (comp. on Job, p. 62); and (2) by the side of the legend of the mere sea-monster, ver. 13, is further added, ver. 14, with distinct purpose, the quite other legend of the half sea, half land monster, which once in the fore-time subdued by God, still always serves as food in its monstrous remains *to a people of savages* (that is לְעָם לְצִיִּים, § 292 a, and Ps. lxxii. 9) *i.e.*, of half-men, who dwell at the earth's ends. Such legends, the reflection of which appears in the translation of the LXX, in *the peoples of Æthiopia*, as well as in B. Henókh, lx. 24, 4 Ezr. vi. 51, and elsewhere, must at that time have been widely diffused. But then this other monster along with Egypt of itself here as elsewhere points to Assyria, *i.e.*, Persia, as is meant more exactly here; and ver. 15 is now no mere repetition of ver. 13 *a*, but points to the deliverance from exile, and is borrowed from passages like B. Jes. xlii. 15, xliv. 27.—Ver. 16*b* from Gen. i. 16; ver. 17*a* from Job, xxxviii. 8. *Turtle* ver. 19, the innocent community, ver. 2; but manifestly from the *HL*; the first הָעֵת merely for the sake of the word-play with the second for חַיָּה (§ 173 *d*). *Covenant* ver. 20, and therefore also the people of the covenant, comp. xliv. 18, Mal. iii. 1; but for מַחֲשַׁבֵּי, which as *dark corner* gives no sense, מַחְשַׁבֵּי is to be expressed in the sense of ver. 8*b*.

Much more collected and composed in the midst of misery are the two following songs, Pss. lxxix., lxxx.; although Ps. lxxx. far excels Ps. lxxix. in tenderness, mildness, and repose as well as in art. For Ps. lxxix. mingles with the mournful description of the sufferings, and with the prayer that instead of permitting the community to be destroyed by cruelty, the foes who scoff at all true religion and Jahvé may be punished,—the recollection of the guilt of Israel, vv. 8, 9; and the wish to see Israel only for the sake of religion (the name of Jahvé) preserved. For this purpose all is more briefly composed, so that the strophé is extended only to five verses, the third and last becomes still shorter. The second turns from the first very strongly against the heathen; and this in particular is the new feature in the song.

1.

1 God! heathen have come into Thy heritage,
 have stained Thy holy Temple,
  turned Jerusalem into ruins;
given Thy servants' corpses
 as food to the birds of heaven,
  to the wild beasts of the earth Thy saints' bodies;
their blood forgotten like water
 round about Jerusalem, without buriers;
we have become a scoff to our neighbours,
 a scorn and disgrace for all round about us.—
5 How long, Jahvé, wilt Thou ever be wrath,
 will Thy jealousy burn like fire?

2.

Pour out Thy wrath on peoples which know Thee not,
 on kingdoms which call not on Thy name,
because they destroyed Jakob,
 and made His pastures desolate!—
Remember not against us the sins of former ones!
 in haste let Thy compassion anticipate us,
because we are very miserable;
help us, Thou God of our salvation,
 for Thy sublime name's sake,
and save us and atone our sins
 for Thy name's sake!

why should heathen say: "where is their God?" 10
let there be known to the heathen clearly before us
the vengeance of the forgotten blood of Thy
servants!

3.

Let the sighs of the fettered come before Thee,
according to the greatness of Thy arm—let children
of death remain,
and sevenfold requite our neighbours into their bosom,
the scorn wherewith they scorn Thee, O Lord!
and we Thy people and Thy pasture-flock,
we will sing praises to Thee ever,
to all ages ever tell Thy praise!

Ver. 6, 7 almost verbally from Jer. x. 25; one does not clearly see why the *plur.* אֱלֹהֵי is here changed into the *sing.*, and the *sing.* seems to be a mere oversight. Ver. 10 a as so much in these songs from Joel ii. 17. *Fettered*, ver. 11, Israel might generally in those circumstances of complete subjection appear; but before the poet's mind there passed, in both members so plainly, the verse cii. 21, that the colour of the language is thence explained.

Ps. lxxx. A modest, tender prayer for the restoration of the utterly ruined state, but so arranged as to be sung in the assembled congregation with alternate voices. While thus the main prayer to be sung by the whole community recurs at the end of the three strophés, the first in general appeals to the Divine help; the second recalls the long duration and severity of the sufferings; and the third and fourth point to the ancient history according to which the community was once so carefully led out of Egypt by Jahvé, and firmly planted in Palestine (verdant like a fruitful vine), and brought to maturity. Shall this pleasant plant of Jahvé pass away through rude hands? Hence the figure admits of the longest and most touching elaboration; comp. earlier Isa. v., Ezek. xv. and xvii.; and hence the language is here doubled, nay quadrupled, for the prayer cannot be urgent enough, as if in the midst of the last despondency. Apart from the two-membered return-verse, the six members of each of the two first strophés are enlarged in the third to twelve: but the recurrent verse is extended, according to its pure sense, now likewise to twelve members. Comp. above the structure of Pss. xcix. sq.

1.

2   Thou Shepherd of Israel O hearken!
    Thou who didst lead Josef like sheep,
inhabitest the Cherub's, O shine forth!
before Efráim and Benjamin, Manasse,
    arouse Thy heroic strength
and come to our deliverance!
O God, restore us again,
    cause Thy glance to shine, that we may be saved!

2.

5   O Jahvé, God of Hosts,
    how long dost Thou still fume at Thy people's prayers?
hast caused them to eat bread of tears,
    made them drink tears to the full measure;
makest us the object of strife to our neighbours,
    and our foes scoff at us:
O God of Hosts, restore us again,
    cause Thy glance to shine, that we may be saved!

3.

A vine Thou didst take from Egypt's earth,
    didst drive away peoples, didst plant it;

Thou madest space before it, 10
    it struck its roots and filled the earth,
mountains were covered with its shadow,
    with its branches cedars of God;
it stretched its tendrils to the sea,
    unto the Flood its sprouts.
Why hast Thou broken through its hedges,
    that all wayfarers pluck it,
the boar out of the forest rends it,
    the brood of the field browses on it?

O God of Hosts, return, we pray, 15
    looking from heaven behold,
    and visit this vine!
For the plant which Thy right hand planted,
    [the son whom Thou didst bring up for Thyself],
scorched in fire is cut down,
    (before Thy glance's menace they perish!)
—so be over the man of Thy right hand Thy hand,
    the son of man whom Thou didst bring up for Thyself!
—We too will not depart from Thee,
    let us live, we will call on Thy name!
O Jahvé, God of Hosts, restore us again, 20
    cause Thy glance to shine, that we may be saved!

Somewhat striking is the statement of the particular tribes, vv. 2, 3. That the poet was a Samaritan (Efráimite) must not be assumed; and just as little, that Samaria was at that time allied with Jerusalem. But Josef and Benjamin appear to stand merely in a general way instead of some old renowned names, because the actual tribe-division has already ceased in these times, but Sion boasts of continuing all Israel, comp. lxxvii. 16, lxxxi. 5, 6, and on Rev. vii. 4-8. שליש, ver. 6, properly a defined measure, the third part of a very great whole, is here more freely translated. Ver. 12: to the Mediterranean Sea and the Euphrates, here and lxxxix. 26, from Ps. lxxii. 8, as ver. 14 is framed from l. 11. But the relation of the individual clauses and members of vv. 15-20 is peculiarly difficult. Were the readings here correct, it must be assumed that the figure of the vine is gradually dropped from ver. 15; with ver. 15 the language bends towards the conclusion, but it is still further spun out in the following words, and the figure first fully explained; *son* ver. 16, would be still in the sense of the figure a young tree, shoot (*pl.* בנות, Gen. xlix. 22), but ver. 18 *b* explains by son of man; as also כַּנָּה is explained by ver. 18 *a*; in ver. 16 the connexion of the פָּקַד with the accus. or with עַל being interchangeable. But in fact much that is improbable lies here; if ver. 16 *b* is struck out as inserted here from ver. 18 *b*, the connexion of all the words becomes much easier, and above all in this way the even structure of the whole song, according to its plainly great uniformity of strophés, is restored. Then the *vine*, described vv. 9-14 (which is given here merely because of the *fem.* gender for the vine-stock) is in ver. 16 also more generally named a *plant* which God's hand had set and planted, but merely in order to describe the devastators of this vine, *i.e.,* of this sappy blooming community, ver. 17 *a*,—after the figures Ps. lxxiv. 3-7,—from another side than was done in vv. 13, 14. And the present condition of this community, vv. 16 *a*, 17 *a*, being once more adduced with the most striking figure, so that here as in a sudden parenthesis ver. 17 *b* the figure is rent through by the expression of the coarsest reality: the prayer is renewed, ver. 18, for the protection of the husbandman, so that about Israel itself this full compassion-deserving man appears as the object of this prayer without further disguise; and the voice of this man finally falls back into the *we*, ver. 19, but the key-note of the prayer may recur for the third time on the whole, and also for the third time in this strophé,— and that with the greater power. The spinning-out of the earlier strophé in the following one we saw already in Ps. xcix.

Ps. cxxxii. and Ps. lxxxix. are so similar in style and contents, that the same composer might be conjectured, who must then be different from the author of the four preceding songs. From cxxxii. 10, and lxxxix. 52 comp. lxxxiv. 10, it is however clear enough who the composer was; for if the two passages be closely considered, we find that the poet himself must have been an Anointed one, a prince,—and therefore a Davîdide, if not ruling, yet called to rule by his descent from the old Davidic kings. A passage like Hab..iii. 13—where the word *Messias* in the second member is interchanged with the word *people* in the first, may not remotely be compared with those of this song. Every living and careful consideration of them anew confirms the hypothesis that here an individual poet with quite peculiar personality is speaking, with the most unique feelings and experiences, peculiar to his life. Indeed it must be said that in the whole composition, nay, almost in every word of these songs, we feel the quite peculiar colouring in which a Davîdide was bound to seize the relations and sufferings of those times. Who this Davîdide was, it is certainly somewhat difficult to make out from other sources: but we know that Zerubabel remained a dweller in Jerusalem; or we might think of a descendant of his. If now both were of the same poet, certainly Ps. cxxxii. is significantly earlier; it is fresher, more powerful, and it has no allusion at all to the great desolation of Jerusalem, and pollution of the Temple.

But in fact notwithstanding all resemblance, in poetic tenor and art and in the stamp of the language there is much diversity between the two; and Ps. cxxxii. plainly stands higher in flight and spirit. Since now we learned to recognize Zerubabel in certain songs of similar flight and of the like time, we esteem Ps. cxxxii. as a somewhat later poem of his, and derive Ps. lxxxix. from his son. For this mutual relation of the two songs their present position also speaks, Ps. cxxxii. as adopted into the above described collection, Pss. cxx.—

cxxxiv., and Ps. lxxxix. along with lxxxv., lxxx., lxxix., lxxiv., xliv.

The poet of Ps. cxxxii., full of the oracle 2 Sam. vii., and several other more ancient in praise of Davîd, and of Sion, unable to conceive and endure that the once flourishing Sion for whose weal Davîd sacrificed himself, should for ever more deeply fall, prays to Jahvé full of hope,—that for Davîd's sake, and the promises given to him, He will be gracious to Sion, the once chosen city, and Davîd's race. Thus, reviewing the ancient history and the present, he prays Jahvé at first to recollect the sacrifice of Davîd, by which Sion became the joyous seat of religion, vv. 1-17. But now it is as if desolate and forsaken of Jahvé, therefore will Jahvé again show Himself in it in His splendour, and hear the Anointed one, according to His promise, vv. 8-12 ; for Sion is once for all, according to ancient oracles the seat of Jahvé, where also Davîd's race shall never cease to shine, vv. 13-18. The first of the three strophés has 14 members, the second closely considered, an equal number, while the last (as frequently) concludes somewhat more shortly.

1.

1 Remember, O Jahvé, Davîd
  all the trouble he endured ;
 he, who swore to Jahvé,
  vowed to Jakob's Strong One :
"I will not enter my house's tent,
  nor ascend the bed of my couch,
"nor give my eyes sleep
  and my eyelids slumber,
5 "till that I find a place for Jahvé,
  I, an abode for the Strong One of Jahvé ! "
and lo, we heard it in Efráta,
  so found we it in the fields of the Forest :
"let us come to His seat,
  do homage at His footstool ! "

2.

O raise, Jahvé, Thyself to Thy resting-place,
 Thyself and Thy sublime ark!
let Thy priests put on gracious righteousness,
 and Thy saints jubilation!
For Davîd, Thy servant's sake   10
 thrust not back the countenance of Thy Anointed!
Sworn hath Jahvé truth to Davîd,
 whence He will never swerve:
" of Thy body's fruit
 will I place on Thy throne!
" if Thy sons keep thy covenant
 and my exhortations which I teach them:
so shall their sons for ever and ever
 sit upon Thy throne."

3.

For Jahvé has chosen out Sion,
 desired it for His own abode:
" this is my resting-place for ever and ever,
 here will I dwell, because I love her;
her food will bless, bless,   15
 will satisfy her poor with bread,
and cause her priests to put on salvation,
 and her saints—they shall shout for joy;
there will I cause a horn to sprout for Davîd,
 prepare a light for mine Anointed,
will cause His foes to put on shame,
 but on Him shall His crown shine!"

The very difficult verses, 6, 7, may—if they are compared with the whole connexion—simply describe the splendid way in which the execution and the result have corresponded to these toils of Davîd: If Efráta, the older, solemn name of

Bethlehem,—here named for David's sake,—denotes by its situation Southern Kánaan, and the fields of the forest, (*i.e.*, Libanon's, the finest and mightiest forest in Kánaan, Isa. xxii. 8, xxix. 17, Ps. lxxv. 7, Hagg. i. 8) denote the Northern, the sense is: "and actually the oath, vv. 2-5, was not in vain; *we* (*i.e.*, the Israelites, as an ancient surviving people generally, in the speech of this time, lxvi. 6) heard through the whole land the joyous words of reciprocal summons to go to the Temple on Sion" (ver. 7 after xcix. 5); and if this is very brief, it is yet entirely suitable. From ver. 8 it does not follow that the poet was at that time in exile and wished that Jahvé and the ark of the covenant might return to Sion. Rather does the poet pray only that Jahvé will with His (at that time lost) ark of the covenant, and in the splendour of earlier times, manifestly show Himself on Sion, and on the whole earth,—or make His presence felt; for in unhappy times He appears to have departed from the holy place. The praise of Sion, vv. 13-18, sufficiently shows that Sion generally was again inhabited, but very scantily and wretchedly; and the historic circumstances here are entirely the same that we find indicated about the same time in the words, B. Jes. xxiii. 18, comp. with xlix. 22, 23, lx. 4, 9-12, Zakh. vi. 10-15. *A light to David,*— his race not only remaining in Sion, but there ever shining in inextinguishable splendour (1 Kings xi. 36, xv. 4 sqq., comp. with 2 Sam. xxi. 17.)

Ps. lxxxix. supplicates in a much unhappier and more woeful tone, quite as in that troubled time we looked upon above; for this song certainly falls with Ps. lxxx. in about the same period; but a somewhat later writer has this song as his pattern in lamentation, for the figures, vv. 41, 42, plainly stand in lxxx. 13 as their original position, and likewise the words vv. 10-14 are not necessarily from the poet of lxxiv. 13-17. The greater must be our admiration of the high spirit and steadfast boldness, which will not willingly despond even in these most unhappy times. As if the poet would with firm resolve, from the midst of all anguish which has long befallen him, cast himself all the more purely and with the greater comfort on the recollection of the Divine grace, he begins a song of thanks and praise to Jahvé, the ever gracious, who promises eternal weal to Davîd and his race; and develops, thus brought under the soothing power of song, in the first instance more assiduously and fully this praise of the greatness of Jahvé and of the happiness of Israel to be *His* people, vv. 7-19. But since to this happiness, according to the ancient view, *this* also belongs,—that Jahvé ever preserves and protects the (Davîdic) prince, who with his people is true to Him: the language then most widely broadens out in the praise of the choice of Davîd long ago, and of the Divine promise therewith given for His posterity, vv. 20-38. And now only at the end, as if drawn forth by this recollection of the glorious past, and its promises, the contemplation of the mournful present so far different from that oracle concerning Davîd, and the most dejected lamentation makes way, vv. 39-52, almost with exhaustion and despondency,—a sobbing discourse, violently constrained and oppressed, scarce finding words to express the injuries of the time and the personal mal-treatment. Thus the end does not answer to the beginning, but while from the first and in the main part rest prevails, with repression of excitement, finally the latter also asserts itself. The main part is almost verbally founded on 2 Sam. vii., only in a few particulars in accordance with the demand of later times and their experience, more fully worked out.—A structure in strophés cannot here be discovered; the poet certainly did not design his song for public singing. On the whole, there appear here as three constituent parts of the long song, (1) Praise, (2) Historical recollection, (3) Lament, and this according to the Massôra in 18, 19 and 14 verses. But the formation in smaller strophés is wanting.

16 *

1.

2   The mercies of Jahvé will I ever sing,
for all times loudly publish Thy faithfulness,
the while I think: eternally is grace built up,
with the heaven itself Thou foundest Thy faithfulness!
" Concluded have I a covenant with the Chosen one,
sworn to Davîd my servant:
5   "for ever will I found thy seed,
for all times build thy throne!" *
And heaven praise highly Thy wonder, Jahvé,
and Thy faithfulness in the Saints' assembly.

For who in the bright height is like Jahvé,
is like to Jahvé among the sons of God?
to God most sublime in the council of the Saints,
and fearful over all round about Him?
O Jahvé, God of Hosts, who is mighty as Thou, Jah,
and like to Thy faithfulness, round about Thee?
10   Thou rulest over the sea's haughtiness,
when its waves are proud, *Thou* soothest them;
Thou didst strike, like one smitten, the Monster,
didst scatter by the arm of power the foes;
Thine are the heavens, Thine also is the earth,
the world and its fulness—*Thou* hast formed them;
North and South—*Thou* hast made them.
Tabor and Hermôn rejoice in Thy name;
Thine is the arm with strength,
strong Thy hand, high Thy right hand.
15   Right and judgment are Thy throne's foundation,
grace and truth Thy glance's fore-runners.—
O blessed the people that knows feasts of jubilation,
Jahvé, walks in the light of Thy glance,
for Thy name every day makes merry,
and of Thy gracious righteousness is proud;

for the ornament of their glory art Thou,
    through Thy favour our horn is exalted;
for Jahvé's own self is our shield,
    the Holy One of Israel our King.

2.

Once spakest Thou in vision to Thy Saint   20
    and saidst: "I have laid help on a hero,
    raised a youth out of the people,
found David my servant,
    with holy oil anointed him,
with whom my hand shall remain firm,
    and whom my arm will strengthen;
a foe shall not be his creditor,
    no son of wickedness oppress him,
dash in pieces will I before him his oppressors
    and smite his haters,
and my truth and grace will be with him,   25
    in my name his horn be raised;
on the sea I lay his hand,
    and on the streams his right hand;
He will cry to me; 'Thou art my father,
    my God, and my salvation's rock!'—
and I also will make him my first-born,
    the highest of the kings of the earth,
for ever keep my grace for him,
    while my covenant remains true to him;
and will make his seed ever-during,   30
    and his throne like heaven's days:
if his sons forsake my law
    and walk not in my judgments,
if they desecrate my privileges
    and keep not my command,
then will I chastising punish their transgression,
    with blows their misdeed,

       yet my grace to him will not break
           and not deny my truth;
35   not profane my covenant
           nor alter the declaration of my lips;
       once have I sworn by my holiness,
           surely to David I lie not!
       His seed shall be for ever
           His throne like the sun before me,
       like the moon subsist for ever,
           with faithful witness in the bright height!"

3.

       And yet Thou hast despised and scorned,
           become wrath with Thine Anointed,
40   rejected Thy servant's covenant,
           profaned low in the dust his crown;
       broken through all his walls,
           turned his fortresses into ruins;
       all who pass by plunder him,
           become a scoff for his neighbours;
       hast raised his oppressor's hand,
           caused all his foes to rejoice,
       yea, didst cause his sword's edge to give way
           and hast not made him stand in battle;
45   hast taken from his glory,
           and cast his throne to the ground,
       shortened his youth's days,
           covered him with shame! *—
       How long, Jahve, wilt ever hide Thyself,
           will Thy wrath burn like fire?
       Remember, Lord, what is life,
           how vainly Thou didst make all children of men?
       who is the man that lives not seeing death,
           who saves his soul from the hand of hell! *
50   Where are Thy earlier mercies, Lord,
           in Thy truth sworn to Davîd?

Remember, Lord, the scorn for Thy servants,
what I bear in my bosom, of all the many peoples,
wherewith Thy foes scorn, Jahvé,
wherewith they scoff at Thine Anointed's steps!

1. Vv. 2-6 : Ever will the poet praise Jahvé, because ever, firm as the heavens and founded in like manner with the heavens themselves (ver. 3, comp. ver. 30, 37, xxxvi. 6) is His faithfulness, the same wherein He once promised the eternal rule of David and his race (vv. 4-5), highly praised by the Angels, the witnesses and nearest in knowledge of Jahvé (ver. 6, comp. Ps. xix., Rev. iv., v., xix. 4). For if the erection of the eternal throne of David was one of the most weighty and gladdening counsels of God, highly furthering the weal of the earth,—so in the solemn moment when this promise was given, this destiny was fixed, the whole heaven must resound with the praise of God, praising His truth whereby He strangely brings about the promise amidst all hindrances. —But the praise which the highest inhabitants of heaven pour forth to Jahvé, leads to the further description and laudation of Jahvé, the incomparable one in heaven itself, vv. 7-9, the only mighty and exalted one in nature and in man, vv. 10-14, ever just and true, ver. 15; so that Israel is to be congratulated which immediately knows and rejoices in Him, as He is the eternal support of the true king of Israel, vv. 16-19. Ver. 9. The last member is very short, but according to the preceding member and to ver. 3, is plain : and whose faithfulness among all round about Thee is like Thy faithfulness ? comp. § 351 a. נשוא, ver. 10, becomes substantive from the *inf.*: self-elevation, pride, as שיא, Job xx. 6, comp. § 153 b. On *Rahab*, see on lxxxvii. 4; but the mythological sense is transparent. *Mercy* and *truth* are (ver. 15) forerunners of Jahvé's arrival, since He whither soever He turns, prepares grace already from afar, quite as lxxxv. 11, 14. תרועה, ver. 15, is the joyous festive jubilation generally ; and we see that Israel at that time again

in peace solemnized feasts, again had long dwelt in Jerusalem. With the words, ver. 19, the poet makes with obvious intention a rapid close to this laudation, in order, according to the preliminary words, vv. 4, 5, to return to the king, the promised genuine descendant, who nevertheless seems necessarily to belong to the Theocracy, and in the following strophe to abide alone by the promise which concerns him. To say, ver. 19, *our* king and shield (xlvii. 10) as if there were such besides him, is not incorrect; because the sentence on the true never-failing king is a general one, which even a Davîdide might thus generally utter,—especially such an one as did not actually rule, but only held fast the inner truth (that termed nowadays the "idea.")

2. With אָז, *at that time*, ver. 20 (therefore not now, comp. מֵאָז, *once on a time*, also of the remoter future, xcvi. 12), plainly enough the old glorious time is indicated, which was touched upon in vv. 4-6. חָזוֹן, taken from 1 Chron. xvii. 15, comp. 2 Sam. vii. 17, is the vision which Nathan saw, who is here named "the Saint of Jahvé." Davîd is, according to the general description, vv. 20-22, set forth as he who is invincible by outward foes (in the time of the poet a vital point, comp. vv. 39 sqq.), vv. 23-25; on the other hand, as Son of Jahvé ruling all, vv. 26-29, finally, as eternally ruling on in his descendant, so that on these severe chastisement might come indeed, but never entire loss of dominion. This is purposely developed to the furthest extent, vv. 30-38. But throughout and especially at the conclusion, the *eternal faithfulness* is brought into relief, vv. 25, 29, 34-38, thus thrice, as if according to the old sacred custom (comp. the *Alterthümer*, p. 151), and even more emphatically. Ver. 23 *b*, almost literally from 2 Sam. vii. 10, where however it is expressed of the whole people; the striking allusion to indebtedness in *a* is explained from the remarks above on cxxxii. 15, 16. Ver. 26 from lxxii. 8, but otherwise than lxxx. 12; the fine image, ver. 27, still more suitably and forcibly from Solomon, 2 Sam. vii. 14. Ver. 30, from 2 Sam. vii. 12, 16; eternal *as the heaven*, comp.

vv. 37, 38 after Ps. lxxii. 5, 7, 17. Job xiv. 12. Vv. 31-33, from 2 Sam. vii. 14, where it is merely of Solomon ; only there it runs more definitely; God will punish him as a sinner with chastisement *of men*, *i.e.*, even as God punishes all men, even the humble, without respect of person; but thereby the inner eternal destination or the right to rule is not to cease. Ver. 34, from 2 Sam. vii. 15. *Once*, ver. 36, because all truly Divine things, once done, endure for ever, not to be improved nor altered, while man may be deceived and hence alter, 1 Pet. iii. 18, Judg. v. 3. On the oath, ver. 38 *b*, comp. § 340 *c*.

3. Vv. 39-46 are very noteworthy in respect of the conception of the misery of the Anointed, mingled imperceptibly with that of the misery of the state and Jerusalem, the two being blended together, as indeed the weal and honour of the two are inseparable. But as in the beginning the personality of the anointed poet comes out, vv. 39, 40, so the discourse returns to this, vv. 45-46; hence too the shortening of the days of youth, ver. 46, to which anew allusion is made, vv. 48, 49, cannot be figuratively understood of the kingdom of Juda. The rest is explained from the fact that the poet would take up the words of that somewhat earlier song, lxxx. 13,—plainly with design, into his own song. מִי הַשָּׁבִית (for in כִּ מִשְׁחֲרוּ according to this pointing is a preposition) : cause to cease, take *from* the thing, thus lessen, weaken it. Vv. 48, 49, as vi. 6, Job vii. 6, 7. That instead of the senseless אֲדֹנִי, אֲנִי must be read, as earlier some scholars (Houbigant, Olshausen) supposed, is shown by the similar beginning, ver. 51. From ver. 47 onwards, the obvious curtness and abruptness in general of the discourse profoundly moved by grief,—rises, vv. 51, 52, to its climax, as if the whole language resounded with sighs. אֲשֶׁר, ver. 52, goes back to the main word חֶרְפָּה, ver. 51. *The steps*, wherever he goes, they pursue him with scorn.

Some light is thrown upon the distresses of that time by the two following songs, quite peculiarly of prophetic-priestly kind, somewhat as Pss. cx., xx. They show that even in those most mournful times hope at last anew germinates. Of these Ps. lxxxv. is the simpler and finer; in it again for the first time a recollection of the great deliverance from exile is found; without question Ps. cxxvi. is present to the poet's mind as a sort of pattern for such prayers. As the poet feels himself called to show the people both genuine prayer and comfort, he puts into their mouth in the first half, vv. 2-8, the most suitable supplication, beginning with thankfully joyous recollection of the great salvation experienced on the return from exile, praying for its renewal and continuance, and causes in the second the Divine answer thereto to be heard, promising consolation and the revelation of near and certain salvation to the faithful, in some of the most florid pictures of the Messianic hopes at that time again powerfully excited. The whole is thus designed for a Temple song, the first half to be sung by the congregation, the second by the priest who after prayer seeks and finds oracles; comp. I., pp. 193 sqq., (*Dichter des A.B.*).

(The Congregation).

2   Thou had'st, Jahvé, favoured Thy land,
       Thou had'st restored Jakob;
    had'st forgiven Thy people's guilt,
       pardoned all their sin*;
    had'st put away all Thy terror,
       ceased from Thy glowing wrath.—
5   O restore us again, God of our salvation,
       and cease Thy indignation with us!
    wilt Thou then ever be angry with us,
       return Thy wrath to every age?
    wilt Thou not again revive us,
       that Thy people may rejoice in Thee?
    Let Thy grace, Jahvé, behold us,
       and Thy salvation may'st Thou give us!

(The Priest).

Let me hear what God Jahve will speak;
  yea, peace will He speak to His people and His
    saints;
  but let them not return to folly!—
" Surely, near to His fearers is His salvation, 10
    that glory may dwell in our land!
" grace and truth meet,
    gracious-right and peace kiss one another :
" truth will spring from the earth,
    gracious-right looks down from heaven;
" both Jahvé will give the best,
    and our land will give its fruits;
" gracious-right will walk before Him,
    and follows His steps' ways."

Ver. 5. שׁוּבֵנוּ short mode of expression from שׁוּב שְׁבוּתֵנוּ cxxvi. 4; comp. lxxx. 4. Vv. 5-9 bear the plainest resemblance to words in Pss. xliv. sqq., and Ps. lx. The transition to the oracle, ver. 9, is truly prophetic, similarly Hab. ii. 1 sqq. Ready to hear oracles, the prophet may indeed expect that Jahvé will,—for He ever intends salvation—also this time renew salvation and comfort; but the first condition for this is that those saved return not again to former despondency and folly. The oracle is then actually favourable and related as only given by Jahvé, so that between vv. 9 and 10 a short pause must be supplied, vv. 10-14. The Messianic glory is briefly but finely described as a perfected harmony between earth and heaven in the renewed race of man; faithfulness, power, fruitfulness from the earth meet the grace of sanctification (צֶדֶק), happiness from heaven, as disposition, state, fruit of the Divine life (Hos. ii. 23-25), in such a way that infinite salvation proceeds from Jahvé, salvation goes before and follows Him. יָשֵׂם, ver. 14, is like שִׁית, take a direction, position (encamp), iii. 7, Ez. xxi. 21; on שָׂם פָּעַם לָדֶרֶךְ=לרגל,

comp. Hab. iii. 5, Isa. xli. 2.—If the resource suggested in I. p. 194 (*Dichter des A. B.*) is not acceptable, it may be assumed that the short answer of the congregation fell away at the end.

Ps. lx. shows on the other hand that poetry in these troubled times calls to its aid the strength and the impulse of ancient poetic art; for on closer investigation it admits no doubt that the words from ver. 7 to זנחתנו, ver. 12, are borrowed from an older and a Davidic song. While all the rest of the words carry us entirely into the style and situation of this late time, the former are in style and stamp, in contents and meaning entirely different; the unlikeness is obvious enough on the face of it. How well our later poet might apply the weightiest words of the old song to the distress and depression of his time, is clear; although at that time the Philistines were not the foes to be feared, yet Gentiles were; and Philistines readily served as an example of all Gentiles. But while the later poet repeated the oracle as the heart and life of the whole,—intact and entirely unchanged, and retains something of the afterword (ver. 11 and the three first words of ver. 12), he gives a quite new introduction, and adds the conclusion for the most part in his own style,—unquestionably because the beginning and remaining end of the old song were hardly suitable for this later time. For other particulars see above, Vol. I., pp. 112 sqq.

We connect immediately with these songs that standing in its neighbourhood, and very similar in contents,

126. PSALM LXXXIII.,

although it may be later by some centuries and in fact shows again a significant loss of poetic force compared with those just commented upon. It falls, according to all signs, in Nehemja's time. Under him there came a new danger upon Jerusalem, when the circumjacent peoples, supported by the Persian governor Sanballat, desired from envy to destroy the

new Jērusalem as it was rising up with greater power, Neh. iv.
1 sqq., vi. 1 sqq.; but owing to the watchfulness and activity
of Nehemja it endured these menaces. In the time of the
first menace of this new evil falls this song. It prays,—since
danger from hostile alliances and concerts draws near from a
distance to the people of Jahvé, yea, even to the sanctuary,—
for powerful uplifting and help from Jahvé, after the examples
of the old history. And this without higher flight: only
where the horrid godless plans of the foes appear, the prayer
rises with new strength, vv. 6, 14. But it plainly breaks up
into four strophés each of four level verses, only the last being
further extended by a half.

1.

God! have no rest,   2
     O be not silent, and rest not, Thou Lord!
for see, Thy foes rage
     and Thy haters have raised the head;
against Thy people they form a cunning plan,
     take counsel concerning Thy clients,
thinking: "go to! destroy we them as a people,   5
     that no more be mentioned Israel's name!"—

2,

For with like heart have taken counsel,
     conclude against Thee the covenant
the tents of Edom and of the Ismaelites,
     Moab and the Hagrenes,
Gebál and Ammon, Amalek,
     Peléschet with dwellers of Tyre;
Assyrians also are allied with them,
     become an arm to the sons of Lôt.

3.

Do to them as to Midian,   10
     as to Sisera, as to Jabin at the Kishon-brook,

who were smitten at Endor,
   who became dung for the ploughed land;
make them—princes like Oreb and like Zeéb,
   like Zébach and like Ssalmuná all the anointed
                                                  ones,
them who thought: "possess we for ourselves
   the pastures of God!"—

4.

My God! make them as whirling dust,
   as stubble before the wind;
15   as fire burns forest,
   as flame kindles mountains,
so may'st Thou pursue them with Thy storm,
   with Thy tempest amaze them!
fill their face with shame,
   that they may seek Thy name, Jahvé!
blush they and be amazed for ever,
   blench they and disappear,
know that Thou—Thy name, Jahvé!—art alone
   the Highest over all the earth!

יִשְׁמְעוֹן, ver. 4, after xxvii. 5. Ismaelites or Arabs, ver. 7, are (Neh. iv. 7, vi. 1, but not 1 Macc. v.) named as most important enemies. *The Hagrenes* are Arabs from the Northwest, not far from Gebal below the Dead Sea; thereabout dwelt earlier Amalek, who here stands merely as an old renowned name beside those at the time better known. *Assyrians*, ver. 9, old name for the rulers in the North, also Persians, Ezra vi. 22, as conversely in 2 Bar. Apocr. (in Dillmann's *Chrest. Æth.*, pp. 6, 12) Persia stands for Assyria; *arm*, help. That the Persian governor was of hostile disposition, is clear from Neh. iv.—Vv. 10-12 after Judges iv., v., vii., viii., where meanwhile Endor is not named; perhaps the poet had yet other historical books. Ver. 14 after Isa. xvii. 13; on גַּלְגַּל, comp.

the Syr. and Arab., dry stalk, prop. what the wind turns over.

127, 128. Psalms lxxviii., lxxxi.

Amidst all these freshly returning distresses it was meanwhile peculiarly the ancient history of the people, now become holy, which could now bestow on the community an ever richer and fuller light; and this in many ways penetrated the songs. We saw the beginnings of this in a few cases above; but while the spirit of the whole community in these anew sinking times plunged ever more zealously into the memories of the ancient high times of Israel,—the poets, in whom ancient words and truths may with reason resound most deeply, do but meet an impulse and a strong tendency of these times, if they intentionally employ the old history as a means of instructing and exhorting their contemporaries. Of this the first great example is given in Ps. lxxviii., a didactic song arranged with design and art, in which the poet seeks in general to warn the Israelites of his later time by the light of the ancient story, and to guard them against the great dangers of their predecessors,—rebellion and unbelief. But along with this he has also the particular object—to deduce the unfaithfulness and the unhappiness of the ancient time from the tribe of Efráim especially, and in opposition to exalt Juda and Sion. This object is too singular to be conceived without a peculiar historical occasion. The song, according to its whole style, carries us into the times before Ezra and Nehemja, when the long-prepared separation between Samaria and Juda had increased to a point past reconciliation; and Juda so little thought to be able to come to terms and unite with the idolatrous Efráim (Samaria) who was of old wantonly ready for revolt,—that it refused her the Temple at Sion, and forced her with a peculiar worship to separate entirely. In this spirit the poet here warns from revolt, above all citing the example of the old (and new) Efráim; the whole ancient history assumes for him a peculiar form and truth, as he reviews it from this point. What would take place if in Efráim were the central point of the ancient Theocracy, he anticipates from the sad period between Josúa and Saûl, when the ark of the covenant stood (for the most part) in the Efráimic Shilo. And since the genuine, undisturbed worship of Jahvé first found its firm seat in Sion under Davîd, he traces the ancient history from Moses to the very point where Sion was glorified as the city of the sanctuary, and by the force of circumstances it was shown that in Efráim the seat of rest and of faith could not be. After the solemn introduction, vv. 1-8,—though the old sins of Israel must generally be mentioned according to the Pentateuch,—yet for the above reasons the Efráimites are named, as preeminently unfaithful, vv. 9-11. Then the first great unfaithfulness in the exalted time of Moses is described, vv. 12-31, and how they, even after the severe punishment not permanently amended, continued to sin, deserving entire destruction had not God's grace prevailed, vv. 32-39; how they from the time of the desert onwards so utterly unmindful of the Divine deeds that were done down to the giving of Kanáan, continued also in Kanáan to sin, vv. 40-58,—so that Jahvé, wrath against Shilo and Efráim, was bound to send severe punishments upon Israel, vv. 59-64; but then again soon, from Samuel's time again gave a salvation to the people which was for ever firmly founded in Juda and Sion by Davîd, vv. 65-72. Comp. below Ps. cvi. and Ps. cv.

This song was not only in its time quite new and creative in kind, but it is as an epic-didactic song composed of two artistic characters, not without a higher vivacity and bounding wit, notwithstanding all the straitness and oppressiveness of the times. Nor is it without artistic completeness, both in the whole arrangement and in detail. It manifestly consists of nine great strophés, each of eight verses; the slight deviations from this in the present verse-division are unimportant. The

wide dilation and restful narration into which it falls, is not
without pleasing effect.

1.

Hearken, O my people to my doctrine,   1
    bend the ear to my mouth's words;
  open will I my mouth in the proverb-song,
    reveal enigmas out of the fore-time!
What we heard and knew,
    our fathers told us,
will we not conceal from their sons,
  to a later generation telling Jahvé's praise,
    His power and wonders, which He did.
For He established a law in Jakob,   5
    a doctrine He gave in Israel,
  which He laid upon our fathers
    to announce to their sons,
that a later generation should know it,
    sons who should be born,
  who standing up should tell them to their sons;
that on God they should place their confidence
    forget not God's deeds,
    regard His commandment,
and become not as their fathers,
    a generation disloyal, refractory,
  a generation without constancy of heart,
    and whose spirit was not faithful towards God!

2.

Efráim's sons it was who slackly stretched the bow,
    turned about on the day of battle,
kept not the covenant of God,   10
    would not go in His doctrine,
  and forgot His deeds
    and the wonders which He had shown them.

Clearly before their fathers He did wonders
   in Egypt's land, Ssóan's field;
dividing the sea He led them over,
   and caused water to stand like a mole,
led them by day with the cloud,
   and the whole night with fire-glow;
15 divided rocks in the desert,
   watered them as with great sea-flood,
drew gushing water out of the rock,
   caused water to run like streams.

3.

And yet they sinned still further against Him,
   provoked the Highest in the dry land,
And tempted God in their heart,
   demanding food according to their pleasure,
blasphemed against God, thinking: " will God be able
   to furnish a table in the desert?
20 " lo, He struck the rock and waters swelled,
   brooks stream over:
will He also be able to give bread,
   or procure flesh for His people?"
Therefore, hearing that, Jahvé was provoked,
   kindled fire in Jakob,
      yea, anger rose against Israel,
because they believed not on God,
   trusted not in His salvation,
So commanded He bright clouds above,
   opened heaven's gates,
rained upon them Manna to eat;
   corn of heaven He gave to them.

4.

25 Bread of the Mighty each one ate,
   diet He sent to them to the full,

causes in heaven the East to break up,
    brought on by His power the South,
rained upon them flesh like dust,
    like the sea-sand feathered winged birds,
caused them to fall into the midst of the camp,
    round about His seats:
and they ate, satisfied themselves greatly,
    their desire He brings to them!
They let not their lust go,   30
    still the food was in their mouth—
then God's wrath rose against them,
    —and He slays in their fat ranks,
    Israel's youths He struck down!—

5.

Through all this they sinned on,
    believed not in His wonders:
therefore He let their days pass in a breath,
    their years in sudden death.
He destroyed—and they asked after Him,
    turned round and sought God,
and thought that their rock was God,   35
    God the Highest their Redeemer:
but deceived Him with their mouth,
    with the tongue lying to Him,
for their hearts remained not firm with Him,
    they clave not to the covenant.
Yet He is pitiful, sin-covering, not destroying
    oft withdrawing His anger,
    not uprousing His whole wrath;
so bethought He that flesh they were,
    fleeting breath, never coming again.—

6.

How often provoked they Him in the desert,   40
    vexed Him in the steppe,

and tempted God ever anew,
    perplexed the Holy One of Israel,
thought not on His hand,
    on the day when He redeemed them from the oppressor,
when He did His signs in Egypt,
    His wonders in Ssóan's field,
turned their rivers into blood, .
    that their running water they drank not;
45 gadflies sent among them, which devoured them,
    frogs, which destroyed them;
gave up their fruit to the gnawing beast,
    their toil to the locusts;
their vine destroyed by hail,
    their swelling figs by the hoar-frost;
their cattle gave over to the pest
    and to the contagions their flocks;

7.

Looses upon them His wrath's glow,
    terror and rage and distress,
    a sending of angels of ill
50 makes for his anger a way,
    snatched not from death their soul,
    and their life gave over to the pest,
and slew in Egypt all the first-born,
    firstlings of strength in Ham's tents;
caused His people to break up, like sheep,
    led them, like the flock, through the desert,
led them safely, without trembling,
    after the sea had covered their foes,
brought them to His holy bound,
    to the mount His right hand had inherited,
55 and drove before them peoples,
    allotted these with the line of inheritance,
    placed the tribes of Israel in their tents.—

8.

But they tempted, provoked God the Highest,
    regarded not His warnings,
fell faithlessly away like their fathers,
    turned round, like a lax bow,
and angered Him by their high places,
    provoking Him by their images.—
Hearing this God was enraged
    and vehemently despised Israel,
and rejected the place of Shilo,   60
    the tent which He had placed among men,
gave captive His glory,
    His pomp into the oppressor's hand,
gave up to the sword His people,
    against His heritage highly enraged;
His youths fire consumed
    His maidens were not sung,
His priests fell through the sword,
    His widows wept not.

9.

But the Lord awoke, like a sleeping man,   65
    like a hero overcome by wine
struck back His oppressors
    allotting to them eternal reproach,
and despised Josef's tent,
    chose not out the tribe of Efráim
but chose Juda's tribe,
    Sion's mount loved by Him,
and built up like heaven's height His sanctuary,
    like the earth which He had founded forever;
and chose out Davîd His servant,   70
    took him from the sheep-pens,

from the milk-ewes He brought him,
to be shepherd in Jakob, His people,
and in Israel, His heritage;
He fed them after His heart's innocence
and with His hands' understanding He led them.

The beginning, vv. 1, 2 entirely from Ps. xlix. 4, 5; but the enigmas which the poet would solve, the ancient history itself yields, as he here presents it with his own explanation. —Instead of saying ver. 4, *our sons*, it here runs forthwith *their sons*, while the long series of later generations is reviewed as in *one* glance; but in *b* follows immediately the more exact expression. *Stand up*, ver. 6, of new generations, Ex. i. 8; Judges ii. 10 comp. Ps. xxii. 31.—If the decisive words in the course of the whole song at the beginning of ver. 9 are compared with ver. 57 and Hos. vii. 16, one is tempted to take רוֹמֵי here not with the old translators simply as in Jer. iv. 29 in the signification of those throwing, shooting, but to understand it as active to the passive קֶשֶׁת רְמִיָּה. The slack bow is the image of the man useless, treacherous at the time when use is expected from him, even as when the warrior in the decisive moment turns before the foe. The connexion of two words referred to the same nomen and reciprocally limiting one another in the *Stat. const.* would thus express: those slackly stretching the bow, prop. stretching (and at once) letting loose, slack. If רוֹמֵי or merely נשְׁקֵי were used, we should have to think according to 2 Chron. xvii. 17 (although there the connexion of words is not quite the same) simply of shooting with the bow. But the doubled word must manifestly introduce something new and gives by its ambiguity a *wit*, and the more so as נשׁק properly only signifies those who *prepare the bow*; how? says with terse wit the following word. For the rest, comp. 'Amr's *Moall.*, v. 58 sqq., *Journ. As.*, 1848, II., p. 215, 1850, I., p. 327 sqq.; indeed, one might be tempted to read נוֹקְשֵׁי (comp. *nakhas*, and *ghyr ankhas*, Hamâsa, p. 441, 9) if the above explanation is not sufficient.—Note how the later poets thus insert the name of a chief city of Egypt, Ssóan, or *Tanis*, vv. 12, 43, which is not found in the Pentateuch in such places: comp. the *Gesch. des v. Isr.* pp. 571 sqq., ii., p. 118 of the third edition.—בְּנוֹ, ver. 13 and נוֹזְלִים, ver. 16, from Ex. xv. 8. *Still further*, ver. 17, is clear from Ex. xv. 24, and other earlier examples. The (ver. 21) merely indicated punishment first follows actually ver. 31 ; for while God foresaw that they had begged for the food merely from desire (comp. cvi. 14) He gives it to them, indeed, to take away their unbelief, but punishes them also at the same time severely so soon as their desire actually was gratified, Num. xiv., comp. ch. xi., Ex. xvi. In this way, ver. 29, יָבֵא is but a witty expression: *their lust*, the same that they from mere evil desire had coveted, *brings He home to them* as it were (on the mode of writing, see .§ 224 b) : now let them see what they will do with the fine things ! But they understand only how to employ them for their greed ! ver. 30.—*Bread of the mighty*, ver. 25, is,—as the manna appears also in cv. 40 *heaven's bread*,—here equivalent to *angels' bread*, with broader representation, *bread of gods*, comp. 1 Sam. iv. 8; but the expression is, vv. 25, 31, from Isa. x. 13, 16.—Ver. 33 after Num. xiv., xvi. Ver. 38 must throughout be taken as our *present*, describing the eternal in God. On ver. 47 comp. Tristram's *Land of Israel*, p. 34 sqq. ; and as here the *hail* is named, the poet, ver. 48 certainly originally meant, instead of בְּרָדוֹ, בָּרָד, which better suits the structure of the members ; and thus some copies read. Ver. 50 after Ex. xv. 17, where as here, the mount near Shilo must be meant. The suffix in יְמִיפֵּם, ver. 55, must refer to the Kanáanites. Ver. 61 after 1 Sam. iii.—v. *Not sung*, ver. 63, because they solemnized no wedding-day. Ver. 66 after 1 Sam. vii., also with regard to the following deeds of David. Ver. 69 ; firm as the heaven and as the earth below, comp. above Pss. xlviii., lxviii., with Ps. cxxv. 1 ; lxxxix. 3.

But no considerable imitators in this new style of narrative didactic poetry were found by this poet. The immediate Temple poetry was at that time too powerfully aroused; and the echoes of the ancient sacred history sounded ever by preference in that poetry. An example of this from that same time is given by

Ps. lxxxi., apparently a general festive song, but especially designed, as it seems (ver. 4) for the most important new and full moon in the year, *i.e.*, the new moon of the seventh month and the feast of Tabernacles. With the autumn-feast agrees also well the mention of the rich fulness of the fair land, ver. 12 *c* and ver. 17; and at bottom the whole song points to this. As these feasts (Ex. xxiii. and other places of the Pentateuch) were derived from the time of the departure from Egypt: the poet repeats, in mentioning their Divine institution, several hortatory and doctrinal particulars from the Pentateuch, quite in its style; so that this song also serves for exhortation. One might be tempted to derive it from the poet of Pss. lxxvii., xcv., were not several particulars, *e.g.*, the notion and the spelling of the word *Josef* יְהוֹסֵף, ver. 6 (comp. lxxx. 2, 3,*) opposed to this.—The song presents itself in its actual arrangement, as breaking into three strophés with five verses each, with an epilogue, ver. 17. In verse 7 *c* we find, indeed, a certain stumbling-block, of which below; and it remains possible that after ver. 7 a whole strophé has fallen away.

1.

1 Jubilate to God, our strength,
shout to Jakob's God;
raise song, strike the kettle-drum,
pleasant cither with harp;
blow at the new moon into trumpets,
at the full moon, day of our feast!

---

* Thus one might be tempted to ascribe Pss. lxxx sqq., to a Samaritan poet did not Ps. lxxx. belong too closely to the remaining above-mentioned songs.

for a law is for Israel 5,
    a due for Jakob's God;
for an ordinance He made it in Josef,
    when he went forth towards Egypt's land,
        I heard the unknown language.—

2.

" I removed his shoulder from the burden,
    free from the basket were his hands;
" in distress thou didst cry, I freed thee,
    hear thee in thunder's covering,
        prove thee at the Quarrel-water! *
" ' hear my people, suffer exhortation,
    Israel, O if thou would'st hear me!
" ' a strange God should not be in thee, 10
    thou should'st not do homage to the strangers'
        God;
" ' I am thy God Jahvé,
    who led thee from the land of Egypt:
" ' open wide thy mouth, I will fill it!' "

3.

" But my people heard not my voice;
    Israel was not willing to me;
" then I suffered her to go in hardness of heart,
    " ' let them follow then their voices!
" ' O that my people had listened to me,
    Israel had gone in my ways!
" ' how soon would I bow their foes, 15
    upon their oppressors turn my hand;
" ' Jahvé's foes would fawn upon them,
    and their happiness be for ever!' "

4.

And he fed them on fatness of wheat,
    and from the rock I refreshed them with honey!

Ver. 4. בַּכֶּסֶה appears to designate prop. the hidden, *i.e.*, *hinder* part, comp. the Arab. *kossey*, hence the second or waning half of the moon, or the time from the full moon onwards, like the Syr. But the full moon most gladly and longest observed is that of the feast of Tabernacles, so that as the new moon is that publicly observed, and therefore that of the seventh month, this song would be composed for the many feast-days of the seventh moon. The two last members of ver. 6 are very difficult. If בְּצֵאתוֹ was to refer to Israel, עַל is inexplicable; it must then still refer to Jahvé; when He went against Egypt, to smite it (Ex. xi. 4). But the third member must necessarily refer to Israel: when *I* (as *we*, cxxxii. 6) *heard the unknown language*, *i.e.*, of the Egyptians, the hated, barbarian tongue, cxiv. 1, comp. Isa. xxxiii. 19, Deut. xxviii. 49. On the other hand it might be said, as the song does not allude to the Pascha, Ex. xii., that here a somewhat later time must be designated than when Israel still heard the strange language about her,—as also actually, ver. 7, the time after the passage through the Red Sea, Ex. xvi. sqq., is depicted. The unknown language would thus perhaps be the voice of the invisible God, so that the words, vv. 7-11, would be thereby introduced. But *lips* and *tongue* point to human speech, not to oracles; and vv. 12 and 17 show that the poet speaks of God in the first person only after the pattern of the speeches in the Pentateuch, and continues in the narrative of His actions down to the conquest of Kanáan. The poet may thus in a wider sense glance at Ex. xii. It is so far difficult to assume a corruption of the text, as there are other quick transitions in this Ps.; but the want of coherence is here too sensible. The *basket*, ver. 7, is the heavy burden-basket on the shoulder, as it often appears on the Egyptian figures. Ver. 8 *a* from Ps. l. 15; on *b* comp. lxxvii. 17-19; *c* just as Deut. xxxiii. 8, so far gives the proof higher strength and certainty, as means of education on the part of the living God. Vv. 9-11 after Deut. v. 1 sqq.; vv. 12, 13, after Deut. xxix. 18, and elsewhere, vv. 13-17 generally, very strongly after Deut. xxxii.

V.

LAST SONGS.

The yet remaining twenty-four songs stand—with the exception of Pss. xxxiii. and lxxxvi. (which, however, according to Vol. I., pp. 28 sqq., are not taken into account)—no longer in the two first of the three Psalm-collections; the second collection might, according to the above (even without exception of Ps. lxxxiii.) be closed about the middle of the fifth century, the first still earlier; and the songs following from this point onwards, may very well be conceived as having arisen in the middle times of the fifth century.

If we look to their contents, it is at once a striking circumstance that we no longer find any song which solved the enigma proposed in the last songs of lament, and no thank-song plainly referring to the plaintive words of these songs. The enigma of nationality is transferred unsolved to further times; thereby the old, free, and serene sense of the people broken, without anything of a better kind being forthwith formed. The song too is ever nothing but the echo and imitation of the earlier mighty voices. Only when it withdraws into the sanctuary of personal reflection is it still great, Pss. ciii. sqq. elsewhere only the Temple-poetry continues to flourish, retaining all the grand conceptions of tne older time, as by a thousand-fold echo, permanently and firmly in the community.

4. *Prayer of an Individual.*

129. PSALM CXIX.

We begin here justly with Ps. cxix., properly a long, but in this uncommon length so new and peculiar a prayer, in which an old experienced Saint pours forth all his truths, feelings, wishes, prayers, and hopes in the completest and clearest manner; but intentionally their tenor is so general, that here and there the didactic element very strongly appears. The psalm is perhaps one of the latest, from the time when Israel again more oppressed from without, adhered only the more firmly to the written law. Thus this song expresses at first the most vivid feeling of salvation by faithfulness to the given revelation; and here the poet only prays for strength, that he may be able fully to understand the whole law, as he inwardly desires, and accordingly fulfil it. The song is noteworthy because of this constant reference to the Pentateuch. But in particular it begs for speedy, great Divine help against the craft, the corruption, the power of the *world*, also of princes; and it is important to note the sharp and salient contrast here between worldly and Divine rule. But the more zealous is this supplication, for faithful perseverance in the excess of suffering seems finally to deserve confirmation.—The poet desiring entirely to exhaust these thoughts, places very artificially together series of eight verses, beginning with the same letter, according to the alphabetic succession. Each of these eight verses is on the other hand very short. Thus there are found twenty-two strophés, according to the twenty-two letters, in each case eight times repeated; and each of these twenty-two parts has a close coherence, the thoughts also following suitably after one another; frequently two verses stand together inseparable in sense. This great song is not devoid of particular flashes of light, although the poet is somewhat fettered by his rule, requiring the filling of twenty-two verses eight times; the spirit of the troubled time weighs heavily also on him.

Who the poet was, and from what peculiar condition of life he thus composed, we may plainly enough recognize from the long words. From such indications as vv. 51, 61, 69, 85, 95, 110, 150, 157, 158, it follows that he as an adherent of the stricter party in the new Jerusalem, led by Ezra, had fallen, into the sorest complexities with the party of the more highminded. In the contest he was (vv, 53, 139) carried away by violence, and was the more readily accused before the heathen magistracy, and despite his fearless defence, imprisoned, vv. 23, 24, 46, 161. Now he feels himself forsaken by the faithful and isolated, vv. 79, 176, and would be extremely unhappy did not his good conscience keep him upright. That he was still young is not to be inferred from ver. 9; rather was he (vv. 84-87) already advanced in years. More nearly we cannot pursue his history to this time, the less because this long song, according to its style, is the one writing that we now possess of his. But this long song itself would have been with difficulty preserved, if it had not been long known that the poet was a man of high merit.

All who walk purely are blessed,   1
    who go in the law of Jahvé :
Attend ever to His precepts,
    with their whole heart seek Him ;
Also never do a wickedness,
    walking in His way.
Appoint didst Thou Thy commandments,
    that they should be kept ;
Ah, would that my ways stood firm,   5
    to keep Thy laws !
And then I shall not blush,
    if I look to all Thy commands,
Aye, with sincere heart will I praise Thee,
    learning Thy just sentences.
As to Thy statutes, I cleave to them :
    forsake me not utterly !

By what way walks purely the youth ?
    by holding it according to Thy word !

10 But I have followed Thee with my whole heart: *
    let me not miss Thy command;
Believe Thy words in my heart,
    that I should not sin against Thee.
Blessed to me, Jahvé, art Thou!
    O teach me Thy laws.
Boldly have I told
    all Thy mouth's judgments.
By Thy doctrines to abide I rejoice,
    as over all treasures
15 Behold Thy commandments always,
    and look to Thy paths!
Beloved are Thy statutes by me,
    I never forget Thy word!

Do well by Thy servant, that I may live
    and hold fast Thy word!
Disclose my eyes, that I may behold
    much wonder from Thy doctrine.
Dwell I as a stranger on earth;
    hide not from me Thy commands!
20 Desire makes my soul to bleed
    after Thy judgments, always.
Denouncest Thou the accursed proud,
    who wandered from Thy commands,
Disgrace, shame, roll from me,
    because I have observed Thy precepts!
Deliberated against me the princes, sitting:
    but Thy servant thinks of Thy statutes:
Delightful are Thy precepts to me,
    Thy judgments my counsellors.

25 Ever cleaves to the dust my soul:
    quicken me after Thy word!

Explained have I my fate, Thou hast heard me ;
   O teach me Thy laws !
Enlighten me to go in Thy doctrines,
   that I may think of Thy wonders.
Exhausted is my soul with grief :
   direct me according to Thy word !
Expel from me the way of lying,
   with Thy teaching be gracious to me !
Elected have I the way of truth,   30
   bethought me of Thy judgments ;
Ever cleaves my heart to Thy precepts ;
   Jahvé, let me not be ashamed !
Ever I traverse the way of Thy commands,
   because Thou makest broad my heart.

Further me, O Jahvé, on the way of Thy statutes,
   that I may finally keep it.
Fit me to keep Thy law,
   and observe it with my whole heart !
Further me in the path of Thy commands,   35
   because it delights me.
For Thy precepts open my heart,
   and not for gain of gold.
From the view of vanity turn my eyes :
   on Thy way quicken me !
Fix for Thy servant Thy word,
   the word : to fear Thee !
Far remove my reproach, before which I am in dread :
   for good are Thy judgments ;
For truly I long after Thy commands :   40
   through Thy righteousness quicken me !

Grace from Thee cause to come upon me, O Jahvé,
   Thy salvation, according to Thy promise,

Gifted with words against my contemner,
    because I trust Thy word!
Get not utterly out of my mouth truth,
    because I hope on Thy judgment,
Given-up to keep Thy law
    for ever at all times!
45 Going the unfettered way,
    because I strove for Thy commandments!
Grant me to confess Thy precepts,
    without blushing before kings!
Grant me to delight in Thy doctrines,
    so greatly beloved by me!
Gladly lift I my hand to Thy doctrines,
    and think of Thy statutes!

Hold promises to Thy servant,
    because Thou hast made me hope.
50 Here is my consolation in my sufferings:
    Thy promise hath quickened me.
Haughty ones scorned me very greatly:
    nevertheless I swerved not from Thy doctrine;
Held Thy ancient judgments before me,
    Jahvé, and consoled myself.
Horror hath seized me because of the wicked,
    who forsake Thy law.
Hymns have Thy statutes been to me
    in the house of my pilgrimage.
55 Have thought by night, O Jahvé, of Thy name,
    and held fast Thy law,
Have gained this,
    that I regarded Thy commands.

I thought, it is my possession, O Jahvé,
    to keep Thy words.

I begged for Thy mercy with all my heart:
    be gracious to me according to Thy word.
I thought on my ways,
    and turned my foot to Thy precepts.
I hastened greatly, not tarrying,   60
    to keep Thy commandments.
I was encompassed around by wicked men:
    but forgot not Thy doctrine.
I lift at midnight my hand to Thy praise,
    because of Thy just judgments.
I am companion of all who fear Thee
    and who keep Thy commands.
Is the earth full of Thy grace, Jahvé?
    O teach me Thy laws!

Jahvé! according to Thy word   65
    Thou hast shown good to Thy servant.
Judgment, true understanding teach me,
    because I believe on Thy commandments.
Just now I keep Thy word;
    but I erred before I learned humility.
Jahvé, good art Thou, showing good;
    O teach me Thy laws.—
Jealous ones patched lies against me;
    I hold Thy commands with all my heart;
Just as fat is their heart swollen;   70
    but my pleasure is Thy law.
Joy for me that I was bound down,
    that I might learn Thy commands!
Justly dearer to me is the doctrine of Thy mouth
    than thousands of gold and silver.

Knit together by Thy hands:
    give me understanding to learn Thy commands.
Know me with joy let them that fear Thee,
    because I hoped on Thy word.

75 Known to me Jahvé is Thy just judgment,
        and uprightly Thou didst cause me to suffer:
    Keep Thy grace for my comfort,
        according to Thy word to Thy servant!
    Known be Thy compassion, that I may live!
        for Thy law is my pleasure.
    Keen shame upon the proud, who oppress me without cause!
        I think of Thy commands.
    Keep at my side all who fear Thee
        and know Thy precepts!
80 Knit my heart into Thy doctrines,
        that I may not be ashamed!

    Languishing for Thy salvation is my soul:
        I hope on Thy word;
    Languishing for Thy promise are my eyes,
        thinking: when wilt Thou comfort me?
    Light have I become like a skin in the smoke;
        but Thy laws I did not forget.
    Live I not too long already?
        when wilt Thou judge those that pursue me?
85 Light-minded ones, not after Thy doctrine,
        have dug pits for me.
    Lovely as truth are all Thy commands:
        idly they persecute me; help me!
    Lightly they would have destroyed me on earth,
        although I forsook not Thy commands.
    Let me live according to Thy grace,
        that I may keep Thy mouth's exhortation!

    Made firm in heaven, Jahvé, stands
        Thy word to everlasting times;
90 Maintains at all times Thy faithfulness;
        founded by Thee stands the earth;

Morning and night wait on Thy judgment;
  for they are all Thy servants.
Me Thy law refreshes; else were
  I already lost in sufferings
My life long I will not forget Thy commands;
  for Thou hast through them quickened me.
Me deliver, I am Thine,
  for Thy commands I sought.
Me to destroy lay in wait wicked men;   95
  to Thy precepts I ever give heed.
Men see an end of all glory:
  but unlimited is Thy command.

Not utterable is my love for Thy law;
  every day it is my thought.
Not to the foe do I yield in wisdom,
  for Thy law remains ever with me;
Not all my teachers are too wise for me,
  for Thy precepts are my teaching;
Not old men are too knowing for me,   100
  for I regarded Thy commands.
Never turned I to ill paths my foot,
  that I may keep Thy command.
Nay, I departed not from Thy judgments,
  for *Thou* hast instructed me.
Not honey is to the mouth so sweet
  as to my palate Thy promises;
Nay, I get prudence from Thy words;
  therefore I hate every path of lies.

O what a lamp to my foot is Thy word,   105
  and to my path light!
Or swore I not, and kept it,
  to keep Thy just judgments?

Oppressed am I very greatly
 Jahvé, quicken me according to Thy word!
O God, in grace take the sacrifices of my mouth
 and teach me Thy judgments!
On my hand increasingly lies my soul:
 but Thy law I forgot not.
110 Of Thy commands not forgetful
 I was ensnared by wicked men;
Of Thy precepts I keep hold,
 for they are my heart's delight;
On, increasingly to the end
 I bend my heart to practise Thy law.

Palterers I hate
 and love Thy law.
Port and defence art Thou to me:
 I hope on Thy word,
115 Profligates, depart from me,
 that I may keep my God's commands!
Provide for me according to Thy promise, that I may live,
 and let me not blush for my hope!
Prop me up, that I, delivered
 may continually look to Thy commands!
Puttedst down all that err from Thy duties,
 for vain is their disposition;
Profligates are, thought I, all dross:
 therefore love I Thy precepts.
120 Plighted to Thee fear shudders through me,
 before Thy judgments I tremble.

Right I practised and duty
 give me not over to tormentors.
Right to execute, be Thou my surety:
 let not haughty ones torment me!

Right and promised salvation from Thee
  waiting for, my eyes fail;
Reprove according to Thy grace Thy servant,
  and teach me Thy laws!
Reveal to me: I am Thy servant,   125
  that I may know Thy precepts!
Rouse Thyself, O Jahvé! it is time;
  they have broken Thy doctrine;
Really therefore love I Thy commands
  before gold and fine treasures;
Regard as precious all Thy commands,
  hate every path of lies.

So wonderful are Thy precepts
  Therefore hath my soul kept them
Streams of light are spread by Thy words' revelation, 130
  making intelligent those who are unintelligent:
See, with wide open mouth I long,
  because I yearned for Thy commands.
Show Thy face, be gracious to me,
  as befits to friends to Thy name
Stepping firmly in Thy word,
  Let not evil rule over me.
Shelter me from the torment of men,
  that I may keep Thy commands.
Show the light of Thy countenance on Thy servant, 135
  and teach me Thy laws!
Streams of water run from my eye
  because Thy law is not regarded.

True art Thou Jahvé, and just,
  straight Thy judgments;
True thoroughly and veritable are Thy doctrines;
  so hast Thou Thyself appointed it.

Troubled was I extremely in my zeal,
   because my oppressors forget Thy words.
140 True entirely is Thy promise found,
   beloved by Thy servant.
Though I be small, despised,
   forget I not Thy commands.
Truth, eternal truth is Thy law,
   and verity Thy doctrine.
Though distress and straitness came upon me,
   yet my pleasure is Thy command.
True are Thy precepts for ever;
   make me wise that I may live!

145 Uplift me, sincerely I call, Jahvé,
   I will keep Thy dues;
Uplift me, I cry to Thee,
   that I may keep Thy precepts!
Unstably, before morning shimmer, I cry,
   hoping on Thy word;
Unstably, I awake before night watches,
   to think of Thy promises.
Ungraciously O hear not my voice,
   Jahvé, according Thy judgment quicken me,
150 Unholy pursuers drew near,
   far from Thy doctrine:
Unto me, Jahvé, Thou art near,
   and true are all Thy commands;
Unfailing of old, Thy doctrines are founded:
   that I knew long ago from them.

Visit me in my suffering, set me free,
   for I forget not Thy doctrine.
Vouchsafe for me, and redeem me,
   for Thy promise' sake quicken me!

Vicious men never gain salvation, 155.
    because they sought not Thy statutes.
Very pitiful art Thou, Jahvé:
    quicken me according to Thy judgments!
Very many are my persecutors, oppressors:
    but I swerved not from Thy precepts.
Vile men I saw with disgust,
    who esteemed not Thy word,
Verily, see, how I love Thy commands:
    Jahvé, according to Thy grace quicken me!
Very full of truth is the number of Thy words,* 160
    eternal is every utterance of Thy judgment.

While princes persecute me without cause
    before Thy word only trembles my heart;
While some rejoice who have gained great spoil,
    I make merry over Thy word.
What hatred and horror have I for lies,
    how I love Thy doctrine!
While I offer seven praises to Thee a day,
    because of Thy just judgments.
Who loves Thy doctrine, enjoys much good, 165
    He stumbles not nor falls.
Well hoped I, Jahvé, on Thy salvation,
    I practised Thy commands.
Well kept my soul Thy precepts,
    and loved them greatly.
Well kept I Thy commands and precepts;
    before Thee are all my ways.

To (*Zu*) Thee, Jahvé, let my sighing penetrate,
    according to Thy word make me wise;
To (*Zu*) Thy seat let this my prayer come; 170
    according to Thy promise deliver me!

---

* Prop. *the head* (the sum) *of Thy word is truth.*

To (*Zu*) Thee let the lips' praise stream!
  for Thy statutes Thou teachest me.
Zest of my song be Thy word!
  for all Thy words are just.
Zealous to help me, let Thy hand come,
  for Thy commands have I chosen.
To (*Zu*) Thy salvation, Jahvé, I yearn,
  And Thy law is my pleasure.
175 To (*Zu*) praise Thee, let my soul live,
  let Thy judgment help me!
To (*Zu*) save a lost sheep, seek Thy servant;
  for I forgot not Thy commands.

Ver. 19 a and vv. 4, 5, from Ps. xxxix. 13.—Ver 20, גֶּרֶם is *be crushed*, be about to pass away, languish, and so identical with כָּלָה, vv. 81, sq., 123, comp. also ver. 131.—Ver. 22. גֹּל *roll* is to be read. Vv. 23, 24, belong closely together, so that in the fine sense the first גַּם (§ 362 a) forms the opposition and the second still more plainly the *apodosis*; *etiam sederint tamen*, &c., and at the end is wanting, after the LXX, צִדְקֹתֶיךָ. —Ver. 26 a is similar to ver. 59.—שָׁוְה, ver. 50, as Isa. xxxviii. 13.—Ver. 38. אִמְרָה, which in other places in this psalm signifies rather *promise*, seems to designate merely *word*, just as vv. 11, 67, 133; on אֲשֶׁר as *namely*, see § 338 b.—Ver. 47. According to the LXX, מְאֹד is wanting at the end, while the words אֲשֶׁר אָהַבְתִּי, v. 48, are incorrectly repeated. The fine image as Job xxxi. 36.—Ver. 53. קִנְאָה = זַלְעָפָה, ver. 139. —Ver. 64. The mode of expression as in xxxiii. 5, civ. 24.— Ver. 73 after Job x. 8.—Ver. 83. כִּי is used as in xxi. 12. —Ver. 91 a. וְהַלַּיְלָה also after lxxiv. 16, must have fallen away at the end, for the words otherwise give no sense; the *standing* in *a* corresponds (as elsewhere so often) to the *serving* in *b*; and the whole strophé brings out at the beginning vv. 89-91, as at the end, ver. 96, the infinity of the Word of God (the Logos) so far as all must serve Him, so that a word from Him may unexpectedly bring every blessing.—Ver. 103, from Job vi. 25, as ver. 109 from Job xiii. 14, and ver. 115 from Ps. vi. 9.—Vv. 118, 119. According to the LXX, תְּרִיָתָם must be read for תרם and הָשְׁבְתָּ֫ for הִשְׁבַּתָּ ; elsewhere, comp. ver. 21.—Ver. 128. I consider פִּקּוּדֶיךָ after LXX and Vulg. to be necessary, whether ך has fallen away because of the following כל, or this כל first arose from ך. The latter is more probable, for the repeated כל has here no significance (otherwise Ez. xliv. 30), and the suffix throughout cannot be wanting. But יִשַּׁר is interchanged with אִשַּׁר, or signifies here rather *esteem right*, like the Arabic *sçaddak, esteem true*, comp. ver. 137.—Ver. 140 from Ps. xii. 7.

How early the true sense of these words of the long song was lost, may be seen from *M.* Aboth iv. 1, Berakhóth ix. 5, at the end, comp. here vv. 99, 126.

B. 130-138. PSALMS CIII., CIV., CVI., CVII., CXI.—CXIV., CXVII.

These are the finest and at the same time the most independent of the congregational songs of this last time. And here in every point of view the two fine songs, Pss. ciii., civ., stand at the head,—songs of thanksgiving and praise which indeed are put into the mouth of an individual, but which manifestly are intended to express the sense of the whole community, as a confession of faith that every one may utter in the sense of the community. They stand in a reciprocal relation:

Ps. ciii. summons men to bless Jahvé especially in so far as He is the Redeemer and Pardoner, as Israel had so gloriously known. That Jahvé is such according to His nature, and on the other hand, according to the nature of the human creation, needing the Divine help and grace, is shown in the middle, vv. 6-18, very fully and beautifully. Hence in the beginning, the call to self to bless Jahvé, as Redeemer, vv. 1-5 ; at the end,—because Jahvé only as world-ruler can show such eternal kindness and redemption,—a summons to all creatures to the act of blessing, from the highest and heavenly down to the earthly and to the individual who here sings, vv. 19-22.

The structure of this as of the following song plainly rests on strophés with four verses or eight short members; the now visible departures from this have no significance. But in the following point both songs are (I., pp. 172 sq., *Dichter des A. B.*) formed quite after the old congregational songs,—that each begins with a short prelude and closes with a similar aftersong; and while both are here connected somewhat closely with the other words, the first and last strophé may thus be somewhat longer. How thoroughly the two songs form at the will of the poet but *one* higher whole,—designed to praise God, according to the two primary forces and effects of His existence as sensible to man (the historical and the eternal) —is clear also from this similar artistic arrangement. The fact that along with this the first is completed in five, the second in eight strophés, is accidental, occasioned by the special contents.

1.

1 *Bless, my soul, Jahvé,*
  all my inward parts His holy name!
 Bless, my soul, Jahvé,
  and forget not all His benefits.
 Who forgave all Thy guilt,
  healed all Thy weaknesses,
 Who loosed from the pit Thy life,
  Who crowned Thee with grace and compassion,
5 Who satisfies Thy spirit with good,
  that, like the eagles, Thy youth becomes new!

2.

 Gracious-right Jahvé ever executes—
  and judgment for all the oppressed;
 reveals His ways to Moses,
  to Israel's sons His deeds;

compassionate and gracious is Jahvé,
    and long-suffering, rich in mercy,
not chiding for ever,
    not for ever bearing grudge.

3.

Not according to our sins did He to us,   10
    not according to our debts did He take us,
but as the heaven overtops the earth,
    prevailed for His fearers His mercy;
as the sunrise far from the sunset,
    He thrust our debts far from us;
as a father pities his children,
    Jahvé pities His fearers.

4.

For He knoweth our frame,
    is mindful that we are dust:
mortal man—as grass are his days,   15
    as the field's flower—so he blooms;
for a wind has passed through him—he is gone,
    no longer his place knows him.
But Jahvé's mercy is from ever to ever on His fearers,
    and His gracious-right to childrens' children,
to those that keep His covenant,
    and think on His commands to do them.

5.

Jahvé has erected His throne in heaven,
    and His kingdom rules over all.
Bless Jahvé, ye His messengers,   20
    mighty heroes who execute His word,
His loud word obeying!
bless Jahvé, all ye His hosts,
    His servants who execute His will;

bless Jahvé, all ye His works,
in all places of His dominion!
Bless, my soul, Jahvé!

Vv. 3-5 plainly contain truths which the individual can only utter for himself so far as they hold good for the whole community; but they might peculiarly thus hold good for the new community.—עֲדִי, ver 5, is understood by the Targ. of age in opposition to youth, but עַד is ever merely duration, time, eternity; it is better understood as a quite different word, LXX ἐπιθυμία, the *spirit*, the *desire*, named from uprising, swelling, comp. the active *ghatha*, Arab., *nourish*, prop. cause to grow; comp. above on xxxii. 9. On the figure of the eagle, comp. Isa. xl. 31, Ter. *Heaut.*, iii., 2, 11, Abulf, *Hist. Anteisl.*, p. 20, 5-8. Ver. 8 from Ex. xxxiv. 6; the hyperbolical, ver. 18, with which similarly the fourth strophe closes, is likewise from Ex. xx. 6, but with respect to the usage in Deut. v. 1, vii. 11, xi. 22, xvii. 19, xix. 9.—Ver. 11 after xxxvi. 6; ver. 12 after Mikha vii. 19; 15, 16 after Job vii. 10, viii. 18, xiv. 2. *Our frame*, ver. 14,—our nature from the creation onwards. Ver. 19 an echo from Ps. xciii. sqq., but with the new word מַלְכוּת. But it is noteworthy that our poet, vv. 20-22, distinguishes as three grades of animated beings from above downwards, (1) the highest angels about the Divine throne; (2) the other angels, as those of the stars, of the winds, etc.; (3) earthly creatures. But these last words on the spirits, from the highest heaven onwards, form a good transition to the following song, vv. 1-4.

Ps. civ. calls men on the other hand to bless Jahvé only in so far as He is the Creator and Lord of the world. As now the whole creation here in all parts and colours freely stood before the later poet as the subject of his song: we have to admire that he, though borrowing from an older type, yet sketched a description, so well chosen, apt, often genuinely poetical and original. His pattern is the description, Gen. i.: but by its high spirit he is himself so inspired that he produces a new and splendid Whole, which recalls the former only in a few traits and indications. For first of all he knows how to interweave in the highest and most beautiful manner with the present as a permanent fact that which in Gen. i. appears as merely past; and every poet most expressively praises God from the Creation as it ever abides and continues. Then he adorns the parts given in detail in Gen. ii. with peculiar touches, in such a way that throughout, the Creation still more stands forth in its infinite greatness, order, and life, and the praise of Jahvé becomes thereby more definite and more intense. Finally he follows the series of particular works of Creation defined in Gen. i., but with poetic freedom and sensuousness, without constraint and empty imitation, rather renewing and altering much in the most happy manner. The six days' work subsides of itself, for the poet has no historical object. If he therefore, vv. 0-4, begins with the light and clouded heaven, as in Gen. i. 3-8, he does it only to praise the Creator from the highest and most invisible side of the Creation, thence to come down gradually to the lower and lesser earthly things. The description of the sea now firmly ordered and bounded from the previous chaos, vv. 5-9, according to Gen. i. 9, 10, is followed by the description of the firm land, vv. 10-18, according to Gen. i. 11, 12, but beautifully transformed here, so that we glance over the firm land immediately in all its glory and animation; also the figure of the heavenly bodies, vv. 19-23, after Gen. i. 14-18, is more nearly referred to the present order of the living; and the poet —having happily interwoven the birds, land animals, and men, Gen. i. 24 sqq., with the previous description,—approaches the end, as if accidentally recalling further the not less wondrous life of the sea (Gen. i. 21-23 in part), vv. 24-30; and then returning to the beginning with blessed wonder, he concludes; but before the last conclusion, suddenly, as if awakening and looking into the actual human world, he is seized by the wish that through such knowledge of Jahvé finally sin may pass away, vv. 31-35.

We cannot fail to recognize how similar our poet is to that of Ps. cxxxix. Only the language sounds somewhat differently; and here particularly when the poet with the greatest brevity would suggest so inconceivably much, it is pointed into unusual conciseness, frequently as by a bound passing over from one topic to another. And yet all down to the great pause at the end of the fifth strophé, ver. 23, is only like a single much-complicated proposition in the praise of *Him who* is so described; all the intermediate words, especially in the beginning of new strophés, vv. 10, 14, comp. vv. 2, 3, 13, continue the description of Him, and pass over, only where the past is to be brought into relief in the beginning of strophés, vv. 5, 19, into the *perf*.

1.

1   *Bless, my soul, Jahvé!*
       Jahvé, Thou my God, very great art Thou,
         adorned with pomp and glory !
       Who in light clothes Himself as in a cloak,
         stretches the heaven out like a carpet,
       Who with water supports His lofts,
         Who makes clouds His chariot,
         Who on wind's-wings walks ;
       Who makes winds His messengers,
         His servants flaming fire !

2.

5   Who fixed the earth upon its foundations :
       it will not tremble for ever, aye.
    Had'st covered it with flood as garments,
       on the mountains stand waters :

before Thy threatening they flee,
  before Thy loud thunder they tremble away—
—mountains rise, valleys sink—
  at the place which Thou hast founded for them;
the bound Thou didst set they overstep not,
  return not, to cover the earth!

3.

He sends forth springs into the brooks,   10
  between mountains they go,
all field-beasts drink,
  wild asses break their thirst;
above them dwell heaven's birds,
  from the midst of the twigs loudly sounding.
He waters the mountains from His lofts:
  of Thy hands' fruit the earth is full!

4.

He causes grass to sprout for the cattle,
  herb for the service of men,
    drawing out of the earth food:
wine, that rejoices man's heart   15
  that his face shines more than with fat,
bread, that sustains man's heart;
satisfied also are Jahvé's trees,
  cedars of Libanon, by Him planted,
where little birds nest,
  the stork has the figtrees for her house;
mountains, the highest, for wild goats,
  rocks a refuge for rock-mice.—

5.

He made the moon for feasts,
  the sun knows its setting:

20 makest darkness—and it is night,
>therein stir all the forest beasts,
young lions roar after spoil
>>and from God to demand their food;
the sun brightens up—they go home,
>lie down in their dens,
man goes forth to his business,
>and to his work until the evening.—

6.

How many are, O Jahvé, Thy works!
>all of them hast Thou wrought with wisdom;
>>full is the earth of Thy creations!
25 Yonder sea, great, broad-sided—
>there is swarming innumerable,
>>beasts, little and great;
there go ships,
>the Monster made by Thee to play with Him.

7.

All wait upon Thee,
>that Thou mayest give their food in season.
Didst Thou give to them—they gather together,
>didst open Thy hand—they fill themselves with good;
Didst hide Thy countenance—they are amazed,
>drawest in Thy spirit—they expire,
>return to their dust;
dost send Thy spirit forth—they are created,
>and renewest the earth's countenance.

8.

30 Eternal be Jahvé's honour,
>let Jahvé rejoice in His works!
He who looks to the earth—and it trembles,
>touches mountains—they smoke.

Sing I to Jahvé as long as I live,
 play to my God as long as I exist!
well-pleasing to Him be my poesy,
 I will rejoice in Jahvé!
May sinners pass away from the earth,   35
 wicked men be no more!
Bless, my soul, Jahvé!

Ver. 2 *b* after Isa. xl. 22; ver. 3 *a* after Am. ix. 6: if the lower heaven appears the firm underpart of the heavenly building, so must the bright watery clouds reaching into infinite heights correspond to the airy lofts or upper rooms of human dwellings. And from these very heights winds and lightnings as servants of Jahvé appear to hasten into the lower world, as was said in ciii. 20, 21. On vv. 6-9, comp. the pattern, Job xxxviii. 8-11; how before the stern threatening command of Jahvé the watery chaos so divides that the water, which but now covered all, quickly collects itself into the depths assigned to it, while now first mountains and valleys become visible in the firm land. Hence ver. 8 *a* must be a parenthesis, for ver. 8 *b* and ver. 9 only complete the image of the sea-water, and admit no other reference. The laudatory fine description thus involuntarily coincides with that in Ovid, *Metam.* i. 43 sq. We must be on our guard against explaining the words of the parenthesis, which thus gives a good sense, from the similar cvii. 26, placing the two in juxtaposition. The latter are not sufficiently alike, and stand in quite another connexion; nor are they by the same poet. Ver. 7 after lxxvii. 17-19.—
Vv. 10-18. Very aptly along with man and his joy arising from the earth's fruitfulness, that of the wild beasts is thought of, which live without needing man, ver. 11 (after Job xxxviii. 26, xxxix. 5), and of the cedars in like manner not tended by man, ver. 16. Most charming is the picture which the poet associates with the change of day and night, vv. 20-23, as also the night is not without fresh peculiar stirring and life, but

the day calling man to toil, scares all rude and wild creatures. Ver. 26. בֹּו must also according to Job xl. 29, stand in close connexion with שִׂחֶק־בּוֹ; *with Him*; in itself it might signify *in it* (the sea), but then עִמּוֹ would stand more plainly as in the some connexion, Job xl. 20; in the first instance the ־בְּ with שִׂחֵק, *play*, must always signify *with*, and probably signifies this in Prov. viii. 30 sq. in a similar description. If this is referred, as the context demands, to God, the sense is: men should guard against playing with the crocodile and similar monsters as with tame domestic animals, but before Jahvé even these monsters are tame and tractable, as immediately, vv. 27-30, is finely described; in like manner ver. 28 is from Job xxxiv. 15. But this vivid description is completely understood only when we consider that according to p. 233 all these legends about such monsters were at that time told in Israel with new vividness; comp. Philo *de Jona*, capp. xlii.-xlv. (II., pp. 604 sq., *Aucher.*) *Bundehesh*, cap. 18.—Ver. 35 is—for the poet so full of God is quickly carried away by indignation at the continuance of sin on earth,—a very similar conclusion to cxxxix. 19.: but as if in a prelude to this the spirit urges him in ver. 32 to throw into the midst of his happy reflection on the surpassing glory and goodness of God the serious counter picture thereof in the thought of the earthquake.

Ps. cvi. and cvii. stand again in reciprocal relation, so that the one receives its full meaning only from the other. Ps. cvi. is, according to vv. 4, 5, 47, the prayer of the Israelites still far dispersed for a long time after the rebuilding of Jerusalem, for final reunion in the holy land and redemption,—under hope indeed of the inexhaustible goodness of Jahvé, but at the same time with lively consciousness of guilt; and if the ancient history in many and painful ways calls the guilt of Israel to remembrance, it also shows the high examples of eternal and Divine grace. Hence there is here developed in recollection of the old history of Israel the consciousness of guilt and consolation of the people of that time; and after the whole community of the still unhappy and dispersed Israelites has introduced the song with prayer, and confession of sin, vv. 1-3, one as a choir-leader carries out further the sense of the community from the ancient history, vv. 4-46, till finally the community concludes briefly with the most weighty prayer, ver. 47, and the Priest with the blessing, ver. 48. The historic presentation is here much less vigorous, and the verse-structure narrower than above, Ps. lxxviii. Also the build of the strophes is less firm; we observe only that the review of the ancient history is carried—(1) down to the wonder at the Red Sea, ver. 12, then down to the sojourn at Sinai, ver. 23, further down to the end of Moses' life, ver. 33, and finally over the time of the Judges, ver. 46. The strophé has thus on an average ten verses, the last a few more.

It is noteworthy in the case of this song that it must have been composed for Israelites outside the holy land, whether they sojourned in Babylon or elsewhere in the land of the stranger. But that here we must think of Babylonia, is certainly evident from cvii. 3, where *the sea* signifies not as in Palestine the West, but as in Babylonia (comp. also B. Jes. xxi. 1) the South. There is actually found in the two songs nothing peculiarly alluding to Jerusalem; and also the style, especially in Ps. cvii., is unusual. The more remarkable are both songs.

(The Chorus.)

Sing praise to Jahvé, because He is good,   1
  because His grace is for ever!
Who will tell of Jahvé's great deeds,
  will make known all His praise?
Blessed they who keep the dues,
  he who practises right at all times!

(Leader of the Chorus.)

Think of me, Jahvé, with Thy people's love,
  visit me with Thy deliverance

5 that I may enjoy the happiness of Thy Beloved,
  may rejoice with Thy people's joy,
   boast with Thy heritage!
We have sinned like to our fathers,
  have failed, done wickedly!
Our fathers in Egypt esteemed not Thy wonders,
  thought not of the multitude of Thy graces,
   rose up at the sea, at the reed-sea:
yet He helped them for His name's sake,
  to make known His power,
and threatened the reed-sea,—it dried up,
  and led them through floods as through pastures,
10 helped them from the hater's hand,
  redeemed them from the foe's hand,
and water covered their oppressors,
  not one remained of them;
then they believed on His words,
  celebrating His glory. — —
Soon had they forgotten His works,
  not staying for His counsel,
and conceived in the desert a lust,
  tempted in the dry plains God:
15 then He gave them their wish
  and sent contagion into their life.
And they were jealous in the camp against Moses,
  Ahron, the holy one of Jahvé;
opening, the earth swallowed up Dathan,
  and covered Abiram's band,
and fire burned up their band,
  the flame scorches wicked men.
They make at Horeb a calf,
  and do homage to the cast figure,
20 changed their majesty
  for an ox-figure, eating grass,
forgot God Who helped them,

who did great things in Egypt,
many wonders in the land of Ham,
    fearful things at the reed-sea;
then had He bidden to destroy them, had not Moses
    His chosen one placed himself in the rent before
        Him,
    to check His wrath, not to destroy. — —
And they despised the land of longing,
    not believing on His word,
and became stubborn in the tents,   25
    not listening to the voice of Jahvé:
then He swore to them with high hand
    to overthrow them in the desert,
to overthrow their seed among heathen
    and to scatter them in the lands.
And they clave to Baal Péor,
    and ate sacrifices from the dead,
and vexed Him by their deeds;
    then the plague broke in among them;
and Pin'has stood and prayed;   30
    then was the plague checked,
and it was reckoned to Him for righteousness,
    for all ages, even for ever.
And provoked Him at the Meriba-water,
    then evil befell Moses for their sakes
because they rose against his spirit
    and he was hasty with his lips. — —
They destroyed not the peoples
    given up to them by Jahvé,
and mixed with heathen   35
    and learned their works,
and served their images,
    which became a snare to them;
and sacrificed their own sons,
    their own daughters to phantoms,

shed their innocent blood, their own sons' and daughters'
              blood,
 they sacrificed to Kanáan's images,
  so that the land was polluted by slaughter,
 and impure they became through their works,
  and fornicators by their own deeds:
40 then was Jahvé's anger glowing against His people,
  and horror He cast on His heritage,
 and gave it over into heathens' hand
  that their haters ruled them,
 and their foes oppressed them,
  they themselves bowed under their hand.
Many times did He save them:
  but they resisted in their own counsels,
  and sank by their own sin deeper;
He saw when they were in straits,
  listening to their complaint,
remembered His covenant with them,
  found repentance in the multitude of His graces;
and caused them to find compassion
  before all their tyrants.

     (Chorus.)
45 Help us, Jahvé our God,
  gather us out of the heathen,
 that we may thank Thy holy name,
 that we may boast of Thy praise!

    (The Priest.)
 Blessed be Jahvé, Israel's God,
  from everlasting and to everlasting!
 and let all people say, "Assuredly!"

Ver. 1 after cxviii. 1-4. Ver. 7 after Ex. xiv. 11, 12; ver. 12, Ex. xv.; ver. 13 after Ex. xvi., Num. xi.; on ver. 15 comp.

lxxviii. 23-30. Ver. 16, Num. xvi. Vv. 19-23, Ex. xxxii.—
xxxiv. Vv. 24-27, Num. xiv. Levit. xxvi. 31 sqq. Vv. 28-31,
Num. xxv. Vv. 32, 33, Num. xx. 2-13. Vv. 34-46, Josúa—
Kings.—The *dead*, ver. 28, are the no-gods, the opposition to
the living God.

Ps. cvii. gives on the other hand the great thank-song of
those assembled about the holy place, after they had come
thither from all distances and a thousand dangers. After the
short introduction, vv. 1-3, follows, as in the roundelay, the
same summons to thanksgiving to all kinds of the redeemed,
those (1) from the desert, (2) imprisonment, (3) sickness,
(4) saved from the sea,—in four strophés, vv. 4-28; until at
last the thanksgiving again becomes general towards Jahvé as
the Friend and Former of mankind, but also the just Punisher
of all the wicked, vv. 29-43. The alternation of the singers is
as in the preceding Psalm, and the main feature consists here
as there of four strophés; but otherwise the arrangement is,
because of the very different contents, a different one. In each
of the four main strophés those summoned to give thanks are
at the outset more closely described in four verses,—a description which becomes in the last, because of the peculiar dangers
and wonders of sea-faring, still more vivid, and is doubled to
eight verses; that the second on the other hand has five is only
a kind of accident. But the summons to give thanks at every
two verses, is here the ever similar echo, into which certainly
the Chorus breaks. The higher after-song is extended however into a longest strophé of ten verses, unbroken, before the
closing word, apparently sung by a priest, ver. 43.

> *Sing praise to Jahvé, because He is good,*   1
>   *because His grace is for ever!*
> thus speak Jahvé's free men,
>   from the foe's hand by Him redeemed,

and by Him gathered out of the lands,
out of the East and out of the West,
out of the North and out of the sea!

1.

They who wandered in the desert, the dry way,
finding no habitable city,
5   in hunger, also in thirst,
their soul fainting in them!
and sore oppressed crying to Jahvé
by Him freed from their distresses,
by Him were led in the right way,
to travel to a habitable city:
*they thank Jahvé for His grace
and His wonders for the children of men,*
that He satisfied the languishing soul,
the hungry filled with good!

2.

10   They who sat in gloom and darkness,
in suffering and iron sore fettered,
because they resisted the words of God,
had despised the Highest's counsel,
so that He by grief bowed their heart,
made them stumble without deliverer;
and sore oppressed crying to Jahvé
by Him freed from their distresses,
were brought out of gloom and darkness,
free, their chains broken:
15   *they thank Jahvé for His goodness
and His wonders for the children of men,*
that He broke asunder iron doors,
broke down iron bars!

3.

They who guilty because of their sins,
grieving for their misdeeds,

loathing in themselves all food,
    already reached to death's gates;
and sore oppressed to Jahvé crying
    by Him were freed from distresses,
while He, sending His word, healed them,   20
    saved them from their graves:
they thank Jahvé for His grace
    and His wonders for the children of men,
and sacrifice sacrifices of thanksgiving,
    tell His deeds full of jubilation!

4.

They that go into the sea with ships,
    are busy on many waters,
there have they seen Jahvé's deeds
    and His wonders in the flood:
how He commanded—and caused storm-wind to come, 25
    which raised its waves;
—towards heaven rising, sinking to the floods,
    their soul melts in ill,
they whirl, stagger like the drunkard,
    all their wisdom is exhausted;—
and sore oppressed to Jahvé crying
    by Him were freed from distresses;
—He brings the storm to a whistling,
    that its waves rested,
and, joyous that they are quiet,   30
    He led them to the haven of their pleasure:—
they thank Jahvé for His grace,
    and His wonders for the children of men,
and praise Him in the people's assembly,
    lauding Him in the council of the Elders!

5.

He turns streams into desert,
    water-springs into dryness,

fruit-land into salt-waste,
 for the wickedness of the dwellers:
35 turns the desert into water-land,
 dry land into water-springs,
caused the hungry there to settle,
 who founded habitable cities,
sowed fields and planted vineyards,
 obtained rich fruit,
and by Him blessed greatly increased,
 —also their cattle He diminishes not,—
but lessened, sank deeper
 because of misery and the pressure of trouble;
40 He pours contempt on the mighty,
confuses them in the pathless waste,
but protects the needy from misery,
 leads as the flock the tribes,
that seeing this upright men may rejoice,
 all wickedness close the mouth:
Who is wise, let him note this,
that Jahvé's graces may be understood!

Ver. 4. The force of the relative clause continues, from vv. 2, 3, ver. 33 from vv. 31, 32; comp. the like above in civ. 5.—Most noteworthy are the images which the after-song, vv. 32-42, sketches: proceeding from the general grand Divine changes of human fate ever according to their desert, and from places like B. Jes. xli. 18, it draws first, vv. 33, 34, the gloomy picture of a land laid waste by men's wickedness, opposes to it, vv. 35-39, that of a land blooming on all sides by human toil (this is the people of Israel of that time!) and causes at the end, ver. 29, to be seen that still many a tear-pearl of grief and loss in human life falls even into this serene picture, but firmly rises, vv. 40-42, above this, with Messianic hopes which are held out by poetic words even of the Book of Job, ver. 40 from Job xii. 21, 24; ver. 41 *b*, Job xxi. 11; ver. 42, Job v. 16;

ver. 43 from Hos. xiv. 10.—Most plainly correspond lvi. 47, and cvii. 3; cvi. 2 and cvii. 43.

Pss. cxi., cxii. form in close mutual connexion, a progressive comparison, carried out not without beauty, of the glory of Jahvé, and that of the worshipper of Jahvé, —so that what is said in the first song of Jahve's praise, greatness, deeds, recurs in the second applied to the praise, greatness, deeds of the saint. With similar verse-structure to Ps. cxix., yet not by the same poet, the alphabet appears twice carried through, in each song proceeding with each member. Here too involuntarily the Messianic element presses in, cxi. 6, cxii. 2. The membering of the verses is here also maintained with such perfect correctness, that only the last two verses are three-membered.

All my heart praises Jahvé 1
    Blesses Him in full assembly of the righteous;
Deeds of Jahvé are exalted,
    Eagerly desired by all their friends.
For ever stands His righteousness:
    Glory and pomp is His work.
High is the fame of wonders which He founded,
    In grace and mildness is Jahvé rich.
Jahvé gave support to His fearers, 5
    Knows eternal truth of His covenant;
Let the power of His deeds be known to His people,
    Making over to them the heathens' heritage.
Naught but truth and right are the deeds of His hands,
    Orderly are all His commands,
Pledged firm for ever, aye,
    Righteously and truly done.
Succour hath He sent to His people,
    True shall His covenant for ever be;
    Unutterably holy is His Name.
Veneration of Jahvé is wisdom's beginning; 10

Well have they understanding who live thereon ;
To (*Zur*) eternity stands fast His praise.

---

1   A man that fears Jahvé is blessed,
By His commands tarrying with joy :
Doth not his seed become mighty in the land ?
Excellent men are blessed ;
Fulness and riches is in his house,
Goodness stands for ever.
Heaven shines on the upright in darkness,
In grace and mildness rich and right.
5   Joy to the man who wishes well and lends ;
Knows how to maintain his causes in judgment !
Live doth he never troubling,
Maintains eternal fame the righteous ;
Never doth he quake before evil lying-mouth,
Over fear, trusting Jahvé, his heart rises :
Pledge-firm is his heart's rest,
Remains till he sees judgment on his oppressors.
10   Spending, he loves to distribute to the needy ;
True stands his righteousness for ever,
Upward ever proudly strives his horn.
Vexed, the wicked shall see it,
Will gnash teeth and pass away ;
To (*Zu*) the ground goes the pleasure of the wicked.

cxii. 4, חנון, etc. is a subordinate clause to לישרים with reference to cxi. 4. One might suppose indeed that the two halves of ver. 4 formed only one clause in the sense : " as light in the darkness, shined upon the upright man the Gracious one," *i.e.*, God, comp. B. Jes., lx. 1 sqq. ; but according to the clear build of these two songs each member proceeding with the alphabet gives for itself a full sense. As for the rest, the poet employs as late songs as Ps. xxxvii. 12, 26 ; ver. 9 *b* is from 1 Sam. ii. 1.

Ps. cxiii. sq. is unquestionably a Pascha-song. For tho the piece, Ps. cxiv. sketches a short, but highly vivid picture, dominating history with genuine lyric power, of the grand time of the going-forth from Egypt, and of the education of Israel to independence. The whole creation is in uproar, all trembling and shaking; in the confusion all is at first full of alarm, so that the question resounds: whence your unrest, ye seas and mountains? But so soon as it has become plain that Jahvé is the author, the astonishment changes into calmness and reverence. This fine fragment which brings out with perfect propriety the fast which the Pascha solemnizes, has not much meaning in itself, if it has not the above particular object in view; and is also by no means entirely self-defined, for in ver. 2 the name of Jahvé is wanting. The piece Ps. cxiii. contains therefore in addition to this historical praise of Jahvé, the main portion of the Pascha-solemnity, the indispensable prelude in the general praise of Jahvé as the infinitely exalted Redeemer, who for that very reason, as the second piece then announces, became in days gone by Israel's Redeemer. The two fragments thus only compose the full song; perhaps between the halves a sacrifice is to be presented. The style too infers the same poet. But this poet was also certainly the same who composed the previous delicate pair of songs; this follows from the manner in which the use of 1 Sam. ii. 1 sqq., begun in cxii. 9 is here continued.

    Praise Jahvé's servants,   1
        praise Jahvé's name!
    Jahvé's name be blessed
        now and to eternity!
    from the sun's uprise to His setting
        be praised Jahvé's name!
    High is over all peoples Jahvé,
        over heaven His power!

5 Who is like to Jahvé our God,
  to Him Who is throned sublimely on high :
  to Him Who deeply casts His glances
   on the heaven, on the earth;
  who out of the dust sets up the lowly,
   raises from dung the needy,
  to rule along with the mighty,
   with the mighty of His people;
  who causes the unfaithful of the house to rule
   as rejoicing mothers of children.

---

1 When Israel forsook Egypt,
  Jakob's house the foreign people:
 Juda became His sanctuary,
  Israel His dominion.
 The sea saw it—and fled,
  Jordan fell back;
 mountains danced like rams,
  hills like the young sheep.—
5 Sea, what ails thee that thou fleest,
  Jordan, fallest back?
 mountains, that ye dance like rams,
  hills, like young sheep?
 —Before the Lord—yea tremble, earth,
  before the God of Jakob;
 who changes the rock into watery swamp,
  flinty earth into a water-spring.

  cxiii. 7-9 almost verbally from 1 Sam. ii. 5-8; but suddenly also here ver. 9, the ancient historical picture turns to Messianic hope with a glance at B. Jes. liv., 1 sqq.—cxiv. 4 after xxix. 6, comp. Hab. iii. 8; ver. 8 after Ex. xvii., Num. xx. 2 sqq. The sea after Ex. xiv. sq., the mountains after Ex. xix.

The shortest congregational song is Ps. cxvii. :

Praise Jahvé, all ye people, 1
praise Him, all ye races of earth !
over us truly His grace prevails,
and the faithfulness of Jahvé is for ever.
Praise Jah !

The stamp of the style of this very short song refers it to this time ; עָלֵינוּ, ver. 1 in this signification, recurs, after the quite isolated use in Ps. lxiii. 4 only in cxlv. 4, cxlvii. 12, and in B. Qôhelet; and the mode of expression, ver. 2 *a*, only in ciii. 11. The הללו יה at the end belongs (Vol. I., p. 16) at least only according to the latest use, to the song itself.

C. 139-142.—PSALMS LXXXVI., CVIII., CXLIII., CXLIV.,

are songs which were in manifold ways composed and renewed from earlier ones, and which we may best conceive as borrowed from a book in which a poet of this time published very many songs of this kind. It was pre-eminently the feeling of oppression both of the individual and of the whole community by the heathen rulers in which in this poet both the urgent supplicatory and the courageously believing ring of the older songs were anew brought to life, and combined in his spirit in new forms.

Ps. lxxxvi. thus contains the prayer of an individual for protection in a time of distress from without, almost solely composed from recollections of earlier related songs, not without delicate feeling. But the situation of the praying one is here quite another than that in the long Ps. cxix. : he feels himself so sorely persecuted only by the tyranny of the heathen. —The strophés are manifestly built on five verses with eleven members; but we must not fail to recognize that the last words, vv. 14-17, might also form a small song of similar contents by itself.

1.

1 Bend, Jahvé, thine ear, listen to me,
    for suffering and helpless am I !
preserve my soul, for I am a saint,
    help Thy servant, *Thou*, my God,
    him who trusts on Thee !
be gracious to me, O Lord,
    for to Thee I cry at all times !
rejoice Thy servant's soul,
    for to Thee, Lord, I raise my soul !
5 because Thou, O Lord, art kind and pardoning
    and rich in mercy for all who cry to Thee.

2.

Hearken, Thou Jahvé, to my prayer,
    observe the loud words of my supplication,
on the day of my distress I cry to Thee,
    because Thou wilt hear me !
Like Thee there is none among Gods, Lord,
    and no works are like Thine ;
the peoples all which Thou hast made,
    they will come, do homage before Thee, O Lord,
    and give honour to Thy name,
10 because great Thou art and doing wonders,
    Thou, God, alone art so.

3.

Teach me, O Jahvé, Thy way,
    let me walk in Thy truth ;
    my heart make one, to fear Thy name !
I will praise Thee, Lord, my God, with all my heart,
    I ever honour Thy name,
that Thy mercy ruled on high over me,
    Thou didst snatch my soul from the deepest hell !

    *   *   *
    *   *   *

Gŏd! insolent ones stand against me
and a band of madmen seek my soul,
not holding Thee before their eyes:
but Thou, Lord, art a God full of pity, grace, 15
long-suffering, rich in mercy and truth.
Turn Thee to me, be gracious to me,
give Thy servant Thy splendour,
help Thou the son of Thy maid!
show me a sign for good,
let my haters see it and blush,
that Thou, Jahvé, didst stand by me and comfort me!

Prayer because of personal misery and great longing for salvation, above all supported on the grace, vv. 1-5, then first vv. 6-10, on the power of the supreme God, reaching over all the heathen. In His ways, the poet, strengthened and led by Him, desires to remain, vv. 11-13 [therefore he will not doubt, though sore oppressed, vv. 14-17]. Ver. 1 after xl. 18; ver. 2 after iv. 4; ver. 4 after xxv. 1; ver. 6 from cxvi. 1; ver. 8 from Ex. xv. 11; ver. 9 from xxii. 28, 29; ver. 11 from xxvii. 11, v. 9, xxv. 4, 5; ver. 14 almost verbally from liv. 5, only בידי for בזדי; ver. 15 from Ex. xxxiv. 6; ver. 16 c from cxvi. 16.

Still more finely selected from old songs and more profoundly striking is Ps. cxliii., which—simply because of its otherwise quite independent origin—cannot be derived from the poet of the songs Pss. cxl.—cxlii. The distress in which the poet thus prayed, came to him as to the poet of the preceding song, from the side of the heathen, and generally the song has much that is related to the preceding. In it three strophés may be distinguished, the second of which proceeds from recollection of the old history; but the measure of these strophés is not strict.

1.

1   Jahvé, hear my prayer, observe my supplication,
       through Thy faithfulness grant me Thy salvation;
   and come not into judgment with Thy servant,
       for no living one before Thee is just!—
For the enemy has pursued my soul,
       trodden down to earth my life
       into darkness cast me like the old dead;
and fainting has my spirit become,
       in my bosom my heart is affrighted.

2.

5   I think of days of old,
       I meditate on all Thy doing,
       I ruminate concerning Thy handiwork;
I spread forth my hands to Thee,
       like a thirsty land my soul strives to Thee: *
haste to hear me, Jahvé! my spirit passes away!
hide not Thy countenance from me,
       that I become like those sunk into the grave!
let me soon perceive Thy grace; for in Thee I trust;
       show me the way I should go:
       for to Thee I lift my soul!
free me from my foes, Jahvé!
       in Thee have I confided!—

3.

10   Teach me to do Thy pleasure; for Thou art my God;
       Thy good spirit will lead me on the level earth!
for Thy name, Jahvé, Thou wilt quicken me,
       wilt through Thy salvation take my soul from
                                               distress,
and wilt through Thy grace destroy my foes,
       bring to naught all oppressors of my life,
   for I am Thy servant!

Ver. 1 comp. lxv. 6; cxviii. 5. Ver. 2 from Job xiv. 3, 4, and seq. Ver. 3 from lxxxviii. 6, or rather immediately from Lam. iii. 6. Ver. 4 from cxlii. 4, lxi. 3, lxxvii. 4. Ver. 5 from lxxvii. 6. Ver. 6 from lxiii. 2. Ver. 7 from xxviii. 1. Vv. 8 and 10, 11, from li. 10-13, v. 9, xxv. 1. פָּצִיתִי, ver. 9, was treated by the Massôretes as if it were *I have concealed*, *i.e.*, secretly spoken *to Thee*. But this is harsh and unintelligible. Better the LXX κατέφυγον, as if it were mis-written for חָסִיתִי. חסה is indeed elsewhere connected with בְּ, yet it might for once stand as well with אֶל like בְמַח, xxxi. 7, lvi. 4.

Ps. cxliv. 1-11 gives, on the other hand, rather a recast composition of older pieces of warlike mood, with which the individual less from his own experience than in the spirit and temper of the whole ancient community may long for the help of Jahvé against heathen. In other respects the character of the whole song shows so surprising a resemblance to the two preceding, that it must for this reason be ascribed to the same poet.

1.

O Thou blessed Jahvé, my rock,   1
   who didst inure my hands to the fight,
   to the war my fingers,
Who art my grace and my retreat,
   my defence and my deliverer,
my shield and He whom I trusted,
   who subjected the peoples to me:
Jahvé, what is man that Thou dost recognize him,
   the son of earth that Thou regardest him?
man—to breath is he like,
   his life is like a shadow that passes away.

2.

Jahvé! bow thy heavens, coming down,   5
   touch the mountains, that they smoke,

lighten a flash, that Thou mayest scatter them,
send Thy arrows out, to scare them,
reach Thy hands out of the height,
draw me and save me from many waters,
out of the power of the strangers,
of them whose mouth speaks only vanity
and whose oath is a lying oath!

3.

God! a new song will I sing to Thee,
with harp of ten strings play to Thee!
10 Thou who givest victory to kings,
who saved David His servant from the evil sword:
draw me and save me from strangers,
from them whose mouth speaks only vanity
and whose oath is a lying oath!

As the first words proceed from the consciousness of the height already won, vv. 1, 2, to prayer for deliverance from the strangers, vv. 5-8, they are connected by the contemplation of the weakness of human life, according to which, if help comes not at the right time to the wretched, it may generally come in vain, vv. 3, 4 But in the joyous recollection of the ancient high days of victory of Israel the poet now begs for the Divine help against heathen, vv. 9-11. The description of the strangers (heathen) as entirely faithless, vv. 8, 11, is here, according to the words, the one new element, where also ימין, *the right hand,* stands noteworthily for the right hand lifted to swear; almost all the rest is from older passages. Vv. 1, 2, 5-7, from xviii. 35, 3, 48, 10, 15, 17; "the strangers," vv. 7, 11, from xviii. 45, 46, only that here throughout instead of David all Israel must be thought of. Ver. 3 from viii. 5; ver. 4 from Job xiv. 2 and elsewhere; ver. 5 *b* from civ. 32; on vv. 9, 15, comp. xxxiii. 2, 3, 12.

The words cxliv. 12-15, fall apart, according to what has been said above, and they certainly formed at first a small song by itself, as this poet constructed it almost entirely from the fragment of an old song, and as it is explained above, Vol. 1. pp. 154 sqq. A closer connexion of sense between vv. 12-15 and vv. 1-11 is also, according to the plain purpose and art of this later poet, inconceivable ; but we saw already in the case of lxxxvi. 14-17 (p. 303) that this poet probably formed also out of older fragments smaller songs of only one-strophé with four verses.

Hence we may justly derive further from this poet Ps. cviii., which is simply a composition from lvii. 8-18, and lx. 7-14,—a few words of high hope and national prayer loosely joined to one another, but distributed into three small strophés as this poet preferred, vv. 2-6, 7-10, 11-14. This last poet found, according to all traces, the two songs lvii. and lx. already in this series and mutual nearness (comp. Vol. I., p. 28), and selected from both the finest pieces for a new song. But he had already cxliv. 2, the words Ps. lix. 11, lxvii. sq., in his eye.

D. 143-152. PSALMS XXXIII., CV., CXXXV., CXXXVI., CXLIV.—CL.,

belong not merely to the latest songs, but also proceed probably from one poet. This is seen in several words and expressions peculiar to it, like the frequent חסידים, the oft-recurring שֶׂבֶר, *hope* (after civ. 27), the now again more frequent שֶׁ for אֲשֶׁר, as well as בְּכֹל, xxxiii. 7, cxlvii. 2, כֹּנֵס, cxlvi. 9, cxlvii. 6, זֹאת, cxlv. 14, cxlvi. 8, etc. Peculiar to the poet further is the long enumeration of all similar things, the many short allusions to particular parts and pieces of the Creation and present world, along with the almost throughout simply artificial collocation of older fragments.—In other respects, there prevails once more a more joyous spirit through these songs which worthily close the long cycle, and this is readily understood from the time from which they plainly sprung. For in the case of Ps. cxlvii. we must obviously think of the first time of the full restoration of the walls of Jerusalem under Nehemjá's vigorous activity, Neh. xii. 27, in the case of Ps. cxlix. of the slight struggles under the same hero, Neh. vi. 1 sqq.; and this very time was the best which under the Persian dominion still cast the gleam of a purer elevation and joy into the heart of the people.—This poet has also once more much elegant smoothness and softness in the arrangement and execution of the songs, but the external completion is already almost predominant.

We begin here with Ps. cv., because in spite of the very different contents, its style infers the same poet, comp. especially vv. 18, 22, with cxlix. 8. But also the manner in which he employs the sacred history is quite in unison with the spirit prevailing in these last songs, and shows how powerfully at last the popular feeling of Israel revived, in opposition to the Gentiles. For it gives, like Ps. lxxviii. and Ps. cvi., a song of praise to Jahvé out of the history of Israel on all its sides; but if that history served in the two above songs to humiliate Israel, and for castigatory instruction, we see here on the other hand the new feature that in recollection of the ancient history only Israel's glory and dignity are brought into relief, and in the peculiar distinction and grace of Jahvé experienced in it towards the patriarchs of the ancient people, a further exhortation only to fidelity towards the Law is found.—Style and mode of presentation are here only slightly raised above that of Ps. cvi.; but the arrangement of the strophés is firmer. After the prelude, vv. 1-6, follow four strophés of nine verses each, with a sudden close, vv. 43-45. Among those four the first leads the history to the time of the three Patriarchs, the second down to the settlement in Egypt, while the two last comprise more narrowly the Mosaic period.

1 Sing praise to Jahvé, call on His Name,
  make known among peoples His deeds

sing to Him, play to Him,
> think upon all His wonders;
boast of His holy Name,
> let the heart rejoice of them that seek Jahvé:
inquire after Jahvé and after His power,
> seek ever His countenance;
think of His wonders which He did, 5
> His signs and His mouth's judgments,
seed of His servant Abraham,
> ye sons of Jakob, by Him chosen!

He is Jahvé our God,
> through the whole earth are His judgments;
He thinks of His covenant for ever,
> of the word that He appoints for a thousand years:
which He made with Abraham,
> and swore to His own with Isaak,
and appointed it for a law for Jakob, 10
> Israel for an everlasting covenant,
saying, " to thee I give the land of Kanáan,
> for the portion of your heritage!"
when they were still easy to count,
> small and only pilgrims therein,
and so wandered from people to people,
> from one kingdom to another land;
He let not men oppress them,
> but chastised because of their kings:
" touch not my anointed, 15
> do not ill to my seers!" — —
Thereupon He called hunger over the land,
> breaking every staff of bread;
had sent hither a man before them,
> sold to be a slave was Josef:
by fetters his feet were plagued,
> into the iron came his soul,

till the time that His word was accomplished,
 the promise of Jahvé preserved him,
20 sending, a king released him,
 a ruler of peoples set him free,
appointed him as Lord for his house,
 as commander through his whole kingdom,
to bind his princes to himself,
 and to master his elders;
so Israel came to Egypt,
 Jakob journed in the land of Ham,
and He made very fruitful His people
 and more mighty than his oppressors. — —
25 He changed their heart, to hate His people
 and to out-wit His servants:
sent Moses His servant,
 Ahron, chosen by Him;
they did among them His wondrous things,
 signs in the land of Ham:
He sent darkness and it was dark,
 and—they resisted not His words;
changed into blood the waters
 and caused their fishes to die;
30 full of frogs their land swarmed
 in the chambers of their king;
spoke—and flies came,
 gnats through all their borders;
gave as their rain-shower hail,
 flames of fire through their land;
and smote their vine and the fig-tree,
 and broke asunder the trees of their borders; — —
spoke—and forthwith locusts came,
 hoppers without number,
35 devoured all herb in their land,
 devoured the fruit of their field;

and smote all the first-born in their land,
firstlings of all their strength,
l d them out with gold and silver,
while none trembled in His tribes;
joyful was Egypt for their exodus,
because their terror had fallen on them;
spread clouds out as a covering,
fire also, for light by night;
They asked—he brought quails,   .   10
and with heaven's bread He satisfied them;
opened rocks—and waters sprung forth,
ran through the steppes like a stream;
because He thought on His holy word,
His servant Abraham, — —
Therefore He led His people forth in delight,
high in jubilation His chosen,
and gave to them heathen-lands,
that they inherited the sweat of the nations,
to keep His statutes,   15
and maintain His law.

Ver. 8 like ver. 42, although this is strongly altered in 1 Chron. xvi. 12. Vv. 8-15 after Gen. xii.—xxv.; ver. 15, Gen. xx. 7. Vv. 16-24, Gen. xxxvii.—l.; ver. 16 *b* after Isa. iii. 1 comp. Ps. civ. 15. Vv. 25-45 after Ex.—Josúa; ver. 28 *b* further explained by ver. 38, comp. Ex. x. 24; ver. 42 goes back to ver. 8; ver. 45 to ver. 1.—A somewhat more bounding language, vv. 18 and 22, is introduced by the change of sense in the repeated נַפְשׁוֹ; *the soul* of Josef, yea, he himself the hero *came into iron* with his noble soul; but as if in recompense for this he had later, at the king's behest, to *bind the princes* of Egypt *to his soul*, that they must do what he bade them out of His soul. The indication in ver. 19 presumes that the poet had read a later history of Josef, where this was represented in a still higher manner than in the present Pentateuch, and of whose existence traces may be found elsewhere.

Ps. cxxxv.: general praise to Jahvé as the great God of Israel—equally in creation and in history, the only true one, in presence of Whom idols and their worshippers are nothing. Three strophés are arranged accordingly, each of seven verses with small members.

1.

1 Praise Jahvé's name,
 praise ye servants of Jahvé,
who stand in the house of Jahvé,
 in the courts of our house of God,
praise Jah, because good is Jahvé,
 play to His name, because He is to be loved,
because Jah chose out Jakob for Himself,
 Israel for his possession.
5 Now I know that great is Jahvé,
 our lord before all gods;
all that He wills Jahvé doeth
 in the heavens and the earth,
 in the seas and in all floods,
who brings up vapours from the earth's end,
 turns lightnings to rain,
 fetches the wind out of his chambers.

2.

He slew Egypt's first-born
 from men to beasts,
 sent signs, wonders into Thy midst, O Egypt,
 against Pharao and all his servants;
10 He slew many peoples,
 put to death numerous kings,
Sihon, king of Amorites, Og the king of Basan
 and all the kingdoms of Kana'an,

and gave gave their land for a heritage,
  a heritage to His people Israel:
Jahvé, eternal is Thy name,
Jahvé, for all ages is Thy glory!
For His people will Jahvé judge,
  concerning His servants have grief!

3.

Heathen images are silver and gold,   15
  work of human hands,
have mouth—and speak not,
  have eyes—see not,
have ears—hearken not,
  no breath at all is in their mouth:
let their framers be like them,
  every one who trusts in them!—
Israel's house, bless Jahvé,
  house of Ahron, bless Jahvé,
house of Levi, bless Jahvé,   20
  Jahvé's fearers, bless Jahvé!
Blessed be Jahvé out of Sion,
  He Who dwells in Jerusalem!

Vv. 1, 2 after cxxxiv. 1, only here said of all Israel; ver. 3 *b* after lii. 11, liv. 9; ver. 4 from Ex. xix. 5; ver. 6 from cxv. 3; ver. 7 from Jer. x. 13; ver. 9 in the middle after cxvi. 19; ver. 14 from Deut. xxxii. 36; vv. 15-20 from cxv. 4-11, only that here, ver. 20, Levi is distinguished from Ahron.

Ps. cxxxvi. is at bottom the same thank-song as the preceding psalm, from which it borrows much in particular points; but it is elaborated in new style in such a way that while in the first half of each verse the praise according to the particular dignities and deeds of Jahvé takes its course, in the second always with the same manner the mention of the *grace* of Jahvé as the conscious ground of His praise recurs; probably the constant echo was to be sung by the whole congregation. But thus appear in conjunction first six times three verses together, then four times two verses together.

1 Thank Jahvé because He is good, *because His grace is for ever!*
Thank the God of Gods, *because His grace is for ever!*
Thank the Lord of Lords, *because His grace is for ever!*
To Him who alone did great wonders, *because His grace is for ever!*
5 To Him who made heaven with understanding, *because His grace is for ever!*
To Him who spread out the earth upon waters, *because His grace is for ever!*
To Him who made the great lights, *because His grace is for ever!*
Made the sun for the rule of the day, *because His grace is for ever!*
Made the moon for the rule in the nights, *because His grace is for ever!*
10 To Him who slew Egypt's first-born, *because His grace is for ever!*
And from its midst fetched Israel, *because His grace is for ever!*
With strong hand and outstretched arm, *because His grace is for ever!*
To Him who cut the reed-sea in pieces, *because His grace is for ever!*
let Israel pass through, *because His grace is for ever!*
15 Pharao and his army overthrew in the reed-sea, *because His grace is for ever!*
To Him who led His people through the desert, *because His grace is for ever!*

To Him who slew great kings, *because His grace is
for ever!*
Put to death mighty kings, *because His grace is for
ever!*
Sihon, king of Amorites, *because His grace is for ever!*
Og, the king of Basan, *because His grace is for
ever!* 20
And gave their land for a heritage, *because His grace is
for ever!*
A heritage to His people Israel; *because His grace
is for ever!*
Who in our depth thought of us, *because His grace is
for ever!*
And from our oppressors freed us, *because His
grace is for ever!*
Who gives bread to all flesh: *because His grace is for
ever!* 25
Thank the God of heaven! *because His grace is for
ever!*

Ps. cxlv. offers praise in light and beautiful style with triple sounding of the greatness, grace, and faithfulness of Jahvé, as of the true eternal *King* of the community of the faithful, in twenty-two two-membered verses after the twenty-two letters. The further membering is that seven times three verses and at last three members stand together.

All Thy praise let me sing, my God and King,   1
and bless Thy name for ever and ever!
Bless I Thee continually,
and praise Thy name for ever and ever!
Deep, unsearchable is Jahvé's greatness,
great is He and greatly praised.—
Each generation praises to another Thy deeds,
telling of Thy powers.

5   For the splendid glory of Thy power
        and Thy wondrous deeds let me speak !
    Greatly be celebrated Thy sublime works,
        Thy great deeds—let me narrate them !—
    Highly men boast the greatness of Thy goodness,
        and exult in Thy righteousness.
    In grace and mildness is Jahvé rich,
        long-suffering, of great love.
    Jahvé is good to all,
        compassionate over all His works.—
10 Known is Thy praise by all Thy works, Jahvé,
        and Thy saints bless Thee ;
    Loudly they speak of Thy kingdom's pomp,
        and announce Thy power,
    Men's sons telling of His mighty acts,
        and His kingdom's sublime pomp.—
    Nay, an everlasting kingdom for all times is Thy kingdom,
        for all ages Thy rule.
    [Oh, faultless is Jahvé in all His deeds,
        loving in all His works.]
    Provide for all the sick doth Jahvé,
        and sets up all the bowed down.—
15 Revert to Thee all eyes in hope,
        and Thou givest them their food seasonably ;
    Spreadest open Thy hand,
        and satisfiest the wish of all life.
    True is Jahvé in all His ways
        and loving in all His deeds.—
    Unto all calling on Him is Jahvé near,
        all who call on Him with truth ;
    Verifies the wishes of His fearers,
        and their clamour he hears and helps.
20 Well doth Jahvé preserve all that love Him,
        and all the wicked He destroys.—

To (*Zu*) Jahvé's praise let my mouth speak,
and bless all flesh His holy name
for ever and aye!

After ver. 13 the verse with ב is wanting, which the poet cannot have omitted. The LXX have a verse which very well fills out the place, comp. ver. 17; the first word is then בָּאֱמֶן. —רצון, ver. 16, to be referred, after ver. 19, to the living; if it was intended to refer as *grace* to God, רצונו might be expected; לכל is therefore dative.

1.

Praise, my soul, Jahvé! 1
praise I Jahvé then, as long as I live,
    play to my God, so long as I exist!
Trust not on princes,
    on man's son, who has no deliverance,
He, when his spirit goes forth, returns to His earth:
    on *that* day his plans are lost!

2.

Blessed he whose help is even Jakob's God, 5
    whose hope is on Jahvé his God!
Him who made heaven and earth,
    sea and all that is therein,
who keeps truth for ever:
who does justice to the oppressed,
    who gives the hungry bread.

3.

Jahvé, who looses the fetters!
Jahvé, who makes seeing the blind,
    Jahvé, who sets up the bowed down,
        Jahvé, who loves the righteous!

Jahvé, who preserves strangers,
  orphans, widows helps up again,
    and turns aside the way of the wicked!—
Rule Jahvé for ever!
  thy God, Sion, for all ages!

Vv. 7 and 8 after Isa. lxi. 1.

Ps. cxlvii. turns rather to the community and Sion, and alludes to the complete restoration of Jerusalem and its walls; a fine song of praise to Jahvé as the only Mighty One, in the creation and in the human world, especially in Israel,—so that this twofold praise recurs in each of the three strophés, but in the beginning of the first and third the immediate circumstances of that time are brought into relief. The song is constructed of strophés with twelve members; but that the last is longer is a less striking fact than the omission of one in the second.

1.

1   *Praise Jah,*
  because it is beautiful to play to our God,
    because it is lovely, praise is seemly!
  Him, who builds Jerusalem, Jahvé,
    collects the dispersed of Israel,
  who heals the heart-broken
    and binds up their griefs;
  who appoints to the stars a number,
    gives them all names:
5 great is our Lord and of great power,
    His understanding unbounded,
  He helps up again the sufferer, Jahvé,
    He bows the wicked down to the ground!

2.

  Sing to Jahvé high with thanks,
    play with the cither to our God!

who covers the heaven with clouds,
    who prepares the earth's rain,
        who causes the mountains to sprout grass;
who gives to the cattle their fodder,
    young ravens that for which they cry;
hath not pleasure in strength of the horse,   10
    nor joy in man's legs:
joy hath Jahvé in His fearers,
    in them who wait for His grace!

3.

Praise, O Jerusalem, Jahvé!
    praise Thy God, Sion,
that He fastened the bolts of Thy gates,
    blessed thy sons in Thee!
He who makes thy borders salvation,
    satisfies thee with fat of wheat;—
Who sends His word on earth,   15
    in haste runs His command:
Who gives snow like wool,
    scatters rime like ashes,
Who casts forth His ice like fragments;
    who will stand before His cold?
then sends His word and—melts them,
    bloweth His breath—waters run!—
Who announces to Jakob His words,
    His judgments and laws to Israel:
to no people did He thus,   20
    and laws—they know not thus.

הללו יה is here, ver. 1, and similarly Ps. cxvii. 2, for the first time somewhat more closely connected with the song, and hence the mode of expression explained in connexion with lii. 11 (Vol. I., p. 267) somewhat otherwise applied.

    Ver. 3 after Isa. lxi. 1. Ver. 4 after Isa. xl. 26; ver. 8 c after Ps. civ. 13; ver. 9 after Job xxxviii. 41; ver. 10 after Ps. xx. 8; ver. 14 c after Isa. liv. 12, b after Deut. xxxii. 14; also vv. 19, 20 after Deut.—Ver. 15. The severe, raw cold wind is meant, which brings forth the things in vv. 16, 17, ver. 18 the mild, warm wind. On ver. 9 b comp. Plin. *Nat. Hist.*, x., 15.

Ps. xxxiii. bears the greatest relationship to the last song, and only appears more as a proper festive song. After the introduction, vv. 1-3, it celebrates both Jahvé the righteous, the Creator of all, of the heathen also, vv. 4-11, and His community which through Him is stronger than through the greatest external protection, vv. 12-19,—which therefore ever believingly hopes on Him, vv. 20-22. The song is accordingly constructed of two great strophés, each of eight common verses, with fore and after-song of three verses each. But each of the two great strophés is halved in the middle.

a.

1 Rejoice, ye righteous, in Jahvé,
    praise becomes the upright!
thank Jahvé with the cither,
    with ten-stringed harp play to Him!
sing to Him a new song,
    play well in sound of jubilation!

1.

For straight is Jahvé's word,
    all His doing with truth;
5 He loves right and truth,
    full of Jahvé's grace is the earth;
the heavens are by Jahvé's word created,
    and by His mouth's breath their whole host;
He gathered the sea's water as in a skin,
    laid up floods in storehouses:

all the earth feared before Jahvé,
    all earth's dwellers quake before him!
for *He* spake—and it came to pass,
    He commanded—and it existed.—
Jahvé hath broken the counsel of the heathen,   10
    hath made utterly void the people's plans;
Jahvé's counsel for ever stands,
    His heart's plans for all ages.

2.

Happy the people whose God is Jahvé,
    the community, chosen by Him for a heritage!
High from heaven looked Jahvé,
    saw all the sons of men;
looked far from His seat of rule
    upon all the sons of earth:
He who together forms their hearts,   15
    who observes all their deeds.
Never doth a king prevail by force,
    a hero deliver himself by great strength;
vain is the horse for victory,
    brings not deliverance although very mighty;
lo, Jahvé looks on His fearers,
    on those who wait for His grace,
to save from death their soul,
    to keep them alive in hunger.

b.

Our soul hopes on Jahvé,   20
    our defence and shield is *He*.
Because our heart rejoices in Him,
    because we trust His holy name,
let Thy grace come, Jahvé, upon us,
    as we wait for Thee!

Ver. 1 as cxlvii. 1. Ver. 7. כי after the expression רב,

mole would lead to Ex. xv. 8 : but not the former wonder in the sea, but the damming-up or closing-in of the sea-water from Chaos onwards, must here, when the Creation is referred to, be spoken of. Comp. Job xxxviii. 8. Hence נאד=נֹד *skin* must be read, also in correspondence with the following "storehouses;" in like manner of the water of the clouds, Job xxxviii. 37, xxii. Ver. 9 after Gen. i. 3. Vv. 13, 14 allude, equally with ver. 10, to the last experienced Divine help (comp. cii. 20), so that ver. 10 and vv. 13, 14 reciprocally complete one another. Ver. 17 after Ps. xx. 8, comp. cxlvii. 10; ver. 20 from cxv. 9-11.

Ps. cxlix. is a song of victory, in which the warlike-religious inspiration, as it was again aroused in the small struggles with neighbouring peoples (Neh. vi. 1 sqq.) appears still more strongly than in the preceding three songs; an echo besides of Pss. xciii. sqq. The song plainly breaks up into three strophés of three verses each, of which the second points to the latest victory, the last on this side gives voice in decisive tones to the Messianic hopes.

1.

1   Sing to Jahvé a new song,
        in the throng of saints His praise!
    in His Creator let Israel rejoice,
        Sion's sons exult in their king,
    praise His name with dances,
        play to him with kettle-drum and cither!

2.

    For in His people Jahvé hath joy,
        adorns with victory the poor.
5   Let saints exult with boasts,
        highly rejoice upon their beds,
    sublime praise to God in their mouth,
        and a two-edged sword in their hand.

3.

To take vengeance on the heathen,
punishment on the nations,
to bind their kings with chains,
their chiefs with iron fetters;
to execute the written law on them;
this is honour to all His saints.

Here Ps. xxx. is strongly imitated, as מָחוֹל ver. 3, בְּבוֹר ver. 5, etc.—רִנָּה ver. 4 as cxlvii. 11.—Ver. 8. Merely echo of Isa. lx. 11; it is to be understood, according to the context, rather as possibility and goal; and constantly the princes of even quite small peoples were termed kings. Ver. 9 according to the passages of the Pentateuch against the Kanáanites, which was frequently understood too literally in later times. This song shows in germ how with the inspiration of that time gradually much that is troubled mixes.

Pss. cxlviii. and cl. appear to form with design the close of collection of Psalms; for they give the most general, exhaustive summons to the praise of Jahvé, as if they desired finally to conclude the infinite thanks and praise of Him. And indeed Ps. cxlviii. calls upon all in the creation, from the highest to the lowest, from the greatest to the smallest, to praise Jahvé the world-creator and God of Israel. The song falls—according to the subject, heaven and earth—into two strophés with six verses each, while an after-word again comprises all the contents.

1.

Praise Jahvé from the heavens,   1
    praise Him in the heights;
praise Him, all His messengers,
    praise Him, all His hosts;
praise Him, sun and moon,
    praise Him, all brightening stars;

praise Him, ye heaven of heavens,
   waters, which are above the heavens;
5 which praise Jahvé's name,
      because He bade—and they were made,
   caused them to stand for ever, aye,
      gave a law that cannot be transgressed!

2.

Praise Jahvé from the earth,
   sea-monsters and all floods;
fire and hail, snow and ice,
   storm-wind, fulfilling His word;
mountains also and all hills,
   ye fruit-trees and ye cedars all,
10 wild beasts and all cattle,
   small creeping things and feathered birds!
kings of earth, all nations,
   princes and all judges of the earth;
Young men and maidens also,
   old men with boys:

3.

Who praise Jahvé's name,
   because His name is alone exalted,
   His majesty above earth and heaven,
and He exalted His people's horn,
   the praise of all His saints,
   of Israel's sons, the people near to Him!

Ver. 2 after ciii. 20, 21.—Ver. 6. The case in which חֹק beside עָבַר stands in the accusative, Jer. v. 22, can have no application; we must rather compare the same words, Esth. i. 19, ix. 27, whence it is clear that this is a short proverbial mode of expression: *a law and man shall not transgress it, i.e.,* one not to be transgressed (§ 294 *b*).—קִיטוֹר,

ver. 8, cannot in this connexion denote *smoke*, unless the smoke of an army were thought of; but the old translations have mostly *ice*, here very suitable; comp. the Syr. *katar*, be bound, curdle, and therefore freeze.

Ps. cv. summons all living things to the worthy praise of Jah with all instruments of praise:

Praise God in His sanctuary, . 1
    praise Him in His sublime welkin!
praise Him for His sublime deeds,
    praise Him according to His full greatness!
praise Him with trumpet-blast,
    praise Him with harp and cither;
praise him with kettle-drum and with dances,
    praise Him-with strings and shalms;
praise Him with clear-sounding cymbals   5
    praise Him with dull-sounding cymbals!
All breath praise Jah!

Ver. 1; on earth, as in heaven, comp. xxix. 9; a conception of the harmony between the two, which, properly carried out in the whole preceding song, is here only briefly again taken up. For, not to speak merely of the instruments, this song suggests the three questions: (1) *where?* (2) *why?* ver. 2, (3) *wherewith* shall God be praised? And because all conceivable human instruments are insufficient for this, the song rightly closes with the brief exclamation comprising all that lives, ver. 6. On ver. 5 comp. Appendix, p. 339.

APPENDIX.

On the Singing and Music of the Songs.

FREQUENT allusion has been made (in the "General Observations on Hebrew Poetry") to the fact that certainly in the case of the poets who must historically be considered the most ancient, all the arts of the Muses—poesy, singing, and playing (music)—formed still an undivided whole. The genuine song is, from its primary origin onwards, not to be conceived as devoid of musical accompaniment; and it has been shown above* that we still even now fancy that we can hear the style of the music sounding out of the dead members of many an old Hebrew verse. The epic singer too, accompanies readily the beginning and end of his verses with musical play.† A consequence of this original and hence ever anew-manifested connexion may, still later, be that Asaf, the sons of Qorach, and other men of the kind, who, according to the historical information, are only singers and players in the narrower sense, are named in the superscriptions of many Psalms as their poets (see Vol. I., pp. 42 sqq.)

But early the separation of these arts of the Muses began, when those who had still greater capacity and pleasure in singing and playing, got hold of the songs once produced by the poet, and further pursued the musical element lying in them after their fashion. In point of fact, individuality is developed more readily and completely by such separation of

---

* *Dichter des A. B.*, I., pp. 108 sqq.

† This may still be observed at the present day amongst the Egyptian public story-tellers, whose character, in a certain point of view, may be compared with that of the ancient Rhapsodes, comp. Lane's *The Modern Egyptians*, Vol. II, 116.

the different powers and capacities; but these may again be united with reference to *one* object; singing and playing, considered as a special art by itself and so practised, will thus only be capable of flourishing freely. That this separation had begun among the Hebrews as early as the pre-Davidic times, is shown by accounts like Ex. xv. 20, 21; also among the Arabs singing arose somewhat early as a special art; the melodies were often given by the singers, not by the poets, and several singers, female and others, were particularly distinguished in this.*

The last separation is that between singing and music, so that the pure playing of the different instruments comes out with greater completeness. Public playing indeed, without any accompaniment of singing, appears to have been little known to the ancient Hebrews, although other peoples standing still nearer to original conditions were acquainted with it; and only among the shepherds of the fields the pure performance on musical instruments may have been by itself developed among the Hebrews at the earliest time; and all the earlier among them inasmuch as they formerly belonged to the pastoral peoples.† But also later, singing was, according to all indications, not so fettered and obscured by the accompaniment of playing, as is often the case at the present day; for, on the contrary, we find everywhere singing predominant. But that playing was actually, at least from Solomon's time, very highly developed as a special art side by side with singing, and that it was freely employed, follows with great certainty from several phenomena. Let us note, in the first place, the great mass of very different instruments which are named in the Old Testament; and we shall not find

---

* We know this most clearly from the close and detailed descriptions in *Kitáb al'aghani*; comp. e.g., the article on the Azzat el Mailá in Kosegarten, *Chrest.*, pp. 130 sqq.

† Comp. שְׁרִיקוֹת עֲדָרִים in Deborah, Judg. v. 16; the Greek συριγί certainly passed further westward from these pastoral peoples.

the Hebrews in their knowledge and practice to have been behind the ancient Egyptians and later Arabs. All these instruments may have been derived by them from other still older peoples, for we do not know that they invented or used any that were entirely peculiar; and we see from Am. vi. 5, that in the ninth century artistic aptitude in the Davidic stringplay passed for something rather novel among potentates; and many, without capacity, still did not think it below their dignity; but it cannot be denied that in this they successfully emulated other neighbouring peoples. But that among such peoples playing was already separated from singing, we know from certain sources.* In general we see this much from the slightly confused, but nevertheless in great part genuine, historical and extremely precious information of the Chronicles, especially from the long descriptions I., capp. vi., xv., xvi., and xxv., xxvi., that music and singing from ancient times flourished to the highest degree among the Hebrews, and accompanied the sublime worship with equal dignity and pomp.† To this may be added such definite testimonies as Ps. lxviii. 26, where, in the description of a solemn procession, the players on strings and the maidens striking tambours are distinguished from the singers; also Am. v. 23, comp. with vi. 5, leads to something similar. It might indeed appear according to 1 Chron. xv. 16 sqq., xxv. 1 sqq., as if the Levitic singers appointed at the Temple also played in David's time instruments; indeed we cannot mistake that the solemn train of singers and players, 1 Chron. xv., is quite otherwise described than in Ps. lxviii., which is most readily explained if

---

* The paintings of the Egyptian tombs show very plainly singers, beating at the same time the time with the hand, along with players; both performing together, see Wilkinson's *Manners and Customs of the Ancient Egyptians*, chap. vi., where will be found also a very rich number of drawings of the ancient instruments; comp. with Champollion's *Gr. Égypt.*, p. 369. On the Arabs in the present day, comp. Lane's above-named work, Vol. II., pp. 59-93. To explain the instruments mentioned in the Old Testament, is only partly relevant here.

† Comp. the discussion on the three masters—Haeman, Asaf, Aethan, Vol. I., pp. 42 sqq.

the two descriptions have two very different times in view. Yet from the most literal explanation of these passages of Chronicles so much would ever be gathered, that in David's time this separation had not yet appeared in its completeness.

But however desirable it might be to form to oneself a more certain and exact notion of the manner in which the songs were sung and played in the actual life of the ancient people, we must here forthwith admit that we are greatly deficient in the means for giving a full and satisfactory answer to such questions. Matters like the mode of singing and playing, change greatly with the times; and even a clear recollection of them passes gradually entirely away, if their form is not retained in the writing by exact indications like our *notes;* but antiquity was entirely unacquainted with such signs in the extensive and accurate way in which we use them. Hitherto no success has followed any of the modern attempts to call anew into life a trustworthy idea of ancient Greek music; and this must still more be the case with the incomparably older Hebrew. In the case of the people Israel there are besides the great agitations and demolitions which its whole status so early endured, and which were bound to have a most prejudicial effect on such arts of life. Whether, on the restoration of the ancient Temple in the sixth century, the ancient Temple-music was also fully restored, we do not exactly know. Certainly it was attempted, and, according to all signs, Temple-singing flourished, the more in the new Jerusalem as now all such sacred externalities were preserved in Jerusalem. The (so to speak) musical style of the books of Chronicles, which may give us a notion of it, however incomplete, is still purely Hebraic. Nevertheless, the high glory of the Temple-music, as it must have been in the times of the bloom and power of the old kingdom, may have suffered much in those late and oppressed times. But then there occurred with the Greek age, manifestly enough for all the arts of the Muses, and especially for music a great revolution; new, purely Greek musical instruments were customary, as the Book of Daniel shows, and new modes of singing and playing might easily obscure the more exact knowledge of the more ancient. In fact, the helpless ignorance with which the LXX neglect and erroneously translate many of the musical artistic expressions and words of the Old Testament, may sufficiently prove that in the Greek period the old musical words and ideas passed away, and therewith also the music itself was entirely changed; and the other ancient translators hardly know how to deal with the subject. A certain and simply ancient mode of singing was retained indeed in the synagogues, and through those in the ancient church; * but a closer investigation is first required as to whether actually more than a slight uniform remainder from the full real substance of that ancient music was retained by the early Christian Church, whether even of that great variety of ancient tunes which the scattered words retained in the Old Testament attest, and of the distinction of particular ones, any reminiscence or other trace has survived. That accentuation which the Massôretes made regular in the three great poetical books, may have arisen from this tradition of the synagogues; but in the first place, it prescribes the same simple mode of singing, as if a proverb of Solomon's were to be sung just as a psalm; and, secondly,—and this is connected with the foregoing,—it has manifestly no further clear recollection of the different old melodies, the traces of which we shall soon see more closely; without taking into account that it subjects also all prosaic sentences and words not originally belonging to the song within the three books of Psalms, Proverbs, and Job to the same law, and only excepts from this the long prose narratives at the beginning and end of the Book of Job.

Hence it might be conjectured that the comparison of the music of the other nearly related peoples, or those that had once come into contact with the Hebrews, must here be of

---

* Comp. Augusti's *Handbuch der Christl. Archäologie*, Vol. II., pp. 58, 107 sqq.

much advantage. But on the side of the ancient Egyptians, and Assyrians the figured representations of musical matters on their monuments are our only sources of instruction.' A description of the music of the Phœnicians or of the ancient Syrians (and such would be here the most instructive) has not been retained. Of the Muslim we possess indeed very many musical writings; but the Arabic music, as it existed from the time of the Caliphs, has no immediate connexion at all with the ancient Hebrew; and for this reason all these writings can only afford us a more remote advantage.* Such musical signs as are found in the psalters of the Ethiopic, Armenian, and other early Christians † is of very different character. And thus we are bound to say that what we possess in the Old Testament, of relics of the Hebrew music, is but a slight fragment very hard to read, from an art which must once have highly flourished, but which already in the Talmudic time ‡ had become entirely unintelligible to posterity.

Nevertheless we need not hesitate to form for ourselves an approximately correct idea of the style of the ancient Hebrew

---

* What is said in the book of Jones and von Dalberg, *On the music of the Indians* (Erfurt. 1802), respecting Arabian music, is very meagre, and entirely different from what is found in the *Kitâb al' aghâni*. The discussion of Villoteau, *De l'état actuel de l'art musical de l'Egypte* in the *Description de l'Egypte,—Et. mod.* tom. xiv., gives indeed extracts from Arabian treatises on music, and an idea of the present musical art of Egypt; but these extracts are insufficient, and the writer has no knowledge of the entirely different musical observations in the *Kitâb al' aghâni*. The work of Lane again on modern Egypt describes only the external features of the new Arabic music. Under these circumstances I expressed the urgent wish in the first edition of this work that the old Arabic music of which in this day we have no ideas, might be more closely investigated in original sources. The edition of the *Kitâb al' aghâni* was then actually begun by Kosegarten, 1840, but not continued; and as a connoisseur of music R. G. Kiesewetter wrote *On the music of the Arabs* (Leipzig, 1842, but without certainly understanding the Muslim works from which he gives extracts, relying only on Hammer.

† To the Ethiopic signs I myself was the first to call closer attention on the D. M. G. Z. 1846, pp. 39 sqq.

‡ Where still are found some individual detached reminiscences of the Temple-music (as M. שקלים, v. 1, התמיד, iii. 8, G. ערבין, ii. 3 bl. 10 sq.) but none in any way sufficiently coherent and clear.

music, especially in so far as it was public Temple-music. Every more exact description of the music of those ancient times is indeed wanting; but many individual words have been preserved which must have had a musical signification. These are the short abrupt words and phrases which were noted against many songs; we find them now attached to very many psalms, but also to the above explained (pp. 161 sqq. *Dichter des A. B.*), song of King Hizqia, Isa. xxxviii., and to the piece Hab. iii., which was designed (p. 84) for public occasions; but further the so-called Psalms of Solomon show the traces of this. We perceive from these instances above all that at least since the eighth century before Christ there was among the ancient people a peculiar musical art for Temple-songs, according to which all such songs were to be produced, and with whose artistic expression such songs might be accompanied. But how highly this art was developed is sufficiently clear from the fact that it possessed its peculiar expressions which, reduced to quite brief verbal signs, yet plainly were held sufficient; so that they may certainly be termed the *musical notes* of those times. But again, quite independently of this, we know that in the Temple from Davîd and Solomon's times there existed a highly developed school of Levitic musicians;* and we have every reason to derive from it also our musical signs.—For us, indeed, these word-signs, because of their unusual brevity and abruptness, are now certainly only as scattered Sibylline leaves from the lost book of ancient Hebrew music; but we must start with the explanation of them so far as is possible in the present day, and then further seek to ascertain what information they yield. For this purpose the books of Chronicles afford us at the present day the most help, because happily so occurs that their last writer, as certainly himself a Latin musician, pays very close attention in his narratives to this side of the status and history of the ancient people, and pursues it, with

---

* Comp. the *Gesch des V. Isr.*, III., pp. 315-317 of the 2nd edit.

personal and most lively sympathy.* If we now apply these and all other means open to us at the present day to the understanding of these artistic expressions, we can still glance with a higher confidence over much that is of considerable importance. The expressions themselves are of three-fold kind, which we must here forthwith distinguish; but with reference to them the preliminary observation must be made, that even the position in which they are found inscribed on the songs, and which plainly is not arbitrary, may also assist towards the recovery of their correct sense.

1. The first word—before every other here pertinent—is the extremely obscure לַמְנַצֵּחַ. It is found in the Book of Psalms always in the very first place in the superscriptions; in Hab. iii. it stands at the end, which, as has been made clear, makes no important difference; altogether it appears fifty-four times. To understand this singular word, we must note above all that it is tolerably often read with the addition בִּנְגִינוֹת, Pss. iv., vi., liv., lv., lxvii., lxxvi.; Hab. iii. 19. For an addition of the same sense עַל נְגִילַת, Ps. lxi., must in all probability be taken, since both prepositions are conceivable.† This word comes from נָצַח, which signifies properly *pure, complete*, then transferred to time, *uninterrupted, continuous;* from the notion of completeness the meaning in Piel is derived: to put something in a perfectly good condition, order something, have the oversight of something; according to this meaning it is connected immediately with עַל, *over*, but may very well be also connected, still more briefly, like all verbs of *ruling, leading,* with בְּ (*Lehrb.* § 217 *f.*) But according to historical usage this word is used in a remarkable manner only of that ordering and conduct which is entrusted to the Levites;‡ in this sense

---

* Comp. the *Gesch des V. Isr.*, I., pp. 254 sq.

† The Massōretes have indeed here pointed בְּגִינַת in the *sing.*: but this is merely one of the many proofs that they were no longer quite certain about these ancient words. But in fact many copies have the ֹו lūr.

‡ Also in such cases as 2 Chron. ii. 1, 17; xxxiv. 12, 13, the words if more closely considered are used only of Levitic oversight of workmen.

it is frequently read in the Chronicles and the Book of Ezra. Therefore הַמְנַצֵּחַ עַל נְגִ׳ or נְגִ׳ בְּנֵי הֵמָן might signify *him who leads* the strings or the string-play, *i.e.*, *the music:* but here we have at once many other points for consideration.

In order then first only to understand how the *strings* נְגִילֹת might here be specially named, we must more fully consider the usage of all the instruments among the ancient people. And here it is above all certain that such a concert of all possible instruments, as has become customary amongst ourselves, was strange to all antiquity.* As the art of each playing instrument proceeded originally from a peculiar local circle, and served for quite special objects, so among those peoples who earliest developed music, each instrument was kept always in its own limits, and found its special use. Least of all, however, may the music resounding to the Temple-songs be conceived as a species of Janissaries' music, and that for the reason that the singing must be heard through, intelligibly and loudly enough, with the individual words. *Wind instruments*, flutes and others, were certainly never employed for the purpose: they are too powerful for singing; and when we find them in the ancient people, they serve quite other objects. The trumpet, with all similar blowing instruments, served for summons, giving of signals, for making announcement and gathering men together; and their use was moreover from the oldest times a privilege of the higher priests,† of which more is said in the body of the work. The flute on the other hand, with all such finer blowing instruments, was greatly preferred at entertainments‡ or for the accompaniment of trains,|| but was never used to accompany

---

* From passages only like 1 Sam. x. 5; Ps. cl., one must not draw erroneous inferences.

† Comp. the *Alterthumer*, p. 330. ‡ Isa. v. 12.

|| Even festive ones, Isa. xxx. 29; but not 1 Kings i. 40, comp. the *Gesch. des V. Isr.*, III., p. 285. Even in Ps. cl. the flutes for good reasons are not mentioned. On their history among the Greeks see Böttiger's *Kl. schriften arch. u. Antiqu. inhaltes*, I., pp. 1-61.

the Temple-song. Of *striking instruments*, the hand-drum* (tabret, tambour, timbrel), this most necessary accompaniment of the dance, was used from the most ancient times quite customarily by female singers for beating the time, and appears in early times even in conjunction with sacred hymns which resounded in this antique fashion :† but for the more artistic Temple-song as the Levites from David's time termed it, it was never adopted. Only in so far as dancing was practised at the sanctuary on certain occasions, it is also mentioned in connexion with the Temple.‡

The main portion of the playing accompaniment to the Temple-song was certainly formed from the days of David and Solomon by *stringed instruments* as the most fit for this purpose. They were from all times the most apt with their delicate sound to accompany singing : upon the perfecting and diversifying of them extraordinary pains and invention were early bestowed, and they must have been developed so highly and in so many forms among the Hebrews as among other Semites, at an early time, that their art along with the name was diffused over Asia Minor, and even among the Greeks. For the Temple-music there were then two different kinds in use, which we recognize also in Greek and Latin terms : the כִּנּוֹר κινύρα and the נֶבֶל νάβλα (ναύλα) or nabhia, only that we do not more exactly collect their significations from Greek and Latin sources at the present day. That the two were very different is certain; and the distinction cannot have consisted merely in the external form or only in the number of the strings.§ We may much more safely assume that

---
* הֹף also historically an archaic word.
† According to Ex. xv. 20, comp. Judges xi. 34 ; 1 Sam. xviii. 6.
‡ Such expressions as Ps. lxxxi. 3 must manifestly be estimated by the similar and about contemporary Ps. cxlix. 3, and especially cl. 4 ; we then see that the hand-tabret stands only in closest relation to dancing, to which at the Temple all other indications point. Also in Ps. lxxxvii. 7 we understand by the הֹלְלִים most correctly *dancers*.
§ What Josephus, *Arch.*, vii., 12, 3 says, that the Kinnor was ten-stringed, the Nabel twelve-stringed, the former played with a hammer, the latter with the

338   APPENDIX.

they took their name from the different materials of which originally their strings were composed: thus the Kinnôr was originally made from hemp-strings, the Nâbel from gut-strings.* With this agrees the fact that the Kinnôr of the two must have been relatively the older,† and certainly it was the inferior and commoner instrument. In German we may at the present day best designate the Kinnôr by a word originally quite correspondent, by *Cither*, and hence the *Nâbel* by *harp*. How developed were these instruments may be estimated from the fact that the Nâbel, which was the more delicate of the two, is always designated as the ten-stringed.‡ But not merely in the older

---

fingers, may be true for his times, but little suits the old times of David, when the נְגִינָה (1 Sam. xvi. 23; xviii. 10; xix. 9) always passed through the hands only, and when on the contrary the Nâbel (Ps. xxxiii. 2; cxlix. 9 and the better reading of Ps. xcii. 4) was ten-stringed. But still more it is a pure fancy of Jerome that the Nâbel, as similar to a ע, took its name from a *pitcher*.

* Since נֵבֶל originally signifies not a pitcher but a *skin*, it might very well also designate gut. Of כִּנּוֹר it is maintained in the *Lehrb.*, § 79 *d*, 118 *a*, *note*, that, as derived from כָּנַת, it was originally identical with the word κάνναβις *hemp*, which is in Sanskrit *bhangá*, and Persian *bandj*, and as an archaic word, with a change of sound elsewhere customary, runs through all these languages (*kannaab* is from the Greek); actually *kenôr* (Syr.) according to a notice, denotes *hemp*, *kinnoreh* (Arab.) at least something similar; and the κιθάρα (comp. the Æ*th*.) would then be another form of the same word. The Kithara is not derived from the Greek, but it might possibly come from another part of Asia to the Greeks as the κινύρα.—Hemp could only be equivalent to thread= string; but it is known that there were and still are strings of flax, hemp, silk, and cocus; therefore for the origin the first signification may be retained.

† The Nâbel is indeed mentioned in 1 Sam. x. 5, but only the Kinnôr and along with it the tambour were, according to such descriptions and modes of expression as Gen. iv. 21, xxxi. 27, 1 Sam. xvi. 16 sqq., the oldest and most favourite instruments; the Kinnôr is also later always much more frequently named than the Nâbel. Only where כְּלֵי שִׁיר *singing-instruments* are spoken of, as Amos vi. 5, 1 Chron. xvi. 42, 2 Chron. v. 13, must both be understood. But in general it is remarkable how widely the Kinnôr was known. Not only the Syrians and (according to Krapf) the Ethiopians have it, it appears even in the ancient Indian legends of the Brahma-born *Kinnaras*, and was transformed in the mouth of the Arabs before Muhammed by a rudely explicable change of sound into *carîne* (Lebid's *M.*, v. 60) and *caran*.

‡ In Assyria too they had them, comp. Layard's *Nineveh*, II., p. 412, and his *Discoveries*, pp. 454 sqq. But also the Egyptians had the ten-stringed harp, comp. the fine figure in Wilkinson's *Customs and Manners*, Vol. II., at the beginning.

narratives of how Solomon instituted the Temple-singing,* and in the books of Chronicles, but also in Ps. lvii. 9 (cviii. 3) and in many later Psalms, they are so named together, that it cannot be doubted that they formed the basis of all Temple-music.

But along with them and in playing certainly combined with them, metal *basins* (cymbals) were in use, always in a pair,† and struck together with the hands; as we can perceive plainly enough from the indications in the books of Chronicles. They were thus the only struck instruments which were to combine with the string-play: and we may conclude from this that their loud clinking sound was intended not so much constantly to accompany the string-play as to beat the time at the right places. But these bowls might well be of various strength, as is further remarked in the body of the work.

If we ask then how these different instruments were played together in the Temple-music, we cannot indeed ascertain all the particulars at the present day. But we see in the first place that, according to these three instruments, there must have been three kinds of Levitic musicians;‡ and this very number of three we meet with in many relations. And secondly, it is obvious that the whole, if it was desired briefly to designate it by one word, could only be named after the predominant element, after the *strings*. If the Temple-music generally was spoken of, it was briefly termed the *playing-instruments*;§ but there was thence formed a still more defi-

---

* 1 Kings x. 12.

† Hence constantly in the dual מְצִלְתַּיִם, although this form of the word is peculiar to Chronicles; the older is צֶלְצְלִים, 1 Sam. vi. 5, and hence at least poetically, in later times, Ps. cl. 5; the word signifies a *tinkling* sound, as when metals are struck against one another.

‡ The description most clear for us at the present day is given by the words, 1 Chron. xv. 16, 19-21, 28, comp. with the less-clear xvi. 5, 32, xiii. 8, xxv. 1, 6, 2 Chron. v. 12, xxix. 25, Ezr. iii. 10, Neh. xii. 27.

§ בִּנְגִינוֹת: we say here more exactly *playing-instruments* but not *strings*, because the strings themselves are in Hebrew מִנִּים; for this word signifies (formed from the Syr. *menta*, comp. Lehrb., § 176a) *hair*, and is so far less exact

nite word for the *string-play*,* *i.e.*, the Temple-music. The leaders of the music gave with the striking of the bowls the time; next to them in dignity followed the players of the Nábel, and then only those on the Kinnôr.† — And thus, according to all this, the name mentioned p. 335, הַמְנַצֵּחַ בִּנְגִינֹת, might mean *him who leads the Temple-music*; and as the verb נִצַּח was manifestly very frequently used precisely in this musical sense,‡ the mere name הַמְנַצֵּחַ must in a y case be shortened from it; and this could not occasion the slightest ambiguity in cases where songs and hymns only were spoken of, as in the annotations of the songs themselves. The difficult point here is only that the לְ before the expression is not explained, and that neither is one single leader of the Temple-music as an all-significant man elsewhere spoken of, nor could we comprehend why he should be here brought into prominence so entirely alone. Therefore the word is most safely regarded as a neuter formation;§ to designate *the conduct of the Temple-music* in direct opposition to the non-Levitic musical performances. A song which is designated, — whether immediately at the beginning, at its

---

than χόρδαι, *i.e.*, *guts*; but for this reason it was seldom used in the higher style, and is found only in the song Ps. xlv. 9, which has in general a peculiar language, and in the quite properly musical song Ps. cl. 4. On the other hand, נגן as strengthened and abbreviated from נבב, and (p. 31 *Dichter des A.B.*) radically related to נגע, signifies quite originally the *touching* or playing of the strings, and is also so worthy consideration from the fact that it presents a purely Hebrew or even (so far as we hitherto know) Israelitish word.

* בִּנְגִינֹתַי in the song of King Hizqia, B. Jes. xxxviii. 20, and in the subscription, Hab. iii. 19 : this word is formed according to *Lehrb.*, § 164 c, and stands happily by the concurrence of these two very diverse passages so firmly that we need neither think of a corrupt reading, nor of corrupt modes of explanation. That ־ does not permit us to think of *my*, the context in both instances shows ; but the LXX do not stumble at the first,—all the more at the second place.

† All this is gathered from a close comparison of the above passages of the books of Chronicles.

‡ So in 1 Chron. xv. 21, where only music is spoken of, and where the word לְנַצֵּחַ, *to lead the music*, is interchanged as synonymous with לְהַשְׁמִיעַ, *to make music*, ver. 19, comp. ver. 16, xvi. 5 (xv. 28).

§ According to *Lehrb.*, § 160 e.

head, or at the end as *for production with the Temple-music*, is thereby sufficiently distinguished from others. But why this designation now stands at the head only of particular though very numerous Psalms, can only be considered more closely in connexion with all the inscriptions of the Psalms.*

2. Next to this phrase there are a few others which, obscure as each is in itself, must yet have a common destination. We may perceive (1) that they always follow after that לִבְנֵי קֹרַח or לִמ׳ בִּנְגִינֹת, and that immediately.† If this phrase, indeed, according to p. 335, is found altogether in fifty-four songs, these further words appear only in twenty-three psalms: but whatever the cause of this smaller number (further discussion of this will be found in the body of the Commentary on the Psalms), it must in any case have a weighty significance that, where they appear, they are ever found in closest contact with the other phrases as if introductory to them. But further they are recognizable (2) by the fact that they are always introduced by the word עַל *after* . . . . .; if אֶל, Pss. v., lxxx.,

---

* That the sense does not admit "*for* the superintendent of the music," as if the poet destined by means of such notice his song for public singing, is certain: no poet could express himself so foolishly; and plainly enough all such inscriptions point rather to the fact that the songs furnished with them were actually once set to music for the Temple-singing.—Still more erroneous are other ancient and modern conjectures on the word. Noteworthy only is the constant translation by εἰς τὸ τέλος; but this seems to be entirely as obscure and unsuitable. But throughout it is inconceivable that the translator should have exchanged the word with the well-known לִבְנֵי: this would be a very clumsy exchange; and besides, it is not εἰς τέλος, as is so often given for this, but εἰς τὸ τέλος: and the translator would not have been able to make anything of a *for ever*. If the words mean in his sense as much as *for consecration* (like τελετή, they perhaps contain further a reminiscence of the original and correct sense of the expression, for by the *consecration* can only be understood the sacrificial consecration or the mysterion which might be sought also in the sacred Temple-song. Where בִּנְגִינֹת or עַל ני (Ps. lxi.) follows, the LXX render εἰς τὸ τέλος ἐν ὕμνοις, which agrees with this sense; and that they do not otherwise understand the words attached to Ps. lxi., likewise well agrees with what was shown above, p. 335.

† The single exception in the case of Ps. xlvi. can signify nothing; the words must here be transposed by an old copyist: and the possibility of this appears in the course of the Commentary.

is interchangeable with this, this is readily explained;* if once, Ps. xxxix., the לְ stands for this, it may be merely an abbreviation; and if the preposition is entirely wanting with one of these phrases, this may be only from an accidental cause. But an essential feature in them is (3) the fact that they very strongly change without a cause of this being observable in their sense; and this both among one another and individually in themselves. Each of the twenty-three psalms has only *one* such phrase in its superscription; but altogether there are only twelve, or rather,—as two of these probably ran only somewhat more briefly than other two,—only ten; and of these two are found four times, two others three times, three others twice, three only once. That all these phrases in general have significance only for the playing, is indeed quite clear from the connexion in which they are found: and the same is confirmed not less by the fact that at least two of them recur in the narrative of the Chronicles, I. xv. 20, 21, in such a way that they can only be referred to musical directions. But their more exact meaning must have been very early lost, so that in ancient and modern times very different conjectures have been put forth with regard to them. Already the LXX were here in the translation of the Psalter devoid of any exacter knowledge, and so give themselves up to the strangest conjectures, without even so much as assuming that the phrases must have a musical sense; in the Chronicles they proceed at least so far more securely that they retain the words merely according to their Hebrew sound, either as unintelligible or as art-expressions.† We must here, however, above all maintain that only three of these ten phrases give a sense in anywise intelligible for itself, the other seven may be abbreviated only from the beginning or otherwise noteworthy sound of songs.

As regards the first three which were here placed together,

---

* From *Lehrb.*, § 217 *i*.
† In the Psalter the LXX render at least the מִזְמוֹר merely by μαιλιθ

it is immediately further remarkable, that two of them are feminine words of reference, and therefore plainly point to something similar in sense; עַל הַגִּתִּית, *according to' the Gathæic*, Pss. viii., lxxxi., lxxxiv., and עַל הַשְּׁמִינִית, *according to the eight*, Pss. vi., xii., 1 Chron. xv. 21. If we now think (as on all grounds is alone probable, see the Comm.) that tunes are meant, these expressions are clear; from the City of Gath, by which always the most renowned of this name, the Philistine, is understood, a tune might travel to the people of Israel, and it may very well have found a home in Israel by David's means.* But by the *eight* we best conceive the eight in a definite number and series of tunes; for of our musical *octave* one could only think in jest.—The third phrase עַל יְדוּתוּן, Pss. lxii., lxxvii., or more shortly לִידוּתוּן, Ps. xxxix., *after Jedûthûn*,† may then likewise designate a tune as at first introduced by Jedûthûn and much used, for we know that he was a very famous old music-master from the first times of the Temple.‡

With reference to the remaining seven phrases, (1) It is somewhat doubtful only in the case of one of them whether it should be reckoned as belonging to the style of the preceding three or not. This is the phrase עַל עֲלָמוֹת as in Ps. xlvi. and 1 Chron. xv. 20, it is punctuated as if it signified *according to maidens :* one might find therein designated a melody like

---

* *Gesch. des V. Isr.*, III., p. 183. The LXX with their ὑπὲρ τῶν ληνῶν conjectured הַגִּתִּית. The עַל they understand in all these phrases as ὑπέρ, i.e., they explain it of the contents of the subjects of the songs.

† That לְ in such cases may denote, more weakly than עַל, about the same thing, is clear from *Lehrb.*, § 217 d.

‡ See on this the discussion on the inscriptions of the Psalter. Since from this results that the name Jedûthûn may be interchanged with Aethan, it might be supposed, according to Ps. lxxxix. 1, that he intended in Ps. xxxix. to indicate the poet or singer himself; the LXX suggest this meanwhile by their translation τῷ Ἰιδθούν, while they, Pss. lxii., lxxvii. give ὑπὲρ Ἰιδθούν which is certainly not clearer. But the baselessness of such an assumption is clear from the whole style of the superscription of these three psalms, as is shown in the case of the Book of Psalms.

one *in maiden-wise* (*nach jung.fern-weise*), or as the Greek παρθένια,* and then the phrase would immediately belong to the style of the three preceding. But the phrase מוּת לַבֵּן עַל, Ps. ix.,† is plainly only its proper longer expression, so that its literal meaning may be most securely defined by this, while it is readily explained how the עַל might fall away before it, whether merely from an error in writing, or because some disliked saying עַל עַל where the first did not appear thoroughly necessary. As now עַל מוּת לַבֵּן?, Ps. ix, is punctuated, the words do not give the slightest sense: but in many copies the two first words are blended into one. If now this עַלְמוּת is expressed, this formed like יַלְדוּת (*Lehrb.* §.165 *b*) may very well, interchangably with עֲלוּמִים, signify *youth* or rather youthful strength; and the full expression *the son has youthful strength* would only, as an abrupt beginning possibly of an old popular song (*volks-lied*), yield sense. In this case it would therefore belong to the following series of these phrases; but that a song or tune may be designated by the first words of famous old songs, possibly also popular songs, is self-intelligible. We have now

2. A quite similar case of abbreviation in שֹׁשַׁנִּים, Pss. xlv., lxiv., with which אֶל שֹׁשַׁנִּים עֵדוּת Ps. lxxx. and עַל שׁוּשַׁן עֵדוּת Ps. lx., interchange. Obscure as are all these words in themselves, they become readily plain so soon as we assume as the full phrase out of which they may have originated a short sentence like כְּשׁוֹשַׁנִּים עֵדוּת; this would signify *as lilies, i.e.,* pure is *the Revelation*, would thus express nearly the same that we

---

* Comp. C. O. Müller's *Gesch. der Griech*, *Lit.* I., p. 351.

† עַל מוּת, Ps. xlviii. 15 might therefore be also brought to this place, as if this stood only once as in Hab. iii. 19) at the end of the psalm, instead of in the superscription. Actually many copies unite it in one word עַלְמוּת, according to which—especially considering the otherwise fixed and great resemblance of Ps. xlvi. and Ps. xlviii.—it might appear to be quite identical with עֲלָמוֹת. But nevertheless the עַל before it might easily be wanting, but not the לַמְנַצֵּחַ; and in that passage, Ps. xlviii. 15, must rather a word necessarily stand which completes the verse-member.

read in Ps. xix. 8, 9, but certainly would allude to an ancient holy song; we might assume a song from Moses' time, for to this leads the use of the word עֵדוּת* not less than the rare fresh image of the lilies and the childlike joy in the confidence of the true word of God. But if the words were once a designation of a tune, one can readily understand that after the עַל the particle כְּ fell away.—To ancient sacred hymns the two following also lead:

3. אַל תַּשְׁחֵת, Pss. lvii.—lix., lxxv.: this can only signify: *Destroy not!* and may be borrowed from the beginning of an old penitential song of the community which began somewhat as follows: *Destroy not, O God, Thy people!* Before this pure indicative expression the particle of protasis כַּל could in no way be used, and might fall away because its sense in such a connexion is readily understood of itself by the resemblance of the other phrases.—The phrase,

4. עַל מַחֲלַת, *after sickness* . . . Pss. liii., lxxxviii., is explained without difficulty if an ancient similar penitential song began with some such words as מַחֲלָה עַמְּךָ תִרְפָּא, *the sickness of Thy people mayest Thou heal!* quite after the old belief, Ex. xv. 25.—On the other hand, the two following phrases may again be borrowed from old popular songs:

5. עַל אַיֶּלֶת הַשַּׁחַר, *after Hind of the dawn*, Ps. xxii.: an old popular song might possibly thus begin: *Thou hind of the dawn*, thou so early wakeful hind, *what scared thee up?* It would thus be very similar to the following:

6. עַל יוֹנַת אֵלֶם רְחֹקִים, *after Dove of dumbness, i.e.,* dumb dove of *the distant ones*, Ps. lvi.: a popular song might begin with such words as *Thou dumb dove of the distant ones* (*i.e.,* of the men dwelling afar, Ps. lxv. 6), *what tellest thou us from the distance?* with allusion to the certainly ancient use of carrier-doves in those parts. We listen here to archaic words and living pictures somewhat of the same kind as have been

---

* Comp. the *Alterth.*, p. 112. 2nd edit.

retained in Ps. lxviii. 14, from such times; as indeed it is generally very remarkable that on this path such entirely abrupt fragments,—but nevertheless readily to be referred again to their original life,—of early Hebrew songs, both of popular and sacred poetry, have been preserved.—Most obscure for us at the present day is

7, only אֶל־הַנְּחִילוֹת, Ps. v.: this word cannot in any way be explained from Hebrew as elsewhere known, because it nowhere else appears, and yet might have its mere sound by very different derivations. Meanwhile it must be admitted that it may belong to the great number of Hebrew words otherwise lost to us, and merely because it has come down to us in so entirely abrupt a form remains hitherto difficult for us to understand. If it arose from an old copyist error, it might be supposed that it was corrupted from the above מחלת, the fourth in the series; and in any case the hitherto obscure sense of this solitary word does not affect the clearness of all the others here explained.

For to all the above must be added the fact that the fuller compass of all those phrases is preserved at least once in Ps. lxxxviii. 1, for it here runs על מ׳ לְעַנּוֹת, to be sung after *Machalâth*. If, therefore, so far from the pure consideration of the words the result was obtained that all these nine or ten phrases are intended to define the mode of singing or tune of the particular song, this is entirely confirmed by this passage, where for once its original and fuller compass has been preserved. Again, it can be no difficulty that in the place where manifestly enough abbreviation is ever further extended, the full phrase is now retained as if accidentally only in *one* place: in the case of the Séla a quite correspondent example will be found.

Again, it cannot be in the slightest degree doubtful that all those ten phrases are to be understood in like manner and thus form something like a whole. By this correct observation the greater number of entirely inapt explanations which have been sought in ancient and modern times of them, falls to the ground. Especially it is extremely incorrect to conjecture in any one of these expressions the designation of a musical instrument, as has often been done, and is still done in later times.*

If we assume, on the other hand, that these short phrases especially designate the melodies or tunes of each song, the old Hebrew music stands in so far in the best connexion with that of the other ancient prophets. That a single tune or melody was first developed in a single place, and in a particular school of song, to its most perfect form, and then the best were collectively used, and along with one another, is shown most plainly by the history of Greek music. As then the Greeks counted five principal and fifteen subordinate modes,† as the Arab musicians distinguished twelve modes,‡ just so in the ancient people of Israel ten to twelve might be in use.§ And as the Greeks added to their own ancient modes the Lydian and Phrygian, Davîd might, according to p. 343, domesticate the Gathacic in Israel; and if at the same time they were performed in a definite number and series, the name of the *eight* (p. 343) is explained.—But certainly the more exact knowledge and free use of them was

---

* Nothing is, e.g., more erroneous than to suppose the word הַמְּחִילוֹת, Ps. v., designates the *flutes*, elsewhere termed חֲלִלוֹת: this assumption is idle in itself because the two words are formed differently, and scarcely agree in the root, and further idle because flutes never accompanied the Temple-song. When the accompaniment of singing by an instrument is named, the particle בְּ *with* is always used, both in poetic and in common style; only in Ps. xcii. 4, a poet once places in one of the two verse-members עַל, *after*, before the name of the instrument, but merely in order (p. 112, *Dichter des A. B.* to produce a slight change in the dance of the members; in non-poetical language, therefore in the annotations of the songs, this עַל would never have been used in such signification.

† See the leading passage in Plato's *Rep.*, iii. 9, 10, comp. C. O. Müller's *Griech. Literaturgesch.*, I., pp. 275 sqq.

‡ Comp. the above-named piece of Kiesewetter's, pp. 38 sqq.

§ It is remarkable that also for church hymnology seven to eight tunes were from ancient times counted; comp, Petri's *Agende*, pp. 95 sqq.

early lost. The Chronicler (I., xv. 20, 21) names only two more as in actual use, as if the Nábel-players used specially only one, and the Kinnôr-players another by preference. And the LXX understand nothing less certainly than these fragments of old Hebrew instrumental art. The irruption of Greek art which (p. 331) ensued comparatively early after Alexander, had certainly here a very withering effect, and completed the overthrow of a far older art, already from other causes seized with decay.

3. Only behind these two first kinds of art-expressions is found the designation of each particular song as either (1) מִזְמוֹר, or (2) מַשְׂכִּיל, or (3) מִכְתָּם, or (4) שִׁגָּיוֹן. That these four designations of a song stand in an opposed relation is undeniable: the same song is always designated only by one of the four names. That they were intended to distinguish more definitely the songs according to the severally possible modes of the mere delivery was shown in pp. 30-32 (*Dichter des A. B.*, I.); but this distinction cannot lie in the mode or tune, because, as shown above, quite other designations serve for this purpose. If we may not then seek the distinction in the singing, we must look to the mere playing and the singing in some way dependent on this: and here is certainly shown a possibly very definite distinction. For we see from the musical song, Ps. cl. 5, that it alluded to double bowls; clear, with more delicate light sound; and dull, with duller and heavier sound; a distinction which was certainly formed by the different metal or weight of these bowls. But if the bowls gave, according to the observations on p. 339, the time for playing and singing, then if either the clear only or only the dull were to be sounded, certainly an important distinction in the effect of the music must result; but perhaps also with the clear bowls the Nábel as the finer stringed instrument was also intended to resound. Thus four possible distinctions resulted, coinciding with those four names: (1) מִזְמוֹר would be any accompanied song, but in the first instance always such

an one as would be accompanied by the collective Temple-music, and this was the customary (it is found before fifty-six Psalms); (2) מַשְׂכִּיל, the clearer; (3) מִכְתָּם, the duller. With the latter name are now found designated only the six songs, Pss. xvi., lvi.—lx., beside the royal song, Isa. xxxviii.; and as Pss. lvi.—lx. stand together, so do those designated by מַשְׂכִּיל, Pss. xlii.—xlv., lii.—lv., lxxxviii. sq., further small coherent series, while this is found sporadically elsewhere only in Ps. xxxii., lxxiv., lxxviii., cxlii. On what principles the musicians thus distinguished these two-sided songs, we do not now know: it may have been a distinction like that in the old comedy by *tibiis paribus*, or *imparibus, dextris*, or *sinistris;** but if a poet once says *sing a fine song*, Ps. xlvii. 8, while this psalm is designated in the superscription generally as מִזְמוֹר, the word is then applied only in a somewhat freer sense. In all these three cases the music should however remain uniform in character through the whole song with its beginning; but if it was to change with the great strophés, perhaps precisely with the high number of strophés, it was (we may correctly further assume) designated שִׁגָּיוֹן. This word designates the wandering, i.e., deviating indirect course, if thought, feeling and music suddenly change with the new strophé; and actually this passionately excited, suddenly changing, and as it were wandering play suits also very well in sense the two cases where a song is so designated, Ps. vii., Hab. iii. As it was customary, further, to designate each song also quite shortly according to this its fourfold distinction, these four names are found in superscriptions of songs also alone, without the two preceding definitions or the more לַמְנַצֵּחַ preceding; this is then just as if in Greek a song was to be distinguished as Iambos or Dithyrambos.†

---

* Comp. Rheinische's *Museum für Philologie*, 1812. pp. 29 sqq. מַשְׂכִּיל is also, by its etymological signification, *bright, clean*, the exact opposite of a word כהם which expresses the obscure, *stained*.

† I do not use these examples at random; ἴαμβος is probably singing with

This is the most probable view at the present day of these four designations; and if they designate purely musical matters, it is explained also how the poetic piece, Hab. iii., might be designated, by עַל שִׁגְיֹנוֹת *after Dithyrambs* (that is, to be played). This expression runs only more definitely than if such a song, as in the Psalter, is immediately designated quite briefly with one of the four musical names. But like the preceding series of musical art-expressions, this also had become entirely obscure to the LXX. They translate only the מִזְמֹר tolerably by ψαλμός, but interchange the שִׁגָּיוֹן with it, and understand the מַשְׂכִּיל quite without sense as συνέσεως, i.e., a song *of* understanding or *doctrine*. It appears most strange that they render מִכְתָּם, Ps. xvi., by στηλογραρία, and Pss. lvi.—lx., by εἰς στηλογραφίαν; but this misunderstanding too may be satisfactorily explained.*

We may rather in conclusion justly conjecture that these three kinds of brief observations taken all together sufficed as a guide for the old musicians, and that fundamentally many further signs and hints, as have become customary in our artistic music, were not required. Thereby was indicated (1) that such a song was generally adapted for Temple-music, and was earlier used for this purpose; (2) after what mode of

---

one (ἴ from ἕν one) set (ἄμβη) i.e., the simplest, διθύραμβος, that *rising as with two doors*, θρίαμβος (*triumphus*) that *with three*, words which certainly refer to a very ancient mode of Greek music. Also the סַבְּכָא in the B. Daniel is as σαμβύκη (from τριαμβύκη), probably originally Greek, as the ἰαμβύκη corresponds to it.

* The translator of the Prophets indeed understood neither in Hab. iii. nor Isa. xxxviii. 9 the musical expressions; the translator of the Psalter, however, thought certainly to explain מִכְתָּם from מִכְתָּב, Isa. xxxviii. 9, and thus pitched upon στηλογραρία, which we now recognize best from the great examples in *C. J. Gr.*, no. 3569 c, 4310, 4379 o. Here we see didactic poems in the alphabetic order of the verses cut into pillars, which might be very aptly termed στηλογραρία. But this suits neither the royal song in the B Jesaja nor the six so-called Psalms, and rests only on a false reading, as is sufficiently shown above. —Comp. on the whole the *Jahrbb. der B. W.*, X., pp. 65 sqq.

singing, and (3) of instrumentation it was produced. Had we still the true key to the most important of these few signs, namely the knowledge of the kinds of the old Hebrew tunes, much would still become vital for us in this field; but unhappily this very knowledge had manifestly been entirely lost among the old translators, and we cannot now by any means discover conjecturally the origin of most of these short designations. For certainly all musical knowledge in the Levites' school had been propagated only by tradition, so that recollection might easily be weakened and lost under quite altered conditions and times.*

Yet there is found, in especial, one further word certainly of musical object but of other position and significance, the famous סֶלָה which stands, never at the beginning, but constantly in the course, sometimes at the end of a song. A musical sense it must surely enough have for the reason that it never belongs to the sense of the verse or song (although the Massôretic accentuation connects it closely with the number against which it is placed), and is ordinarily found only in such songs as bear the other previously explained musical signs.† The literal sense of this sign seems indeed to be very obscure, for this word is not found in any other connexion; but we have a further passage, Ps. ix. 17, where the phrase has been more fully preserved, and from which we must necessarily

---

* Here suitably the Kitâb al' aghâni may be compared, which I have deeply investigated in MS. It states with every more important song the music very exactly and somewhat circumstantially; but it seems nowhere further to define the mode of singing, except that it names the first who sang a song artistically, with some further art expressions, which only yield a solution to those acquainted with the matter.

† We read סֶלָה from once to four times on the following forty songs: Psalms iii., iv., vii., ix., xx., xxi., xxiv., xxxii., xxxix., xliv., xlvi.—l., lii., liv., lv., lvii., lix.—lxii., lxvi.—lxviii., lxxv.—lxxvii., lxxxi.—lxxxv., lxxxvii.—lxxxix., cxl., cxliii., Hab. iii. Of these merely eight have no לַמְנַצֵּחַ at the beginning or at the end, viz., xlii., xlix., l., lxxxii., lxxxiii., lxxxvii., cxliii. Meanwhile these bear at least the name מִזְמוֹר, p. 349. It is very noteworthy that with the translation διάψαλμα it is found also in the so-called Salomonic Psalter. xvii. 31. xviii. 10.

start. Here runs the musical intermediate observation, הִגָּיוֹן סֶלָה.

The first of these two words signifies according to the clear connexion of the sense in one verse, Ps. xcii. 4, as much as the *artistic play*, properly the meditation, musing and reflection, *music*, in the same way as the word Music is gradually used especially of Instrumental Music. סֶלָה is regarded according to this punctuation most safely as derived from a substantive סַל, whence סלל *ascend*, whence סֻלָּם the scale, which word is likewise applied in the musical sense; סֶלָה (*Lehrb.* § 216 c) is thus equivalent to *to the height! up!* which in things of sound can only be equivalent to *loud! plainly!* If then the full phrase runs *Music, loud!* it is thereby expressed from the other side that the singing is to cease while the Music alone loudly breaks in. Here then we observe immediately the use, indeed the indispensableness of this sign. For usually music accompanied the singing to all appearance somewhat softly and low: but there might be cases where it was to break in more strongly during the silence of the singing, and this, according to all preceding musical signs, must be marked by a peculiar sign in the course of the song. By what reasons indeed the artists were guided in particulars, has become to us with the whole ancient music an enigma, the solution of which can hardly be expected. Meanwhile we have thus a tolerable explanation why the word almost always stands only at the end of a verse,* indeed very often at the end of a strophé, for unquestionably in such passages the music may well strike in most strongly; hence it is certainly of some weight in seeking for the strophés. Yet from all this it is also clear how wrong it would be to regard the word in and for itself, as a sign of the pause or of the end of a strophé; this would neither suit the literal sense of these two words nor to the passages collectively where they are found.—For the rest, pre-

---

* At the end of a middle verse-member it stands in Ps. lv. 20, lvii. 4.

cisely. this word in later antiquity appears to have longest remained clear, for the translation of the LXX διάψαλμα probably contains a good reminiscence of the original sense.*

---

* If, that is, the Greek word is about equivalent to *intermediate play of strings*, where the string-play alone breaks in ; comp. on this rare word in the Greek writers elsewhere the old Lexica and the passages in Augusti : *Handb der Christl. Archäologie*, Th. 2, pp. 81, 124, who, for the rest, erroneously supposes the formula Hallelujah may be compared with Selah.—To criticize other explanations of this word is at the present day scarcely worth the trouble.

INDEX.

Psalm	i.	Vol. I.	p. 318	Psalm	xxix.	Vol. I.	p. 91
,,	ii.	,,	,, 147	,,	xxx.	,,	,, 187
,,	iii.	,,	,, 141	,,	xxxi.	,,	,, 302
,,	iv.	,,	,, 144	,,	xxxii.	,,	,, 136
,,	v.	,,	,, 259	,,	xxxiii.	Vol. II.	,, 322
,,	vi.	,,	,, 183	,,	xxxiv.	,,	,, 90
,,	vii.	,,	,, 74	,,	xxxv.	,,	,, 50
,,	viii.	,,	,, 103	,,	xxxvi.	Vol. I.	,, 267
,,	ix.	,,	,, 320	,,	xxxvii.	,,	,, 328
,,	x.	,,	,, 320	,,	xxxviii.	Vol. II.	,, 56
,,	xi.	,,	,, 71	,,	xxxix.	Vol. I.	,, 204
,,	xii.	,,	,, 197	,,	xl.	Vol. II.	,, 60
,,	xiii.	,,	,, 185	,,	xli.	Vol. I.	,, 191
,,	xiv.	Vol. II.	,, 143	,,	xlii.	Vol. II.	,, 23
,,	xv.	Vol. I.	,, 84	,,	xliii.	,,	,, 23
,,	xvi.	Vol. II.	,, 10	,,	xliv.	,,	,, 227
,,	xvii.	,,	,, 4	,,	xlv.	Vol. I.	,, 165
,,	xviii.	Vol. I.	,, 117	,,	xlvi.	,,	,, 218
,,	xix.	,,	,, 97	,,	xlvii.	Vol. II.	,, 212
,,	xx.	,,	,, 158	,,	xlviii.	Vol. I.	,, 221
,,	xxi.	,,	,, 160	,,	xlix.	Vol. II.	,, 17
,,	xxii.	Vol. II.	,, 33	,,	l.	Vol. I.	,, 310
,,	xxiii.	Vol. I.	,, 179	,,	li.	Vol. II.	,, 77
,,	xxiv. 7-10.	,,	,, 79	,,	lii.	Vol. I.	,, 265
,,	xxiv. 1-6.	,,	,, 82	,,	liii.	Vol. II.	,, 143
,,	xxv.	Vol. II.	,, 90	,,	liv.	Vol. I.	,, 271
,,	xxvi.	Vol. I.	,, 296	,,	lv.	,,	,, 252
,,	xxvii.	,,	,, 174	,,	lvi.—lviii.	,,	276-289
,,	xxviii.	,,	,, 300	,,	lix.	,,	,, 290

INDEX.

Psalm	lx.	Vol. I.	p. 112	Psalm	xcvi.	Vol. II.	p 194
,,	lxi.	,,	,, 272		xcvii.		1.9
,,	lxii.	,,	,, 200		xcviii.		1.9
,,	lxiii.	,,	,, 274		xcix.		193
,,	lxiv.	,,	,, 262	,,	c.		198
,,	lxv.	,,	,, 232		ci.	Vol. I.	.. 81
,,	lxvi.1-12.Vol.II.		,, 213	,,	cii.	Vol. II.	. 6
,,	lxvi.13-20.Vol.I.		,, 195	,,	ciii.		.. 281
,,	lxvii.	Vol. II.	,, 199	,,	civ.		.. 284
,,	lxviii.	,,	,, 200	,,	cv.		.. 310
,,	lxix.	,,	,, 66	,,	cvi.		. 290
,,	lxx.	,,	,, 65	,,	cvii.	,,	.. 2 5
,,	lxxi.	,,	,, 85	,,	cviii.		.. 309
,,	lxxii.	Vol. I.	,, 333	,,	cix.	,,	. 72
,,	lxxiii.	Vol. II.	,, 126	,,	cx.	Vol. I.	., 107
,,	lxxiv.	,,	,, 230	,,	cxi.	Vol. II.	.. 2 9
,,	lxxv.	Vol. I.	,, 216	,,	cxii.	,,	.. 294
,,	lxxvi.	,,	,, 226	,,	cxiii.	,,	.. 301
,,	lxxvii.	Vol. II.	.. 133	,,	cxiv.	,,	.. 301
,,	lxxviii.	,,	.. 255	,,	cxv.	,,	., 181
,,	lxxix.	,,	,, 233	,,	cxvi.	,,	,, 183
,,	lxxx.	,,	., 235	,,	cxvii.	,,	,, 303
,,	lxxxi.	,,	,, 264	,,	cxviii.	,,	.. 177
,,	lxxxii.	,,	., 141	,,	cxix.	,,	.. 267
,,	lxxxiii.	,,	,, 252		cxx.		.. 148
,,	lxxxiv.	,,	., 30	,,	cxxi.	,,	.. 150
,,	lxxxv.		,, 250	,,	cxxii.		.. 162
,,	lxxxvi.	,,	,, 303		cxxiii.	,,	.. 151
,,	lxxxvii.	,,	,, 170		cxxiv.	,,	.. 159
,,	lxxxviii.	Vol. I.	,, 307	,,	cxxv.		.. 161
,,	lxxxix.	Vol. II.	,, 242		cxxvi.		.. 163
	xc.	Vol. I.	,, 208		cxxvii.		. 164
,,	xci.	Vol. II.	,, 215	,,	cxxviii.	,,	.. 166
	xcii.	,,	,, 188		cxxix.	,,	.. 160
	xciii.	,,	,, 190	,,	cxxx.		.. 152
	xciv.	,,	,, 138	,,	cxxxi.		.. 173
	xcv.	,,	.. 196		cxxxii.		.. 238

Psalm cxxxiii.	Vol. II.	p. 167	Psalm cxliii.	Vol. II.	p. 305
,, cxxxiv.	,,	,, 168	,, cxliv. 1-11.	,,	,, 307
,, cxxxv.	,,	,, 314	,, cxliv. 12-15.	Vol. I.	,, 154
,, cxxxvi.	,,	,, 315	,, cxlv.	Vol. II.	,, 317
,, cxxxvii.	,,	,, 173	,, cxlvi.	,,	,, *319
,, cxxxviii.	,,	,, 186	,, cxlvii.	,,	,, 320
,, cxxxix.	,,	,, 218	,, cxlviii.	,,	,, 325
,, cxl.—cxlii.	Vol. I.		,, cxlix.	,,	,, 324
		p. 240-250	,, cl.	,,	,, 327

* Before the translation of Ps. cxlvi. the following words should be supplied:—

"The three following songs give praise and thanks to Jahvé as the true Helper, especially emphasizing the truth that external human power does not bestow victory. Ps. cxlvi. expresses this rather as the feeling of each individual, with strong imitation of Pss. ciii. sq. The short song unfolds in three small strophes, of seven members each. The verse-division is manifestly inapt, vv. 6, 7."

www.ingramcontent.com/pod-product-compliance
Lightning Source LLC
Chambersburg PA
CBHW020218240426
43672CB00006B/349